Telling Complexions

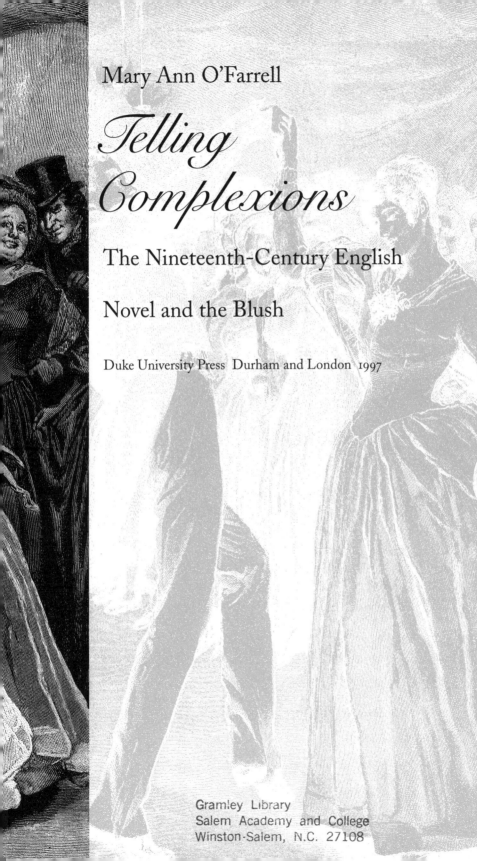

Mary Ann O'Farrell

Telling Complexions

The Nineteenth-Century English

Novel and the Blush

Duke University Press Durham and London 1997

© 1997 Duke University Press

All rights reserved

Printed in the United States of America on acid-free paper ∞

Typeset in Adobe Caslon with Snell Roundhand Script display

by Keystone Typesetting, Inc.

Library of Congress Cataloging-in-Publication Data

O'Farrell, Mary Ann.

Telling complexions : the nineteenth-century English novel and the
blush / by Mary Ann O'Farrell.

p. cm.

Includes index.

ISBN 0-8223-1903-9 (cloth : alk. paper). — ISBN 0-8223-1895-4
(pbk. : alk. paper)

1. English fiction—19th century—History and criticism.
2. Blushing in literature.   3. Austen, Jane, 1775–1817—Knowledge—
Psychology.   4. Gaskell, Elizabeth Cleghorn, 1810–1865—Knowledge—
Psychology.   5. Women and literature—England—History—19th
century.   6. Dickens, Charles, 1812–1870—Knowledge—Psychology.
7. Psychology in literature.   8. Emotions in literature.   I. Title.

PR868.B58O34   1997

823'.809353—dc20   96-38211   CIP

For Margaret C. O'Farrell and
Edward J. F. O'Farrell

Contents

Acknowledgments

*T*he help of colleagues and friends has brought to the privacy of thinking about blushing the sociability that is so often attendant on blushing itself. I thank the following for offering attentive readings, spontaneous encouragements, well-placed words, good stories, and happy distractions: in earliest days, John Bishop, Carol Clover, Deborah Dyson, Ralph Rader, Kerry Walk; more recently, Nancy Armstrong, Joseph Litvak, Eve Kosofsky Sedgwick, and the always smart and consistently generous readers for Duke University Press; more locally, Harriette Andreadis, Margaret Ezell, Samuel Gladden, Melanie Hawthorne, Howard Marchitello, Pamela Matthews, Krista May, J. Lawrence Mitchell, Robert Newman, Larry Reynolds, James Rosenheim, and Lynne Vallone; Gillian Brown, Ian Crump, Helen Emmitt, Howard Horwitz, Judith Remmes, Carol Siegel, Lynn Wardley; Gwendolen Albert, Jay Baer, Maureen and Mike Bellotti, Jack Bodden, Sean Chadwell, Maggie Landis, Deshae Lott, John Loughlin, Patricia Loughlin, Gabriel McWhirter, Joshua McWhirter, Amy McWilliams, Margaret O'Farrell, Nancy Tubbs; and Ken Wissoker, who, as editor, has struck the perfect balance between supportive patience and the polite suggestion that I might put the damn thing in the mail. Time and stimulation provided by the Interdisciplinary Group for Historical Literary Study at Texas A&M University have facilitated the completion of this work. A version of Chapter 1, "Austen's Blush," appeared in *Novel* 27 (1994): 125–39. I thank the editors for permission to reprint it here.

Audrey Jaffe and Leland Monk have long been best companions in novelistic pleasures; Jeffrey Cox has been the most generous of colleagues and friends. D. A. Miller recognizes himself, I know, in those parts of this text that are engagements with him, and I trust he knows, too, that I would not have written without him. David McWhirter's Sunday dinners, along with his mastery of the transition, have been only the most obviously material forms of his support, which—as intelligence and conversation and company—is sustenance made into buoyancy. First thanks and last are offered to my parents.

"Oh!" cried Jane, with a blush and an hesitation which Emma thought infinitely more becoming to her than all the elegance of all her usual composure.—Jane Austen, *Emma*, 1816[1]

> Josh: Stop it; you're making me blush!
> Cher: See, now; I need make-up for that.
> —Television promo for *Clueless*, 1995[2]

*O*nly half overcoming rivalry in reserving to herself the joys of estimation, Austen's Emma Woodhouse registers the attractions of the somatic blush. If the blush of Jane Fairfax proves "more becoming" than her habitual composure, this is because it rejects the monolithic singularity and self-containment of elegance in favor of the duplicitous flirtation and semiosis of intermittence, of advances and retreats, comings and goings. Here, at this point in *Emma*, Austen's blush is a site of pleasure.

Oddly enough, in this pairing of references, it is Cher's response to Josh in *Clueless*—the 1995 movie that reimagined Austen's Emma as a high-fashion Beverly Hills teen with very little to distress or vex her— that touches more directly on the responsibilities of the blush. Though Cher's exchange with Josh takes place in the early stages of a flirtation, this flirtation occurs in the context of that familiar narrative in which an older and wiser boy educates a sweet but misguided girl into an admission of her defects as prerequisite to a humbled recognition of her worth. If Cher is empowered in this relation by her ability to make Josh blush (or by her ability to elicit his statement that she might), she is nevertheless also startled by these abilities into a complementary confession: though *Clueless* will suggest that Cher is not in fact a jaded denizen of mall culture (revelation: she's clueless), she thinks herself one, and the inability to blush without Shiseido might betoken a hardened and unfeeling self, unable to register with the intermittent colors of physiology the moral sense that, in some quarters at least, makes a blush a grace.

Contemporary American culture continues to explore and sometimes to entwine both of these strands—the line of pleasure and the line of moral obligation—in its use of and dependence on the blush. Commerce embraces and reconfigures (the better to eroticize) the uncommitted insubstantiality of the fermented rosé, using advertising for the blush wine to assert its preferences in song ("Your smile is fine anytime, but I love to see you blush"), while a cosmetics print campaign commands that women "Just Blush," confining us to the exercise of this single obligation within a realm of similarly eroticized legibility.[3] The corporation humanizes itself by attempting incorporation, using the language of color to suggest embodiment and authenticity as it asks, "Have you ever seen a bank blush?"[4] But if the corporation's transparent bashfulness seems ineffective and nearly harmless, the white-supremacist use of the blush as determinant of Aryan status enlists the blush in order to alibi invidious distinction and authorize a bloody violence. In his book on "the evolution of the racialist right in American politics," James Ridgeway reports the conversation of Laverne, a Nebraska farmer: " 'What's the saying, "blood in the face?" ' asked a visitor. 'If you can blush you're not a Jew,' Laverne nodded."[5] Extending its search beyond the usual suspects, the white-supremacist demand for blood in the face embodies and interrogates even the presumed privilege of white manhood, which, if it must not fail in producing on demand what has been called a "mild erection of the head,"[6] still proves most satisfying when it performs its inadequacy.

Though the culture at large is merely less extreme in its conception of somatic display as a task to be performed—without exempting privilege, assigning that task most often to women and workers, to gay men and to the racially othered[7]—it is also able sometimes to conceive of somatic testimony as an expressive pleasure; certainly envy characterizes Cher's answer to Josh, but it is he who, as a flirting white boy, identifies and announces (in case you had missed them) the marvels of his responsive complexion. And when African American daytime talk-show host Bertice Berry points to her palm and introduces a sexy segment with a report that she's blushing ("See?"), the cultural work performed is quite sophisticated in the simultaneity with which Berry accedes to legibility's demands on her body and mocks them with the ambivalent power of her self-consciousness.

In both its notion of the blush as an expressive pleasure and its use of the blush as an instrument of watchful estimation, contemporary culture displays as a disintegrating legacy remnants of the nineteenth-century novel's striking and persuasive understanding, representation, and exploitation of the blush. As a movie of manners, *Clueless* was exceptional in enjoying the status of this lineage: "Actually, the movie is a very loose reworking of Jane Austen's 'Emma,'" wrote the *New York Times*,[8] and the film's writer and director explained, "It's Jane Austen with f——me socks";[9] but the influence of the nineteenth-century novel on the twentieth-century blush in American advertising, television, music, film, and language remains most visible in the work of unexamined attitudes and unacknowledged dependences, in the evidence of convention, and in the sense of loss that characterizes popular culture's reference to its blush. In telling here about the nineteenth-century novel's intimate relation to the blush, I mean in part and by implication to understand and to tell about the formation of the well-mannered literary subject, whose pleasures and discomforts in the face of the blush have everything to do with contemporary manners and contemporary aggressions. But in doing so, I recognize that even the self-consciousness that insists upon such acknowledgment accepts and participates fully in an inherited fantasy of the blush.

The attractions of the blush for writing are visible along the two courses (of pleasure and of legible utility) I have begun to outline. As an event of the body, the blush is a temporal phenomenon that has been taken to imply causality; when I read a reddened complexion as blushing, I interpret it already as a response to embarrassment or even to embarrassed delight, rejecting matters of digestion and health, for example, or the urgings of alcohol and anger as its inspirations.[10] And as an act of interpretation, identifying the blush entails imagining it as the writing of the body and, thus, as the product of somatic agency, a means to dispel the alternative fantasy that the obdurate body is obstinate in its refusal to speak. The blush can seem, then, to partake of both body and language—

supplementing language with an ephemeral materiality—and novelistic usage would even suggest that, by means of the blush, body and language are identical and simultaneous in function and effect; the heroine of Harlequin romance, for example, might be seen to speak with her body ("No, no," she blushed), while Dickens's Podsnap may be understood to embody his assertion (" 'A gentleman can have no feelings who contracts such a marriage,' flushes Podsnap").[11]

In responding to the blush's hybrid allure, the nineteenth-century English novel seizes upon its imagined demand for interpretation and, attempting to answer that perceived demand, responds also to the blush as to an invitation to narrative. In its efforts to manage within the confines of a readable sign system both the challenges posed by the body and the anxieties the novel itself imposes on particular bodies, the novel finds in the blush an implicit promise to render body and character legible. The blush's efficacy in fulfilling its pledge for the novel depends upon its seeming, by means of its involuntarity, to evade the constructive capacities of gesture, disguise, and will. Like Emma Woodhouse, the novel seizes upon blush and context to evaluate character: "When she saw that with all the deep blush of consciousness, there had been a smile of secret delight, she had less scruple in the amusement, and much less compunction with respect to her.—This amiable, upright, perfect Jane Fairfax was apparently cherishing very reprehensible feelings" (243). Reading the deep blush against the delighted smile and against her information about Jane Fairfax's acquaintance among men, Emma reads the blush in social and somatic context, determining its nature by that context. But reading the blush (reading it *as a blush*) is always reading context, and always asserting against context fancies and *doxa* about those sets of circumstances in which a blush is warranted, demanded, made.

The example of Emma Woodhouse, of course, destabilizes the blush's utility as legible self-evidence, for Emma's readings of Jane Fairfax are gloriously wrong. If reading the blush means—as it means for Emma—reading the wrong story, it has also meant for the novel making up the story one may have thought one merely read, even seeking and using the blush as incitement or as alibi for both the licit and illicit pleasures of narration.[12] With Emma, Frank Churchill prepares to observe Jane Fairfax, while preparing for purposes of his own to excite Emma's imagination with the fluctuations of Jane's complexion: "You shall see how she takes it;—whether she colours" (222). In suggesting an event to be accounted for or explained, the blush in fact or in prospect offers to "a mind lively and at ease" (233) such opportunities as facilitate and excuse the exercise of a writerly imagination.

The experience of blushing for those who blush also proves narratable and useful for the nineteenth-century English novel. When Emma fears that, with "her heart . . . in a glow," "her face might be as hot" (328), her fear depends on her belief in the capacity of her complexion to reflect a readable self: legibility is as much a fantasy for those of us who blush as for those of us who watch the blushing. Like *Clueless*'s flirtatious Josh, Emma might deflect with apparent anxiety a *desire* to be read; within sentences, she relies on the expressivity of her face to thank Mr. Knightley for his kindness to her neglected friend: "Though too distant for speech, her countenance said much, as soon as she could catch his eye again" (328). By means of its attentions to blushing as a perceived event of the body, the novel suggests that—in seeming involuntarily and reliably to betray a deep self—blushing assists at the conversion of legibility into a sense of identity and centrality. The novel values this sense of identity, even or especially when it is produced by the pains as well as the pleasures of mortified self-recognition and self-revelation; the painful blush lends the credible support of the body to the self that is generated, recognized, and revealed in all the felt if ostensible uniqueness of its discomfitting mortifications. Construed in this way, the blush—as an act of self-expression—performs a somatic act of confession.

This last of course begins to sound a little as if it has been suggested by the work of Michel Foucault. Writing of confession as "one of the West's most highly valued techniques for producing truth," Foucault can resemble the smart novelist of manners in seeing confession as an obligation felt as an urge, in seeing confession as (with the force of the *de rigueur*) what one does: "One goes about telling, with the greatest precision, whatever is most difficult to tell. One confesses in public and in private, to one's parents, one's educators, one's doctor, to those one loves; one admits to oneself, in pleasure and in pain, things it would be impossible to tell to anyone else, the things people write books about."[13] Foucault's notion of power's productivity (as opposed simply to its prohibitions) has been useful for this study, which develops the notion that, as a productive response to circumstance, blushing is precisely a social obligation felt as an urge, an act of somatic confession that dazzles with its promise to establish unique identity by revealing the body's truth.

My argument about the nineteenth-century English novel and the blush, then, takes place within the larger discussion by literary and cultural critics of the novel's work as an instrument of coercive (if also sometimes seductive) ideology.[14] Like some of the other critics who have been engaged in this argument, I acknowledge most obviously my debt to Foucault. Within a rigidly Foucauldian frame, the blush would be seen as an instrument by which the body is enlisted in the production of legibility in order to serve at surveillance's creation of domesticable bodies, and the novel's use of the blush would be seen as institutionalizing that service. And so, in part, I do see the blush and the novel. But, as articulated in Foucauldian terms, all confessions can come powerfully but inescapably to illustrate and to tell the same story: the always interesting but perhaps incomplete narrative of their extraction. The Foucault of my book is a Foucault whose totalizing, terrorizing, and even ventriloquizing authority and allure are tempered by a sense of the real pleasures generated by (and only sometimes in tension with) the novel's coercions.

The source of these pleasures is a Barthesian reading practice that, in rewriting such coercions, admits and exploits for pleasure (as Foucault cannot) the opportunities afforded by fantasies of the legible body, which in offering itself for reading and interpretation also offers to itself the experience of *being read* as its own pleasure. Seen as affording such opportunities, the novel is able sometimes to engender perversities that complement most precisely the disciplines it would enforce.[15]

What this entails as practice is a concerted attempt to retain or to restore the textures and differences that an unbending adherence to the Foucauldian narrative of the blush in the novel could sweep dismissively aside as the glittering distractions made always available to divert a magpie narcissism. In wanting both to respect and to manipulate these textures, I want to supplement Foucauldian discipline (understanding discipline both as a subject pertinent to consideration of the blush and as the governing narrative of power that articulates an account of the blush's social work) with the Barthesian vision of reading as an *ars erotica*. In valuing a pleasure-privileging writerly reading, I do not mean to oppose it to what might seem to occupy here the place of its obvious obverse in a Barthesian evaluative binary: a Foucault-inflected approach that could be seen as readerly in a pejorative sense. Indeed some of the last decade's most attentive readings of the novel have been engendered by Foucault. Rather I want to locate the inspiration of Barthes's writerly reading—as some of these same attentive readers have done—within the realm of Foucauldian operations, to pursue the pleasures of narrative within an examination of the novel as an institution.[16] This betwixt and between methodology is suited to the double-faced (not to say duplicitous) nature of the blush, which supplements the discipline of its (on-again/off-again) commitment to legibility with the flirtatious intermittences characteristic of an erotic art.

Cultural notions about the blush, now as in the nineteenth century, register the blush's utility for both legibility and erotics in fantasies about its circulatory properties. Whether understood as the effect of contagion or as effecting a polite intercourse between bodies, the blush's circulation between and among persons is expressive of social relation. But while it may announce most clearly the subscription of the blushing body to the code of an extensive social network, the blush in the nineteenth-century English novel can also work the work of local resistance, embodying with a flush relations—not always fully articulable in the nineteenth-century novel—that cross or evade the strictures and compulsions of class and gender and the marriage plot.

The resistances wrought by the blush, that is, take sometimes the form of permissions: for all that it both records and advances the public project of the blush as incorporate enforcer of moral regularity (the blush as product of discomfort and of tension), the novel graces the blush with its solicitous attentions, acknowledging and encouraging the blush as well in its issuance of well-mannered license to gratification and release. When, in the midst of a self-indicting self-examination, Emma Wood-house catches her imaginist's mind wandering in forbidden directions,

Jane Austen writes that "she stopt to blush and laugh at her own relapse" (137). Blushing and laughing, Emma seems to enjoy her blush, and Austen couples it with what might seem most inimical to the sometimes painful experience of blushing. Her laugh makes Emma's blush a welcomed interruption of self-correction, enhanced by a leisurely indulgence (she "stopt" to blush and laugh). But it also unveils this blush as a kind of triumph for the English novel; though in the next moment Emma will take up again the "more serious, more dispiriting cogitation" and "unmirthful reflections" her actions may have warranted and that will send her to bed "with nothing settled but the conviction of her having blundered most dreadfully" (137), for this moment, the novel permits her to embody and permits itself to entertain the ephemeral vision of a blush that—without escaping it—refuses the sovereignty of a socializing mortification. Like Emma's laughing blush, the English novel, while constructing well-mannered textual bodies and well-mannered reading bodies with the help of the blush, manages sometimes also to fantasize the bodies it has made in animating resistance to the constraints imposed by their construction.

In beginning my discussion of the nineteenth-century English novel and the blush with a consideration of works by Jane Austen, I want to identify the novel of manners as the form that—in part by teaching the legible blush—teaches the body to behave itself in public, and I mean to recognize that the compelling pleasures of reading Jane Austen enforce manners lessons. These pleasures prove an enduring, forceful, and difficult inheritance for the nineteenth-century novel, which—when it confronts issues of materiality and textuality—seems inevitably to have to deal with Austen's recognition and use of the body's potential for significatory excess as represented in the blush. In a way, then, this history of the blush in the nineteenth-century English novel is also a history of the novel's response to the legacy of Austenian manners and their construction of the body. In confronting the challenges posed by Austen's manipulation of the mannerly blush, nineteenth-century novels turn back to the body as a source of supports (the swoon, the scar, the blunder) that—taking the place of the blush—might signify character more stably. The novel's management of the blush, I suggest, participates in the novel's modal procession from manners toward (it will not seem so far) self-consciousness.

Chapter 1 watches "Austen's Blush" at work in *Pride and Prejudice*, where it functions as a stable and reliable index of character. Austen's blush exploits the body's credible and involuntary (credible because involuntary) testimony to supply ready somatic support to manners' interest in regulating the body. But, discovering that pleasures are to be taken with the pains of blushing, Austen recovers a sense of the body in manners. Her erotics of mortification works the perverse conversion of the sign of manners into the sign of desire, though it does so finally in service of the marriage plot's subordination of the body to its social work.

Writing *Persuasion*, Austen undergoes a crisis of faith in her recuperation of the blush from legibility for erotics, and the signs of Austen's mannerly pleasures threaten to collapse into conventionality. Chapter 2, "Mortifying Persuasions, or the Worldliness of Jane Austen," argues that, having redefined mortification as the erotic in *Pride and Prejudice*, Austen recognizes and pursues the risk her erotics of mortification necessarily entails: that mortification might end (as it is commonly supposed to) in insensibility rather than sensation. Exploring mortification, Austen articulates its centrality to a set of associations (narrative, knowledge, sophistication, self-possession) that define themselves against the lessons of mortification.

Austen's remarkable negotiation between the pressures of erotics and manners, and her creation of a satisfying and legible blush, prove challenging to Elizabeth Gaskell. In trying to contain the novel of manners within her industrial novel *North and South*, Gaskell confronts class issues that the novel of manners permitted Austen to evade, and Gaskell's own anxious fantasies about class and about the status of the body in fiction compromise her use of the blush. Chapter 3, "Gaskell's Blunders," considers Gaskell's attempts to find a fit substitute for the blush. Her search for a reliable somatic sign that will suit and reflect character leads Gaskell to experiments involving other potential indices of character and virtue (the blunder, the swoon, and even the suitable death) with which she can replace the blush. Though Gaskell's provisional recastings prove finally unsatisfactory, they nevertheless lead her to articulate for the novel its fantasy that the body is the anxious author of its own signs and that somatic events are records of the body's marked intentions.

If Austen's achievement is that, coincident with her satisfaction of the demands of legibility and manners, she recuperates the blush's significatory excess for erotics and pleasure, Dickens's trouble lies precisely in the realm of Austen's triumph. Chapter 4, "Dickens's Scar," suggests that, moving from manners to melodrama, Dickens foregrounds the blush against the scar, attempting by his physical graphics of mortification to install stability and fixity in the place of instability and intermittence. But Dickens's anxieties about the blush are merely displaced onto Rosa Dartle's scar in *David Copperfield*, which proves—in Dickensian fantasy— elusive of Dickensian authority. The marked body in Dickens comes to be associated with a mode of speech that evokes the body while refusing the commitment of legible meaning.

The final chapter, "The Mechanics of Confusion," departs from the practice of attending closely to a single novel, surveying a number of texts in order to address various ways in which novelists later in the nineteenth century evince dissatisfaction with the blush, even while taking regular recourse to its assistance in delineating character. Through readings of works by Mary Elizabeth Braddon, Anthony Trollope, George Eliot, and Henry James, this chapter registers the increasingly self-conscious tension in the English novel between the sense that the blush is expressive of character and a developing recognition (a recognition acknowledged in more and in less sophisticated forms) that the blush is an inevitable and mechanistic response to and product of circumstance. The nineteenth-century English novel's recurrent fantasy that blushing effects a dissolution of boundaries and a confusion of bodies articulates the mechanistic structure of social relation, as the English novel understands it. In *The Sacred Fount*, Henry James eliminates dependence on the blush as a legible sign of character, while preserving through the novel's central image the structural relation between bodies that the blush has elsewhere helped to outline. Turning in conclusion to the work of Salman Rushdie and to contemporary popular culture, I consider the trajectory of the novel toward self-consciousness, abstraction, and disembodiment as a literary mode, and the direction of the blush toward announcement ("you're making me blush") as its popular form. Even thus diluted, the blush continues to articulate and to reveal cultural fantasies about the attachments of embodiment and the imperatives of social obligation.

In exploiting the blush for its suggestiveness about character, the nineteenth-century English novel is itself touched by what colloquialism calls the blush's contagion; the colors of the blush reflect upon the novel, rendering it legible and recording its best pleasures. The novel's dependence on the blush, then, enacts the novel's own expressive fantasy; the complex network of social relations that is constructed (made, that is, but also understood) by the persuasive fictions of the novel is visible—like Jane Fairfax's feelings—in the traces of "a blush which showed . . . how it was all connected" (420).

Chapter One Austen's Blush:

Pride and Prejudice

*I*n a 1796 letter to her sister Cassandra, Jane Austen reports on the status of her flirtation with a young man Austen biographers have found among the most plausible of Austen's possible love interests. Austen writes first of what she and Tom Lefroy have done together:

You scold me so much in the nice long letter which I have this moment received from you, that I am almost afraid to tell you how my Irish friend and I behaved. Imagine to yourself everything most profligate and shocking in the way of dancing and sitting down together. I *can* expose myself, however, only *once more*, because he leaves the country soon after next Friday, on which day we *are* to have a dance at Ashe after all. He is a very gentlemanlike, good-looking, pleasant young man, I assure you.[1]

That Tom Lefroy and Jane Austen have paid each other public attention constitutes a public exposure the pleasures of which Austen seems about to forgo only with regret. Evidence suggests, as Austen goes on in the letter, that the days remaining them are unlikely to consist of private intimacies:

But as to our having ever met, except at the three last balls, I cannot say much; for he is so excessively laughed at about me at Ashe, that he is ashamed of coming to Steventon, and ran away when we called on Mrs. Lefroy a few days ago. (1)

Austen critics and biographers, always ready to fix Austen in some plain relation to the marriage plot, have been eager to find in Tom Lefroy love lost and long regretted—to identify him as, in Austen's mind, the one that got away. Of Lefroy, John Halperin writes: "The available evidence suggests that he recovered more quickly than she from whatever disappointment there may have been. A major theme of *Persuasion* is that woman's love is more enduring than man's; it is likely that Jane Austen never entirely forgot Tom Lefroy."[2] If Austen biographers love the idea of this romance, they use its luster as Lefroy did—as one might, given the chance—to add some romance to stories of youth: "Years later the old Chief Justice told his nephew that he had once been in love with the famous Jane Austen, but 'he qualified his concession by saying that it was a boyish love'" (62–63). Austen's appeal for the older Lefroy seems in part to have been her fame, as his appeal to critics seems to be his success; critics enjoy referring to his status in later life, the appeal of his title being, presumably, the suggestion that its bearer could have been smart enough for Jane Austen.

Austen's discussion of Lefroy's runaway behavior late in his visit prompts recollection of a story told by a character in Hitchcock's *Rebecca*. When Maxim de Winter abandons without ceremony the tea he has been taking with Mrs. van Hopper, the overbearing American to whom Joan Fontaine plays companion, his departure prompts Mrs. van Hopper to reminisce: "I remember when I was younger there was a well-known writer who used to dart down the back way whenever he saw me coming. I suppose he was in love with me and wasn't quite sure of himself. Well, *c'est la vie.*"[3] The film ensures that Mrs. van Hopper's unselfconscious account of repulsion as attraction is to be read as patently ludicrous by its use of Florence Bates's body, so stout as to seem stoutly armored: the movie wonders who, facing a body like hers or, in a different sense, like Rebecca's even in outline,[4] could be "quite sure of himself." As I mean this parallel to suggest, if only in part, the sure business of "the future Chief Justice of Ireland" (Halperin, 61) may indeed have been, like that of the "well-known writer," ensuring his getaway from what, attracted or repelled, he found daunting. That one is also tempted not to read Lefroy in this way may just be testimony to the evident desire of her readers to make Austen into an Austen heroine; but some empathetic joy in her audible delight in telling this story may also result from the story's familiarity to readers of Austen's novels, from which they have learned that avoidance, separation, awkwardness, and a "general incivility" ought to be understood as "the very essence of love."[5]

Austen's turn to incivility and its associates, embarrassment and confusion, as signs of love is a resort to involuntarity as a basis for the credibility of expressed feelings. The voluntary speech or gesture might forward the lie based in politeness or interest, or, more often the case in

Jane Austen, might find itself contained within the strictures of mannerly code. Worldly Charlotte Lucas, explaining Jane Bennet to Elizabeth Bennet, gives shape to the uses of incivility by laying out the limitations of good manners. When Elizabeth rejoices that Jane's "composure of temper and uniform cheerfulness of manner . . . would guard her from the suspicions of the impertinent" about her feelings for Bingley, Charlotte replies: "It is sometimes a disadvantage to be so very guarded. If a woman conceals her affection with the same skill from the object of it, she may lose the opportunity of fixing him; and it will then be but poor consolation to believe the world equally in the dark" (21). If Jane Bennet "smile[s] too much" (16), the excess in question inheres in the inability of her smiles, in their frequency and uniformity, to particularize or distinguish themselves or their object; if smiles at Bingley and at Sir William Lucas look alike, so then, bizarrely, do the two men come to resemble one another. Along with her smiles, Jane's "serenity of . . . countenance" (197) and the "complacency in her air and manner" (208) act in opposition to felicitous resolution of the marriage plot: Jane is caught in the trap of the good girl who would succeed in the world of courtship; her good manners won't get her a man.

Having used Jane Bennet to outline a provisional opposition between appropriate, well-mannered behavior and the success of the marriage plot, Austen turns to the body as the clearest source of an incivility that is yet recuperable in the world of manners. In its involuntarity, the incivility of the blush—as apparent sign of the body's separable will and of the body's willful intrusion into social order—seems to exempt the blush from the limitations imposed on love in the system of manners, from, that is, the vagaries of the lie or the comprehensiveness of the code. In the plotting of marriages, the involuntary blush exceeds the voluntary smile in uncovering a truth yielded against one's well-behaved will. But the tension between manners and the marriage plot is apparent rather than actual, and Austen's use of the blush facilitates the real work of manners: including the body in social order and teaching it to behave itself in public. So used, the blush in manners arranges bodies in marriageable pairs assigned the exercise of desire in marriage. But in invoking the involuntarity of the body in even its most delicate form, Austen necessarily invokes what about the body is most inimical to manners, what makes manners most vulnerable to disruption. In *Pride and Prejudice,* she works to make-over the unstable blush; the blush in the novel of manners, legible and reliable index of character, comes to seem almost voluntary in the rigor of its obliged association with moral status; as Austen uses it, the blush enforces mannerly ethics, but it proves nevertheless and of course to be so much linguistic paint.

Pleased as he is with the complexity and interest of the portraits he says Jane Austen paints "without employing any but the commonest of colors," George Henry Lewes is nevertheless dismayed by what he misses in the body of her work: though the reader may be interested, he writes, "the reader's pulse never throbs."[6] While contemptuous of the contempt of "Currer Bell" for Austen even as he quotes it, Lewes would seem to agree with her that in Jane Austen one finds "no glance of a bright vivid physiognomy," for Austen misses, says Lewes in his own voice, "many of the subtle connections between physical and mental organization" (160, 158). Lewes is just one among those who note that Jane Austen "minimizes the bodily dimension."[7] Yet if readers of *Pride and Prejudice,* as Lewes contends, believe despite everything in the written Elizabeth Bennet as a "flesh-and-blood heroine" (165), it is because, I will argue, they have been convinced by Austen's frequent indications that the colors of that flesh and the blood seen through it are white and pink, that the countenances described in *Pride and Prejudice* are practiced in blanching and in blushing.

Throughout *Pride and Prejudice,* Jane Austen notes with frequency the blushes and colorings of her characters. Austen's blushes seem sometimes to work as natural and involuntary signals of embarrassment, vexation, or love. Jane Bennet, for example, blushes the warmth of her feelings for Bingley even while verbally denying their strength. ("You doubt me," cried Jane, slightly colouring; "indeed you have no reason. He may live in my memory as the most amiable man of my acquaintance, but that is all" [134].) It may seem to Jane when she blushes—as it may seem to all of us who are self-conscious, when we blush—that her body tells the truth to spite her. The body that blushes so is a body that betrays, even while betraying a truth, a body that involuntarily obtrudes itself on the propriety of Jane's assertion that she has yet this blessing, "nothing" with which "to reproach" the man who has abandoned if not seduced her (134).[8]

Yet social propriety is of course also served by blushes, even by blushes such as these. The blush that reddens the white lie, that unfounds the verbal construct, is a blush that reassures in delivering on the promise implicit in the possibility of embarrassment: legibility. Jane's blush offers Elizabeth the reassuring promise of a feeling self beneath the self-denials of good manners, even if the cost of reassurance demands the expense of sympathetic pain: Elizabeth, reassured, can know what Jane feels; she can know that she has been right in knowing it all along; she can love and praise Jane the more for the ineptitude with which she masks her continuing attachment;[9] better, she can know her sister physically incapable of dissembling.[10] Jane's very body tells despite her the truth of her integrity.

More efficient and more dense in the processes by which they signify in *Pride and Prejudice* are those blushes blushed for others. For her mother, for example, Elizabeth Bennet "blushed and blushed again" (100). And when Lydia and Wickham return from their wedding, the enthusiastic Lydia and her new husband fail to register the colors evidently appropriate to elopement as occasion. Austen writes of Elizabeth that, receiving the Wickhams in the breakfast room, "*She* blushed, and Jane blushed; but the cheeks of the two who caused their confusion, suffered no variation of colour" (316). Austen's writing makes and enforces a social and physical law: for her characters, it is as if in this room, at this time, so much blushing must occur; if those responsible for the pressure of its imperatives do not respond to that pressure, response then becomes the social obligation of those who recognize the insistence of its pulse.

Yet how is this sense of obligatory blushing to be reconciled with blushing like Jane's that can be thought to prove something precisely in being involuntary? Elizabeth and Jane cannot blush here, as they might smile somewhere else, willingly, eagerly, appropriately;[11] voluntary coloring requires the assistance of a covert pinch or powdered brush. It seems rather that the bodies of Jane and Elizabeth are written by Austen as thoroughly socialized bodies, bodies so schooled in their obligations that these bodies respond to circumstantial pressure, anticipating or obviating consciousness of obligation. When Elizabeth and Jane blush, their blood tells, as we are told blood will, their knowledge and their socialization, even as it tells the failures of Lydia's socialization, tells what I am unable quite to call Lydia's "innocence." The constraint of my discourse ("unable quite") is the constraint exercised by Austen's narrative on the urge to read as proof of Lydia's innocence Lydia's failure to blush; not blushing, Lydia could be imagined not to know she is supposed to, not to know, that is, the social code by which her actions are read as something less than virtuous. And the rush of blushes to the faces of her sisters might seem to give those faces, after all, a somewhat more knowing look. Schooled and socialized myself in the narrative code by which I know to read Elizabeth as heroine, I have learned to want from her the blush by which I may read virtue and innocence, but I am vexed by its appearance; innocence, after all, is compromised by the knowledge that raises the blush. And yet Elizabeth's blush, duplicitous as it might be in showing a socialized innocence as inevitably curtailed by the knowledge that constitutes socialization, is finally, too, a gesture of reassurance. Like the act of confession, the blush of embarrassment supports and perpetuates the social scheme within the novel and the narrative scheme that is the novel in their promise to offer and control the flirtations of vice and virtue by permitting the fluctuations of red and white.

Austen's notorious flirtation with her readers' abilities to assess vice and virtue in the case of Darcy and Wickham depends on the fluctuations of color between men rather than on one man's cheeks. Describing Wickham's first meeting with Darcy, in *Pride and Prejudice*, Austen outlines in color "the effect of the meeting." "Both," she writes, "changed colour, one looked white, the other red" (73). Correct assignment of colors to characters (correct reading of somatic signs) has sometimes proven difficult for readers of this passage, especially, perhaps, for first-time readers ignorant (not to say innocent) of the prejudicial knowledge they will come to acquire or less practiced in working the codes by which one recognizes a novel's hero; one need not know at this point in the novel that Darcy's is the righteous, angry blanching, Wickham's the embarrassed blush.[12] When "one looks white, the other red," blood circulates within a single social body; one countenance drains of blood, it seems, that the other might register blood's rush. That color in this passage is not specific to character eliminates the distraction of individual subjectivity and evacuates it of significance; readerly ineptitude here serves at the display of the social body: every blush is the blush of the social body, every change in color an indication of its health in giving bashful assent to social obligation. In establishing this circulatory property of embarrassed or righteous blood, Austen creates the circumstantial and systemic obligation that the obliging Jane and equally obliging Elizabeth answer, in the breakfast room, for the unembarrassed newly wed.

Austen describes an unchanged Lydia, returned to the Bennet family circle: "Lydia was Lydia still; untamed, unabashed, wild, noisy, and fearless" (315). With Lydia "Lydia still," the good Austen reader is asked to mime the reactions of the good Bennet sisters in being, like Elizabeth, "disgusted," like Jane, "shocked" (315). Indulging with smug piety my disgust and shock as such a reader, I face what my apparent distress signals I want, sadistically, from this scene: I want, it seems, Lydia tamed, abashed, silenced; I want Lydia's "ease" of manner disrupted (317); I want Lydia blushing, Lydia mortified, Lydia stilled. But the sadistic pleasures of good reading will not have to cease in satisfaction since I want what Austen assures me I will never have to have. "It was not to be supposed that time would give Lydia that embarrassment, from which she had been so wholly free at first" (317). Given that Lydia herself seems contentedly married to "dear Wickham" ("he did every thing best in the world" [318]), reader distress apparently *for* Lydia turns out to be self-motivated, self-interested, compensatory. As an uneducated body, Lydia can seem to possess that "better" contentment Darcy later identifies for Elizabeth: the contentment of ignorance (369). The mortified pity for Lydia that Austen manages to induce is envy at Lydia's ability to escape the somatic coercions of social knowledge with which devoted readers of Jane Austen remain possessed; such pity is the pity of the knowing for themselves. Unlike Lydia—possessed of her own strong and unblushing body ("Oh!" said Lydia stoutly, "I am not afraid; for though I *am* the youngest, I'm the tallest" [8])—devoted readers of Jane Austen put their devotion to work in a display of the self-consciousness acquired as part of the mannerly inhabitation of social and textual spaces.[13] Decorous comportment within these spaces permits a kind of reciprocal inhabitation: responsive to pressures within the social and textual spaces I inhabit, learning to blush for parts of the social body or the reddening text, I submit my body to inhabitation by them; emptied by circumstance of all that circumstance does not demand, I may answer its dictates with myself, having become—unexpectedly, appropriately—"all amazement" (260), "all politeness" (26), all mortification.

Austen's prognostication for Lydia, though, is finally less a source of disappointment than—again—of reassurance. More or less sadistic in my reading pleasures, perhaps, than I have allowed myself to think, I do not want Lydia to have learned embarrassment; Lydia stilled represents an obstruction to narrative. That Lydia, unembarrassed, is still "untamed, unabashed, wild" permits and encourages the embarrassed pleasures of social circulation. Like Mary Bennet, "impatient for display" (25), I have become perverse in learning to enjoy the flush by which I blush for Lydia still. The text that engenders embarrassment offers and teaches as a pleasure indulgence in mortification's textually modulated pain.

It is appropriate that embarrassment should be among the pleasures of reading Jane Austen, since embarrassment is the site of those somatic pleasures Austen's novel is willing to acknowledge.[14] Embarrassed reading mimics the signs by which love is legible in *Pride and Prejudice,* signs that *Pride and Prejudice* itself has taught are to be read as signs of love rather than embarrassment. Late in the novel, Elizabeth, finding Jane and Bingley together in the Bennets' drawing room, is foiled herself in trying to foil again her mother's attempts to leave them alone. Austen describes the scene made and unmade by Elizabeth's entrance, highlighting what will indicate that a proposal has been made and been accepted. Elizabeth, Austen writes,

saw, to her infinite surprise, there was reason to fear that her mother had been too ingenious for her. On opening the door, she perceived her sister and Bingley standing together over the hearth, as if engaged in earnest conversation; and had this led to no suspicion, the faces of both as they hastily turned round, and moved away from each other, would have told it all. *Their* situation was awkward enough; but *her's* she thought was still worse. Not a syllable was uttered by either; and Elizabeth was on the point of going away again, when Bingley, who as well as the other had sat down, suddenly rose, and whispering a few words to her sister, ran out of the room. (346)

Entering, Elizabeth registers averted eyes, confusion, awkwardness, coloring, separation, silence, embarrassment. Separating from his beloved and running from the site of his embarrassment, Bingley runs from Jane's account of their betrothal as Elizabeth has twice run from Lydia's account of her wedding. Bingley's action stages Austen's erotics of embarrassment.[15] While Bingley the runaway is embarrassed by the erotic and would escape its revelation, Jane Austen in making him so produces a scene in which embarrassment *is* what's erotic. The text in which it is separation that represents desire is also, here and throughout, a text that takes its pleasures where it is able to find them, confusing for pleasure's sake the blush of embarrassment with the flush of arousal.

No surprise that the heroine of this novel is sensible to the pleasures embarrassment arouses, finding them first, untainted and unalloyed by the charms of Darcy or of his estate, at the ball at Netherfield. Elizabeth's first two dances are with Mr. Collins, and Austen writes that in these "dances of mortification" Mr. Collins gave to Elizabeth "all the shame and misery which a disagreeable partner for a couple of dances can give" (90).[16] And yet, for Elizabeth, the dances, if apparently not Mr. Collins himself, offer another gift: "The moment of her release from him was exstacy" (90). Elizabeth's joy, not to say *jouissance,* when freed of association with her partner, is produced by the hydraulics of embarrassment: release is the consequence of mortification's restraints; ecstasy is the end to which, if by way of shame and misery, the dances of mortification have led.

Elizabeth's ecstatic response to her dances with Mr. Collins invites articulation of what goes largely without saying in *Pride and Prejudice:* why Elizabeth does not love Mr. Collins. If eroticism in the novel is signaled by embarrassed blushes, then Mr. Collins surely ought to be beloved. And by the novel and its readers, in some way, he is. Yet his insensible participation in the dances of mortification ("often moving wrong without being aware of it" [90]) prevents him from experiencing with Elizabeth either mortification (even hers) or the ecstatic release that is its product. Mortified by the dances—by pure figure—Elizabeth does not suffer her mortification at the hands of Mr. Collins; exposed by Austen, exposed to readers, she is not exposed to him (characteristically he is "apologising instead of attending" [90]) as chastening by Collins would seem to require.

As part of her erotics of embarrassment, Austen conceives, in the novel's central relationship, a process by which mortification might come to be experienced as mutual, its dances partnered. Elizabeth's first account of Darcy sets up a relationship in which he is all pride, she all mortification: "I could easily forgive *his* pride, if he had not mortified *mine*" (20).[17] Later, noting the extent of Darcy's attention to her one evening at Netherfield and unable—in light of what she has overheard—to construe that attention as admiration, Elizabeth believes instead that Darcy watches her "because there was a something about her more wrong and reprehensible, according to his ideas of right, than in any other person present" (51). Reading Darcy, Elizabeth imagines herself in his regard occupying the most special place possible for the mortified: if not the most approved, she must be the most reprehensible. The temptation to believe Elizabeth's imaginings mistaken is itself mistaken: in just a few more sentences Darcy is shown to be occupied with worry about preserving himself from mortifying association with "the inferiority of her connections" (52). The unequal relation here between Darcy's elevation and Elizabeth's abjection will have to be balanced, according to Austen's erotics, in a sort of bleak reciprocity.[18] As Elizabeth is conclusively mortified, proven wrong by Darcy's letter's "mortifying . . . reproach" (209), and led by that mortification to be able to love Darcy, Darcy is himself conclusively mortified by Elizabeth's reproach that he has not been the gentleman he has thought himself.[19]

Pride and Prejudice demonstrates the finally inevitable association of mortification with the narratives that generate knowledge, learning, education. The moments at which characters experience mortification are moments at which they are forced to recognize themselves in retellings of themselves—as merely "tolerable," as inferiorly connected, as ungentlemanly, as proud or prejudicial. As objects of one another's narrations, Darcy and Elizabeth suffer the abuse of being disabused. The revised notions of the self constructed in these mortifications find powerful support in the ready responses of the socialized body. Reading from within a culture as much made as represented by Jane Austen, I believe—or wish—these responses involuntary (in polite company, their intrusions are said, reassuringly, to be ill-mannered and antisocial), and I believe the discomfitting sincerity of mortification as I cannot believe the uncomfortable posturings of best behavior and best manners; the body's support of mortification permits the welcome "recognition," in mortification's stories, of a bad self, a self that if bad is nevertheless knowable, credible, potentially self-possessed. When Elizabeth claims that her mortification by Darcy is "self-attracted" (209), she as much values as blames her self for its achievement. Prizing in love, as in mortification, what is "self-attracted," the reader who learns love from Jane Austen learns to believe in mortification's testimony as the testimony of the body, which still serves as phantasmatic ground for a self unknowable in manners except through the body's irruptions. In *Pride and Prejudice,* love is a response to being known and, further, of being known in the way finally most credible—as that which one might not want to be known to be. The beloved's pleasure in such knowledge is the same as the pleasure to be taken in embarrassment: the thrill of being known, the *frisson* of exposure. And, provided by embarrassment—or by love, as it is learned from Jane Austen—exposure seems the logical extreme to which heightening sensation might push embarrassment's fantasy of legibility. Blushing or loving, in such terms, means wanting to know oneself legible, and wanting to know oneself so by the only imaginable proof of that legibility: the exposure of whatever discomforts, disappoints, pains, subjects, mortifies.

In *Pride and Prejudice,* exposure is achieved by the society of accomplishment's encouragement of display. As Mary Bennet's delight at displaying her musical accomplishments turns into the nightmare of having delighted long enough, her own father tells her she must "let the other young ladies have time to exhibit" (101). Exhibiting intransitively, young ladies will seem inevitably to exhibit reflexively, and, for the mannerly in the novel, witnessing such exhibition will yield "agonies" and "painful sensations" (100). The extent of Mary's delights is not, of course, her own nightmare; it is her sister's. It is Elizabeth (in her resistance to playing and singing, socially *just right*) who experiences Mary's exposure, as she experiences Lydia's, and her family's: "To Elizabeth it appeared, that had her family made an agreement to expose themselves as much as they could during the evening, it would have been impossible for them to play their parts with more spirit, or finer success" (101–2). The exquisite agonies of perfect embarrassment by her family permit Elizabeth to indulge in conspiracy theorizing. Out to expose themselves, the Bennets must be out to expose her. But what Elizabeth construes as unfortunate nevertheless functions in some way *for* her: unlike Mary and Lydia—able, despite or because of their insensibility to social pressure, to feel the manifest pleasures of display—Elizabeth will be able to feel its pleasures only in alloy, as exposure. Further, until she is mortified by Darcy, she will be unable to experience even exposure in her own person. She needs the Bennets (the mannerly need the ill-mannered); and so does the even-countenanced sister for whom she cares so much. In her efforts to keep Jane Bennet decorously separated from the returned Bingley, Elizabeth *would* keep them separated. In this novel of manners, the well-behaved and conscious sister would hinder the marriage plot, while the gauche sister, eager to open the secret of Darcy's role at her wedding, facilitates its progress. Impeding exposure, good manners impede the warm pleasures exposure generates.

When Elizabeth tries to persuade her father to keep Lydia from traveling with the regiment, Mr. Bennet advises her that "Lydia will never be easy till she has exposed herself in some public place or other" (230).[20] What seems wrong about this nevertheless testifies to its astuteness: Lydia, who has never seemed anything but easy, has also never not seemed to expose herself. Mr. Bennet's speech is astute, as well, about the erotics of the novel, in which happiness, contentment, satisfaction, ease are produced by the pleasures of exposure. But existing only in ease and exposure, Lydia unexpectedly resembles the frustratingly good Jane, who can seem, in parallel, to exist only in manners and smiles. Lydia's ease, suggestive as it is of a kind of vacancy, seems unerotic beside the tensions and releases that constitute Elizabeth's mortified sensibility.

Mr. Bennet's stipulation that a condition of exposure is its occurrence "in some public place" could seem to evacuate novel-reading of exposed pleasures; the ease of novel-reading might reside, after all, precisely in the safe isolation of its exposures. And yet, like some other privacies, that of novel-reading seems to involve not solitude but an intimacy born of the precariousness of separation and identification, an exposure in which one feels, if most sheltered, also most vulnerable. When Wayne Booth writes of the Jane Austen narrator in *Emma* that "we accept her as representing everything we admire most" (265), he articulates the position of an awed and vulnerable readership, naked and notorious in the tenacity of its devotion to Jane Austen.

After reading Jane's epistolary revelation of Lydia's elopement and chastising herself for failing to prevent it with revelations she has withheld, Elizabeth contemplates the way in which, with Darcy, "her power was sinking" (278). Austen describes the means by which Elizabeth attempts to elude self-reflection with the distractions afforded by the elements of Lydia's plot:

> But self, though it would intrude, could not engross her. Lydia—the humiliation, the misery, she was bringing on them all, soon swallowed up every private care; and covering her face with her handkerchief, Elizabeth was soon lost to every thing else; and, after a pause of several minutes, was only recalled to a sense of her situation by the voice of her companion . . . in a manner, which though it spoke compassion, spoke likewise restraint. (278)

Elizabeth's escape from self in Lydia's story (this is a scene of reading) seems perversely to return her to a self-consciousness the privacy of which is made public by the handkerchief that is its cover. Alone but not alone, Elizabeth is roused from immersion and loss of self, as from a book, by a voice which, like that of the narrator who offers companionship in the intimacies of reading *Pride and Prejudice*, extending compassion likewise secures restraints.

Thanks to Mr. Collins, to Mrs. Bennet, to Mrs. Bennet's younger daughters, to other Austen characters who delight in embarrassing; thanks to the contagious responses of Elizabeth and Jane; thanks to Austen's highlighting of those spaces that might be colored with a reader's blush; and thanks even to what identifies readerly failures; readers of

Jane Austen have ample opportunity to exercise their faculties for embarrassment. Blushing like Elizabeth again and again, readers may learn to blush ever more readily in response to social and textual pressures felt and functioning as physical ones. Blushes blushed—repeatedly—at Austen's behest are pulsings and pressures, now incorporated, that echo, in displacing them, the more conventionally corporal rhythms of chastening, chastising mortification.[21] Embarrassment's colloquial relation "mortification" describes with punning aptitude the process by which the socialized body draws repeatedly to its surface its own blood.

When Lewes writes, then, of Jane Austen's flawed sense of the body's relations, he fails to see that its "connections," as she registers them, are more "subtle" than the connections he imagines she misses. If Jane Austen minimizes the bodily dimension, her mode is mortification's own mode of diminishment by reminder. *Pride and Prejudice* describes, evokes, demands the bodily response that is blushing; and when the novel gets the response it demands, it does so because it understands—because Austen understands—that those of us who blush believe, with pain and pleasure, in the tales their blushes tell. And, in turn, our belief that our blushes are able to reveal our truths supports the social and textual systems that generate them for circulation. Finding pleasure in embarrassment and mortification, we seem to find it in the romance of the involuntary; but, like *Pride and Prejudice* itself, we may have learned to take our pleasures where we find them—even if in the satisfying and reduplicating self-consciousness of our suspicion that the tale told by our blushes may be only the narrative of our bodies' inevitable fulfillment of their social obligations.[22]

It has most recently seemed new to discover the constitution by manners of a social aesthetic that, as aesthetics do, promulgates and enforces certain ethical values. Yet recuperable is an understanding as well that the manifest content of manners is most often the management of somatic response, the behavior of the body. It makes sense, then, that in support of the mannerly effort to contain events of the body within a system of signification, Austen chooses to work with and on the blush, which event of the body, in its comings and goings, is most suggestive and provocative of signification. It is the wonder of Jane Austen that, in engendering an adaptation to the condition she helps put in place, she has also invented a perversity that simply *is* the display of good manners—of having the grace to blush: Jane Austen discovers pleasures in the ability of embarrassment's pangs to recover a sense of the body in manners; readers of Jane Austen may discover those pleasures and acquire a habit of mind that, reading sometimes perversely, reads nonetheless with perverse accuracy.

Chapter Two Mortifying Persuasions, or
the Worldliness of Jane Austen

*M*y last chapter argued that in *Pride and Prejudice* Jane Austen
puts in place a system of social support grounded in the blush.
While using the blush as a stable and reliable register of character in *Pride
and Prejudice,* Austen also manages to manipulate the blush in a way that
seems more subversive of social order than the blush's ostensible stability
and reliability might suggest. Austen's blush—her perverse adaptation to
the system of socially recuperable legibility that the novel of manners (*her*
novel of manners) puts in place and maintains—is the crucial component
of her erotics of embarrassment, an erotics that offers and takes perverse
pleasure in its conversion of the sign of good manners into the sign of
desire. Nevertheless, though recovering a sense of bodily presence in
manners, Austen's blush performs this recovery in order to do the social
work of including the body in manners by arranging for the manageable
exercise of desires within marriage: Austen's blush works invariably in
service of the marriage plot.

In writing *Persuasion,* however, Austen writes a novel the plot of
which simply *is* the acknowledgment (envisaged as a threat) that not all
plots end in marriage,[1] and in which her systemic employment of the
blush is endangered by the barely contained risk involved in nudging the
erotics of mortification toward an anxiogenic and always recognizable
extreme: mortification in *Persuasion* always might end in insensibility
rather than sensation, numbness rather than *frisson.* As if robbed, by
some imp, of faith in her perversions, Austen confronts in *Persuasion* the
danger of conventional definition: while in *Pride and Prejudice* Austen
has managed to reconstrue separation as the very sign of erotic presence,
in *Persuasion,* engagement with the plot depends on separation's seeming
always about to mean *separation,* indeed estrangement; and while in the
earlier novel, mortification reminds the well-mannered body of the pleasures as well as the pains of the somatic condition, in the later one,
mortification threatens by the boredom of repetition to diminish the

body's pleasures as it weakens its pangs. The energies produced by mortification's use in the novel of manners circulate between such reminder and such diminishment; *Pride and Prejudice*'s exploitation of somatic reminder seems at first to have given way in *Persuasion* to the heroine's interest in harnessing the energies of somatic diminishment. Anne Elliot's sophistication in the ways of mortification, and her wistful hope that its pains harden and habituate an untouchable self, allow Austen to amplify and to resolve her contradictory sense of mortification and to explore more widely a world of issues that always revolve around mortification as she writes it; questions of knowing and narration, of sophistication and self-possession—for Austen as for some later nineteenth-century English novelists—are most visible and articulable as responses to the fact or the prospect of mortification.

"Anne haggard"

In his early-nineteenth-century treatise on blushing, Dr. Thomas Burgess writes of an entire family suffering under what he calls a "diseased sensibility," a tendency to blush too much.[2] Citing Burgess, later in the century, in his own discussion of blushing in *The Expression of the Emotions in Man and Animals,* Charles Darwin, too, writes of this "father, mother and ten children, all of whom, without exception, were prone to blush to a most painful degree."[3] Darwin's brief discussion of the family includes a report that (ultimately unsuccessful) attempts had been made to cure this tendency in the children by sending them to travel around the world so that their "diseased sensibility" might be worn away. Though the logic by which travel might be imagined to effect an abrasive cure remains unexplained in Burgess's text and in Darwin's, Austen's *Persuasion* offers proleptically two accounts of mortification that make a kind of sense of the blushing family's expeditious efforts to disable the blush, and thinking about the blushing family helps me articulate the methods of mortification in *Persuasion.*

The first of these accounts of the way the sensible family might imagine travel as a cure for blushing and mortification (I reserve the second for somewhat later in my discussion) is ultimately a psychological account. In the context of his citations of doctors', missionaries', and traders' recuperative stories of distressed encounters with blushing as they witness it in "all the races of mankind,"[4] Darwin's allusion to travel as a potential cure for excessive blushing invokes a notion of travel as constituted by a series of embarrassments. Respondents to Darwin's survey about gestures and expressions they have noted during their travels are invited and enabled by Darwin's questions to project embarrassment onto those bodies they have been asked to survey, but responses to Darwin's questions serve also as a registry of the particularities (embodiments of sex and race, embodiment itself, indifference to British values)[5] that embarrass and mortify the surveillant imperial traveler, whose ostensible exemption from enduring surveillance is revoked in performing it; in making the observations that inform their answers to his questions, Darwin's respondents might (incorrectly) be imagined to evade the surveillance they perform upon others, but, as he uses it, the information they provide Darwin reveals the circumstances that produce embarrassment (and the habits that constitute it) for his imperial travelers as much as it reveals the embarrassed situations and blushing habits of the world inhabitants they have encountered. Continually shocked and embarrassed, the traveler is habituated to what shocks and embarrasses, and, in fantasy at least, ceases to experience embarrassment. Traveling is imagined thus to accommodate the traveler to the scandalous fact of the world (more mortifying than any of its particularities), and to sophisticate the traveler's response to it. Made both literally and colloquially more worldly by their travels—as if having been *there* provocatively indicated they might actually have done *that*—the blushing family would exorcise naiveté by indulging it; mortification, working by this account from inside out, would (though it doesn't) teach a jaded response to travel that sends phantasmatically home an insensible family, exhausted, unblushing, and even perhaps haggard.

Anne Elliot's complex and perverse relation to mortification in *Persuasion* inheres in her desire to exploit its capacity to refine and to render insensible. "Nobody" to her father and sister, or at best "only Anne,"[6] she has had to accustom herself to mortification and, having done so, comes to see herself as having earned peculiar recourse to its assistance. Described sometimes as "hardened" or as hardening her nerves, Anne tries to manage her feelings by willful invocation of insensibility and indifference. Awaiting the unsought return of her nevertheless lamented suitor Wentworth, Anne resolves upon a way to handle her irritation at the stimulating inanities of her companions: "To hear them talking so much of Captain Wentworth . . . was a new sort of trial to Anne's nerves. She found, however, that it was one to which she must enure herself. Since he actually was expected in the country, she must teach herself to be insensible on such points" (52). So, repeating to herself for their painful and salutary value Wentworth's remarks about her worsened appearance, Anne "began to rejoice that she had heard them. They were of sobering tendency; they allayed agitation; they composed, and consequently must make her happier" (61). Anne's replication of her mortification by Wentworth's words makes of mortification a tool to hand, which if it is unable to respond to the pressure of Anne's insistence (the words *must* make her happier) is yet able to assist at the exquisite and sophisticated pains and pleasures memory makes available to her: "when pain is over, the remembrance of it often becomes a pleasure," Anne later explains to Wentworth, describing what might be called her erotic life "with a faint blush at some recollections" (184).

While Austen imagines Anne as using mortification for such pleasure as she can find, she also continues to imagine her (as I have imagined the traveling family) using mortification, with at least some small success, in the search for insensibility. Anne's ability to make mortification a pleasure in private recollections depends on the danger (for Austen, if not for Anne) of its sometimes ending in numbness. Though she notes the "imprudence" of her family's preference over her of the freckled and vulgar Mrs. Clay,[7] for example, "Anne herself was become hardened to such affronts" (34); so, teaching herself "to be insensible," Anne might actually attain insensibility.

In discussing Austen's interest in Anne's attempts to become insensible, I find myself using the language of precariousness ("danger," "threat") in order to create a sense of impending novelistic disaster. But what disaster, really? Austen's carefully cultivated atmosphere of familial abjection, in which it is a consolation that "to be claimed as a good, though in an improper style, is at least better than being rejected as no good at all" (33), suggests that Anne has ample need of what protection she can find. Insensibility would seem to offer merest sustenance when the "usual fate of Anne" attends: "having something very opposite from her inclination fixed on" (14). But insensibility is a value for Anne only so long as she remains disentangled from the erotic and from the plottings of courtship and marriage; in writing Anne's realized (rather than simulated) indifference, her achieved (rather than wished) insensibility, Austen would be writing interference with her own aims, the realization of which (Anne's success in the marriage plot) is dependent on Anne's attractions. Austen's comic attentions to Sir Walter Elliot, in fact, and their apparent dismissal of his thinking, anticipate and perhaps distract readers from the impending recognition that *Persuasion*'s plot, no less than Sir Walter's toilet, demands unceasing attention to appearance. Austen's mockery of Sir Walter's obsession with his appearance and with everyone else's ("every face in the neighborhood worsting" [6] but "such a number of looking-glasses!" [128]) signifies the fractious kinship that delights in distinction; despite this mockery, Austen is far from being so cheerily bromidic as to offer or accept the dictum that looks don't matter. And Anne has a problem, as one might once have said, in the looks department.

For if Anne's sad attempts to render herself insensible to the pain of mortification are matters more of resolve than of execution and tend finally to be unsuccessful—her need for their recourse seems endless—her mortified self-abuse succeeds in mortification's more traditional aim; Anne's frequently noted loss of youth and bloom signals that she has achieved some measure of dislocation from her body. If mortification, despite Anne's skilled attempts, is useless at deadening her affections, what it evidently has done is alter her complexion. Though Anne "had been a very pretty girl," Austen writes, "her bloom had vanished early" and left her "haggard" (6); "an early loss of bloom and spirits" is the consequence of her "attachment" to Wentworth and of her "regrets" (28); worse, "the years which had destroyed her youth and bloom had only given [Wentworth] a more glowing, manly, open look" (61); and even in more hopeful moments, as an "elegant little woman of seven and twenty," Anne has only "every beauty excepting bloom" (153).

Austen's project, then, in writing a heroine beset by mortification's diminishments and by its potential failures in the realm of the complexion must be the recovery of that heroine for feeling and the restoration of her to materiality. Austen's projected makeover of Anne's complexion will offer Anne the gift of objectification and will suggest that, like Anne, Austen enjoys sophisticated consolation, preferring that her heroine be claimed as a good than that she be thought no good at all.[8]

Centrifugal Forces

Anne Elliot's welcoming embrace of mortification distinguishes her from the worldly and sophisticated characters with whom Austen surrounds her. If sophisticated in the ways of mortification, Anne is an unsophisticated player in the world at large. But Anne's centrality to and periodic abjection within a world of characters who would claim privileged access to sophistication (members of her family, Lady Russell, Mr. Elliot, Mrs. Smith) permit Austen to consider mortification alongside a most distinctly Austenian narratological trait—sophistication—and in relation to that compound of knowledge, behavior, speech, and display that *Persuasion* in particular might want to call worldliness.

Late in the novel, Anne watches as her patroness Lady Russell extends her head to watch the progress of Captain Wentworth, the lover Anne had given up in compliance with Lady Russell's persuasions.[9] Drawing back her head, Lady Russell responds to Anne's unspoken question, "Now, how would she speak of him?"

"You will wonder," said she, "what has been fixing my eye so long; but I was looking after some window-curtains, which Lady Alicia and Mrs. Frankland were telling me of last night. They described the drawing-room window-curtains of one of the houses on this side of the way, and this part of the street, as being the handsomest and best hung of any in Bath, but could not recollect the exact number, and I have been trying to find out which it could be." (179)

That Lady Russell's lengthy account of her viewing habits is a more or less smooth attempt to cover with bluff banality the mortification of being seen to look after Wentworth seems clear enough, there being no real reason to testify that one *was* looking at curtains (handsome and well-hung) except to explain that one was *not* looking at a man. But D. W. Harding's quarrel, in the footnotes to his edition of *Persuasion*, with R. W. Chapman's seemingly incontrovertible reading of Lady Russell as "prevaricating" suggests that for at least one reader Lady Russell makes her excuses with aplomb.[10] The surprise of Harding's response lies in the refusal of the urbane critic who isolated Austen's "regulated hatred" to exercise on Lady Russell his otherwise habitually suspicious faculties.[11] Harding's eager protectiveness of Lady Russell at this point in the text seems less concerned with a particular reading of Lady Russell than with an unwillingness to disrupt a certain fantasy of class and sophistication, and of sophistication's ability to cover and to cover for mortification. Reading *Persuasion* with some interest in the secondary characters, I feel always as focused on something I have learned from Jane Austen as on Jane Austen herself—focused, that is, on the extent to which sophistication is bound up with mortification. Sophistication's work, reading Austen can suggest, is to defend against the recognitions that comprise mortification.

Austen characteristically associates mortification with the aggressive import of what she calls (with breathtaking understatement) "spontaneous information" (60) arising from story or, most famously in Austen, from overheard conversation. It is Anne Elliot's sister Mary who forces upon Anne recognitions about her altered looks, imposing spontaneously upon Anne the information that Wentworth has noted the change: "Captain Wentworth is not very gallant by you, Anne, though he was so attentive to me. Henrietta asked him what he thought of you, when they went away; and he said, 'You were so altered he should not have known you again'" (60). Anne's submission to Mary's narrative in "silent, deep mortification" signals that she is hurt, obviously and of course, by what she seems to learn here about her personal appearance. Hurt to think she has become unattractive, Anne imagines that Wentworth, when in her presence, looks at her only to trace in her face the "ruins" of what he had once found pleasing.[12] But Mary's attack on Anne also involves Mary's easy but effective assumption of epistemological advantage. Anne's unattractiveness must seem to Anne to have been a secret from which *she* has been excluded, but which Mary, Henrietta, and Wentworth have been in on together. Even worse, Mary's callous dropping of the secret ("perfectly unsuspicious of being inflicting any particular wound") tags it as, to her as to Wentworth and Henrietta, knowledge so common that Anne needn't be protected from it; in being told this way, Anne is granted not even the sad privileges custom accords the last to know.

Mary's revelation that Wentworth found Anne altered beyond recognition is encrypted, if barely so, in a narrative of his intimacy with Henrietta Musgrove. Hurt by the comments about her and hurt by the romantic content of that narrative, Anne is also mortified by her merely secondary place in it. Mortified by her status as character in the story of Wentworth's confidences, Anne is dispossessed of the least narrative of which she might fancy herself the subject—the story of her failed attractions. Hearing her sister's story, Austen writes, "Anne fully submitted in silent, deep, mortification" (60–61). In her submission (to the account of her looks, to the reign of appearance, to the version of herself Wentworth's comments and Mary's story construct, to mortification), Anne yields authority (submits) to her sister's narrative, empowered as it is by its exploitation of mortification's persuasive sway. In writing so powerful a description of Anne's submission, Austen articulates a version or a fantasy of the narratee, whose submission to the intrusions of narrative upon naiveté is always a mortification and whose submissions themselves constitute painful or pleasurable admissions; in submitting to narrative and mortification, Anne opens and surrenders her self to narrative's possession, surrenders self-possession.

"'I know it all, I know it all,' cried Mrs. Smith," anticipating the next steps in Anne's story of Mr. Elliot's abandoned flirtation with Anne's sister (200). Though in her betraying eagerness she fails to do it cool justice, Anne's former schoolfellow wields sophistication's stiletto in defense against mortification's persuasions. Nothing more deflates the storyteller than the sophisticate's refusal of submission: "I know" or (more subtle) "I heard." Most recognizable when "knowing the score," the sophisticate is the one who, never a know-it-all, nevertheless knows it all already. Sophistication responds to the threat of being made a character (the threat of characterization) by assuming the position of knowledge or of telling. Beside the liveliness of Elizabeth Bennet, who with greater success or at least with greater appeal assumes a pleasing and knowing sophistication in telling for laughs the story of being slighted by Mr. Bingley's wealthy friend ("I believe, Ma'am, I may safely promise you *never* to dance with him"),[13] Anne Elliot's sad eagerness to replay her mortification by watching for Wentworth to trace her faded features can seem dispirited and weak; but, touching in its determination, it remains a strong and private attempt to reclaim narrative. Seeking and seeing Wentworth's displeasure, she would tell for herself the story of her losses and of his.

Among the most essential of submissions articulated for Anne Elliot in *Persuasion* is this one: "to feel that another lesson, in the art of knowing our own nothingness beyond our own circle, was become necessary for her" (42). Taught this lesson by each removal to Uppercross from her family home at Kellynch, Anne wishes its "advantage" on her father and eldest sister (for their neglect, the reciprocation of Anne's gracious aggression?), who might learn from it, as she has, "how unknown, or unconsidered there, were the affairs which at Kellynch-hall were treated as of such general publicity and pervading interest" (42). But the implications of this lesson extend beyond Anne to Austen and to Austen's readership. The demands of reading Jane Austen have generated notorious alliances between writer and readers and in doing so have produced a devoted readership practiced in the ways, and sophisticated in the acknowledgments, of an Austenian universe. Truly to have learned, from Austen or from other venues, the art of knowing one's nothingness beyond one's circle is, of course, to have learned one's abjection; but it is perhaps also to have learned a strategy with which to manipulate one's abjection into centrality. One's nothingness beyond it makes one's circle all important; to travel beyond it is to risk confronting the mortification of one's nothingness. But Austen's formulation suggests the centrifugal value of that mortification to the desperate maintenance of community. Sophistication inheres in knowing one's circle; in the display and circulation within it of one's knowledge; in knowing, too, one's nothingness beyond the circle; and in behaving as if that knowledge has no consequence.

On the scale, then, of text rather than of character, *Persuasion*'s submission to its nothingness inheres in its recognition (so difficult for Darwin's correspondents) of the fact of the world and in its daring if limited admission of the world to a place of consequence in the novel. Referring both to that social *monde* from which Mrs. Smith and Mr. Elliot have emerged and to that larger entity in which the text's naval population have claimed prizes for Empire and home, *Persuasion*'s "world" links the social with the geographic entity as alike in empiric yield; both are sources of sophisticating experience.[14]

"She had lived very much in the world," writes Austen of Mrs. Smith, as a way of accounting for "the dissipations of the past" (153). This association of world and dissipation—so immediate that one simply explains the other—tells something about Mrs. Smith (if charming, she is also worldly and therefore suspect), but also about a certain fantasy of the worldly world as dissolute and even enervating. When she describes her past friendship and that of her late husband with Anne's cousin Mr. Elliot, Mrs. Smith tells *what she knows,* and in asserting this epistemological privilege over the mortification of *not* knowing, Mrs. Smith portrays all the better a friendship so worldly as to permit a special confidence and intimacy between Mr. Elliot and herself:

"I know he was invited and encouraged, and I know he did not choose to go. I can satisfy you, perhaps, on points which you would little expect; and as to his marriage, I knew all about it at the time. I was privy to all the fors and againsts, I was the friend to whom he confided his hopes and plans, and though I did not know his wife previously, . . . yet I knew her all her life afterwards . . . and can answer any question you wish to put." (200)

The dangers of such intimacy ("He told me the whole story. He had no concealments with me" [201]) might be among those dissipations that simply mean sophisticated worldliness in *Persuasion*. But if "dissipation" evokes a sense of dissolute practices (considering Mr. Elliot, Anne "saw that there had been bad habits" [161]),[15] it also denotes a breaking up, and the bad feeling or bad blood between Mr. Elliot and Mrs. Smith denotes the rupture of the Smith/Elliot circle, which—although, like any sophisticated alliance, it may have been produced for its centrifugal defense against social mortification—proved finally unstable in the presence of those embarrassments (financial ones) determinative of social nothingness.

For all that Mrs. Smith, by way of her past pleasures, is the figure of sophistication in the book, she is introduced as a faded version of that figure, expected to be less a source of pleasure than a claimant on obligation: of Anne, Austen writes that Mrs. Smith "had the two strong claims on her attention, of past kindness and present suffering" (152). Indeed, crippled by illness, bereft of husband and fortune, cast out by her circle, Mrs. Smith inhabits a smaller world than she had once known and moves within it with difficulty if at all. Austen describes her "cheerless situation" (153):

She had been very fond of her husband,—she had buried him. She had been used to affluence,—it was gone. She had no child to connect her with life and happiness again, no relations to assist in the arrangement of perplexed affairs, no health to make all the rest supportable. Her accommodations were limited to a noisy parlour, and a dark bed-room behind, with no possibility of moving from one to the other without assistance, which there was only one servant in the house to afford, and she never quitted the house but to be conveyed into the warm bath. (154)

It will prove to be her charm that, though she might exploit it, Mrs. Smith would not render this account of herself, which seems inadequate preparation for the lively, active, gossipy invalid, whose "elasticity of mind" attends upon the rare blessing of a "disposition to be comforted" (154). Yet in evacuating Mrs. Smith's circumstance of health and even of mobility, and in articulating so precisely the spatial limitations and physical constrictions of her sphere, Austen makes an airless experiment by which to determine whether the centrifugal utility of worldliness can be maintained without a world.

As character, Mrs. Smith answers that it *can* be. The attitudes of sophistication and the modes of the world remain for her, in the incapacitating present, the valued residue of a more expansive past. Using these remnant resources, Mrs. Smith extends her world through gossip and network. Her nurse, the invaluably connected Mrs. Rooke, finds a market for Mrs. Smith's "little thread-cases, pin-cushions and card-racks" among her "large acquaintance" (155). And if the ladies who purchase Mrs. Smith's gewgaws pay as much for her story as for her products, Mrs. Smith, who "had seen too much of the world, to expect sudden or disinterested attachment any where" (154–55), is happy enough to acquire their stories with their money to even the exchange: "Call it gossip if you will; but when nurse Rooke has half an hour's leisure to bestow on me, she is sure to have something to relate that is entertaining and profitable, something that makes one know one's species better. One likes to hear what is going on, to be *au fait* as to the newest modes of being trifling and silly" (155). Both cynical and cheerful in thus franchising her narrative for fun and profit,[16] Mrs. Smith is both cynical and unabashed in revealing the financial plans that underwrite the silence of her plotting. Only when convinced by Anne's acknowledgment of a "somebody else" (197) that Anne would refuse the eminently suitable Mr. Elliot (with him, Anne would be "safe in all worldly matters" [196]) does Mrs. Smith acknowledge, explain, and relinquish her plans to profit by her friend's rumored betrothal. "Let me recommend Mr. Elliot" (196) roughens into a denunciation of him as a man "black at heart, hollow and black!" (199).

"There is always something offensive in the details of cunning," Anne tells Mrs. Smith. "The manoeuvres of selfishness and duplicity must ever be revolting, but I have heard nothing which really surprises me" (207). While Anne comments directly on Mr. Elliot's plot to keep Sir Walter Elliot from marrying his title and inheritance away from Mr. Elliot, her remarks also reflect with unselfconscious aptitude on the cunning labors of Mrs. Smith: Mrs. Smith has been caught plotting.[17] Even in yielding her well-laid plans to use Anne's distaff assistance in the recuperation of position and fortune, though, Mrs. Smith refuses the mortification of discovery and remains cheerful, sanguine, self-consoling. Despite Mrs. Smith's assurance that among women "every man is refused—till he offers" (196), Anne's resolution against Mr. Elliot proves to be genuine, and Mrs. Smith successfully recoups her practical losses and personal disappointments by taking a narrator's position. Mrs. Smith outfaces discovery by telling Anne not only the story of the Smiths' ruin, but the story of her complicity in Mr. Elliot's disrespectful determination to reject or to exploit Anne's family. If Anne's decision about him "changed the face of every thing" for Mrs. Smith, it nevertheless, Austen writes, "left her at least the comfort of telling her whole story her own way" (211).

Join with that narrative comfort another of the gifts with which Austen describes nature as having blessed Mrs. Smith: "that power . . . of finding employment which carried her out of herself" (154). Mrs. Smith combats the visible limitations of her world with such sharp fragments of sophistication as enable her to construct and to tell her own story, with the powerful consequence of being taken—by her own efforts—outside of herself. Extricated from circumstance as a precept and united in a novelist's practice, the comforts (telling her own story, moving beyond herself) with which Mrs. Smith wards off the mortifying awareness of her nothingness beyond the constrictions of a decreased circle become one's comforting ability, perhaps, to tell one's story as if it were someone else's, as if it were not one's own.

This is also and of course precisely what Anne Elliot manages to do as the novel approaches resolution. Anne's famous discussion with Captain Harville about women's constancy is a generalized and third-person claim that her feelings have exceeded Captain Wentworth's in depth and in duration:

"We certainly do not forget you, so soon as you forget us. It is, perhaps, our fate rather than our merit. We cannot help ourselves. We live at home, quiet, confined, and our feelings prey upon us. You are forced on exertion. You have always a profession, pursuits, business of some sort or other, to take you back into the world immediately." (232)

In making—within Wentworth's hearing—her argument that any woman's limited world becomes an emotional hothouse, Anne mounts a defense of herself which, in its plurality ("we cannot help ourselves"), enables her to tell her own sad story with the appealing restraint of its seeming not her own: "All the privilege I claim for my own sex (it is not an enviable one, you need not covet it) is that of loving longest, when existence or when hope is gone" (235). In claiming for her sex the painful privileges of constancy (along with the more satisfying privileges of being thought constant), Anne would refuse the pathos of such privileges for herself. But after all, any appreciation of the difficult dignity with which she discusses so near a subject is dependent on the sense of what that dignity costs her; as the voice of Anne's experience announces itself in her dismissal of inexperienced covetousness and envy, Austen takes care to note that Anne speaks "with a faltering voice" (233) and stops speaking with "her heart . . . too full, her breath too much oppressed" (235). Having used self-conscious Mrs. Smith to arrive at a consoling precept, Austen reserves for Anne, and permits her unselfconscious access to, its saving graces: "Anne was startled at finding [Wentworth] nearer than she had supposed" (233). Beside the mortifying needs and worldly narrative fulfillments of the widow, Austen sets the becoming disavowals of the heroine, disavowals becoming even to a heroine so besieged.

Finding a way of telling your own story as if it were someone else's: this hedge against discovery, this sophisticated consolation for the mortification of recognizing the nothingness of your circle and your own nothingness beyond it, this refusal of consequence to such recognition, this manipulation of abjection into centrality, sounds like nothing so much as the consolation of the house-bound novelist. But, *chez* Jane Austen, consolation for what mortifying knowledge, what truth universally acknowledged? The acknowledgment with which she begins *Pride and Prejudice* may serve Austen less in assessing the disposition of single men than in surveying the extent of the novelist's world: "It is a truth universally acknowledged, that a single man in possession of a good fortune, must be in want of a wife" (*PP*, 3). Her notorious irony in this most famous sentence makes as clear as irony is able Austen's understanding that not only this one but any truth she asserts as of universal acknowledgment constitutes the creed of only "3 or 4 Families in a Country Village."[18] "Let the Portmans go to Ireland," writes Austen to her niece of characters in that aspiring writer's draft of a novel, "but as you know nothing of the Manners there, you had better not go with them" (*Letters*, 269). Advising Anna Austen Lefroy to limit the scope of her mannerly surveillance, Austen embraces the fiction of a conservative travelers' advisory which would caution sagely against the intrepidity of venturing beyond the horizons of the known world.[19] The humor of the figure disguises neither the curtailing wisdom (urged however gently to unpack her bags, Anna would feel the firm compulsion to revise) nor the wistful sadness of a resigned and voluntary detainee: "we think you had better not leave England" (*Letters*, 269).

But if the nothingness beyond it of her sustaining sophistication in the ways of any three or four families in England is the fruit of mortifying self-knowledge for Austen, consolation for this desolation is built into the mode of her acknowledgment. Austen's willing admission of only a provincial's access to the world is yet paired with the worldly assertion of centrality that is the other component of her iridescent irony. Though irony refuses the universality of Austenian truths, irony grants them safe passage; knowing my truths are not universally acknowledged, I get to claim them anyway. How ironic, really, that the strong acknowledgment of provinciality is the force that creates and maintains for Austen a circle of readers reliant—for sustenance in the world beyond her novels—on Austen's dominant fiction of a world governable by a sophisticated and knowing wit that invites mortification and fends it off.

Fit to Be Seen

In *Persuasion* Austen figures her sense of worldliness as *attitude* by exploring the senses in which worldliness might be understood as a matter or consequence of *place*, making reference to the idea of the geographic world in her portraits of self-possession and of mortification. Rendered by their travels literally more worldly than those sophisticated beings Austen describes as having "lived in the world," the sailors and their wives who populate the novel, having defied already any aunts who would have kept them in England, return there, by the time the novel begins, to exchange the ranked hierarchies of England's navy for the distinguished ranks of its social order. (In this, Austen's sailors are not unlike Austen's sophisticates, whose tenure in the world is always expressed in a past tense; if they have lived in the world, Austen hints, they have now retired from it to her novels. Making this suggestion, though, she modestly underrates or strategically understates the worldliness of her domestic concerns.) Bringing her sailors home, Austen refuses to go with them into the world, knowing nothing—as she might say—of the manners there; her interest in rendering the effects of naval travels contains those effects within her understanding of the social order as determined by English manners and understood in indexical relation to the blush. Austen's delighted creation and use of *Persuasion*'s naval characters depends upon the fetishized domestic status of worldly skin.

Sir Walter Elliot, of course, is the means by which Austen enacts her obsession, even if she does not permit him to reproduce precisely the subtleties of her devotion. Considering with initial ill-will the possibility of a naval tenant for his embarrassed estate, Sir Walter discusses the "rough and rugged," "weather-beaten," and "mahogany" complexions of sailors ("all lines and wrinkles"), whose faces are, under and according to the habitual observation of Sir Walter, "about as orange as the cuffs and capes of my livery" (20–22). "A sailor grows old sooner than any other man" (19), concludes Sir Walter, his extraordinary vanity implicated in the sailor's disregard for aging; "I know it is the same with them all: they are knocked about, and exposed to every climate, and every weather, till they are not fit to be seen" (20). The condition of any sailor's skin seems most obviously to offer Sir Walter an opportunity to indulge his smug self-regard; Sir Walter's love of his person, in its ability to unite and display "the blessing of beauty" with "the blessing of a baronetcy" (4), can only be gratified beside the sailor's presumed inadequacies of class and comeliness. Insofar as a sailor's face reminds Sir Walter of his livery, it recalls his congenital attainment of "good looks and . . . rank" (4). Like Sir Walter's entry in the baronetage, a sailor's face might provide "occupation for an idle hour, and consolation in a distressed one," a site where, "if every other leaf were powerless, he could read his own history with an interest which never failed" (3).

Yet if a sailor's face also notably offends Sir Walter it is perhaps because, reading it as registry of a sailor's history rather than his own, Sir Walter reads in it only one story; for Sir Walter, insofar as it can trace a sailor's narrative while reflecting Sir Walter's own estimable charms, the sailor's complexion records the simple fact of a naval history: his complexion identifies a sailor as a sailor without otherwise articulating his responses to the vagaries of manners by means of a variable blush. Sir

Walter misprises, though, the value and embodiment of a naval history; *Persuasion*'s sailors often cut coveted and dashing social figures, the demand for their stories inextricable from the demand for their most desirable persons: "the two Miss Musgroves . . . seemed hardly to have any eyes but for [Wentworth], as to the manner of living on board, daily regulations, food, hours, &c." (64), and even Anne's snobbish sister "had been long enough in Bath, to understand the importance of a man of such an air and appearance as his" (226). Still the illegibility of the sailing complexion disturbs Sir Walter, who misconstrues the significance of that illegibility; unable to see beneath opaque mahogany how a sailor thinks and feels, Sir Walter thinks him obviously unfeeling. The roughened skin of navy men affronts Sir Walter Elliot's aristocratic sensibilities and aesthetic fancies, even as it suggests to him the way its roughening occurs; climatic naval mortifications, he thinks, produce insensitive clods.[20]

The modest cure that active fantasy has suggested travel might work for Burgess's blushing family depends on a similar account of travel's physical mortifications. Travel, if it involves exposure *to* climate and weather, necessarily entails as well a physical exposure *of oneself* to these potentially abrasive forces. Darwin's understanding of the blush as embarrassment's ornamental and protective veil against exposure to observation[21] is anticipated and literalized by the travel cure: reddened and roughened by wind and weather, the textured skin of Burgess's and Darwin's blushing family and of Austen's naval families is tanned—colored; beaten; hardened and proven against vulnerability—by exposure and against exposure. This fantasy of the travel cure, then, works from outside in. Try to look like you're having a good time, magazines advise the party-nervous; in no time you'll find yourself having one. The weather-beaten, by a similar logic, are seen to have undergone a physical mortification that roughens sensibility by roughening skin; traveling, the sensitive family might come to be able to hear with unvarying maritime color what one otherwise might think would make a sailor blush.

Austen's exploitation elsewhere (in *Pride and Prejudice,* for example) of the productive nature of blushing might seem to be in some tension with that which would conceive of the blushing family as needing help at all. To imagine its members ailing is to pathologize the sensible family and to think of curbing their blushes. To what end though, one wonders, curb blushes, given a social system—the system of legibility articulated in *Pride and Prejudice*—that is stoked by the mannerly blush? The blushes of the sensible family (inherited rather than circumstantial,[22] excessive rather than responsive) fail manners in failing to distinguish. In the face of the blushing family, the sources of mortification and of smug satisfaction look too much alike; the indexical capacity of the blush is thus revealed to be fantastical, and the members of the blushing family might seem to endanger legibility in gloriously evading it, finding refuge perhaps in some odd privacy beneath the inscriptions that redden their skin.[23]

So suppose a sailor *were* blushing. Or suppose his wife were. Suppose, that is, feeling and sensibility beneath an illegible and unvarying complexion. Not just a tree-in-the-forest hypothetical for Austen, this supposition determines the nature of *Persuasion*'s Mrs. Croft, the naval wife notable for her happy accompaniment of a seafaring husband on extensive travels and for her acquisition of a sailor's complexion. Austen introduces Mrs. Croft with an account of her appearance: "She had bright dark eyes, good teeth, and altogether an agreeable face; though her reddened and weather-beaten complexion, the consequence of her having been almost as much at sea as her husband, made her seem to have lived some years longer in the world than her real eight and thirty" (48). Giving as it takes away, Austen's description balances its sense of Mrs. Croft's "agreeable face" with its assent to Sir Walter's expectations: her weather-beaten countenance shows a single and aging shade. But the delineation of Mrs. Croft, an aspect of Austen's valorization of the naval life, disputes the sense that personal insensitivity attends upon the roughened complexion. Having lived in the geographic world, Mrs. Croft succeeds with admirable and unexpected aplomb at living in the social one. She listens with "good humour" to the exasperating Mrs. Musgrove (230), and expresses appropriate caution about the Musgrove sisters; she passes the Lady Russell test, while perhaps administering an examination of her own (the two are found to have been "very well pleased with each other" [128]); in the canceled chapter of *Persuasion,* she seeks domestic excuses (the demanding shoemaker, the needful mantuamaker, meteorologically vulnerable windows) to leave Anne felicitously alone with Wentworth at a crucial moment (263–64); and she can even write a letter to suit Anne's finicky sister ("addressed to me, just as it ought" [164]). Most important for *Persuasion*'s readers, her appreciation of Anne's merits distinguishes her from Anne's neglectful family and permits Anne the rare pleasure of "fancying herself a favourite" (126), with the reciprocal consequence that, pondering her lost attachment to Wentworth, Anne imagines that only the spousal devotion of the Crofts might have rivaled it. Her comparison takes as its basis precisely what Sir Walter would find distressing and distressed: "no countenances" could be "so beloved" (64). Mrs. Croft functions ably and kindly in the world of manners, her efforts no less effective or agreeable for her rough stay in the world.

Having described the "squareness, uprightness, and vigor" of Mrs. Croft's "form" and the weather-beaten nature of her complexion, Austen extends her attentions to Mrs. Croft's affect and attitude (48). Despite the climatic mortifications she has undergone in travel, Mrs. Croft seems unaffected by the mortifications of her place as Sir Walter's tenant in the mannerly domesticity to which she has returned: "Her manners were open, easy, and decided, like one who had no distrust of herself, and no doubts of what to do; without any approach to coarseness, however, or any want of good humor" (48). In following immediately upon reference to her "reddened" skin, this balanced account of Mrs. Croft's manners ("open" and "good humour" deflect "decided," while "decided" answers "easy") responds to Sir Walter's reflexive anticipation of insensitivity yet retains a notion of self's continuity with skin. By their failure to register her embarrassment, Mrs. Croft's rough cheeks exempt her from the evils of self-consciousness, even as her exemplary manners refute the fantasy that coarseness of skin implies coarseness of feeling. Rejecting the notion that coarseness moves along a continuum, Austen does not reject *tout court* the idea that dermatology determines character. The characterization of Mrs. Croft introduces to Austen's novel the concept that the roughened and reddened skin of the experienced traveler might afford personal and social protections beneficial in the regulated realm of manners. Neither simply coarse nor conventionally well-mannered, Mrs.

Croft is unselfconscious and unselfconsciously gifted with an enviable self-possession that follows both upon her worldliness—*not* this time Mrs. Smith's charming and amoral sophistication but an informed sense of life beyond her circle[24]—and upon her well-traveled complexion.

Self-possession's derivation from an unvarying complexion is dependent on a notion of the blush as a submission, an admission, a giving over: the oscillating demands of social obligation become the systemic requisitions of a body in the possession of its blush. If Mrs. Croft is a woman without self-distrust and without self-doubt, it is because she is troubled by and responsive to neither the flutter nor the heat of capillary action. *Persuasion* understands the inadequacy of Mrs. Croft's skin to the demands of the social body as constituting—instead of a vulgar and incapacitating inability to live in the world—an enabling evasion of legibility and a dignified refusal of somatic possession, a miraculous retention of self.

The surprise, in reading this novel after *Pride and Prejudice,* is that Mrs. Croft's legibility is not insisted on and that, even if a complexion unvaried by the disruptions of the blush is seen finally not to look so bad, its looks are not what matters. If Anne Elliot "hoped she had outlived the age of blushing" (49), I have hoped for her more than this prospect of a pallid survival. But the example of Mrs. Croft corrects me, suggesting that animating pleasures are still to be felt and taken—if not displayed—at eight and thirty and beyond. Mrs. Croft's service to *Persuasion* is as figure of what Anne Elliot could or would become as a naval wife, and, within the scheme for a naval domesticity, Mrs. Croft models the look or the fantasy of a heroine who has matured, who has lived some years in the world, and who is excepted from the marriage plot by having assumed already a defined and settled relation to it.

Persuasion needs to record the price at which self-possession is achieved, since its very matter in considering Mrs. Croft is the marking of distinction between self-possession and insensitivity; and marriage, not surprisingly, proves the ground against which the negotiated exchange of sensitivity for self-possession is displayed. As Austen's fantasy for Anne, the portrait of Mrs. Croft is not unfraught. The delights of marriage in Austen are most often reserved in potential for participants in the marriage plot; the settled confront issues all their own. In domestic navigation and in marital relation, the Crofts enact a fantasy of the couple as machine, their marriage a vehicular adventure. The novel prizes, as it teases, their evident pleasure in attachment. "Their country habit of being almost always together" (168), most commonly represented as their traveling together, is effectively mocked but pleasantly modeled by their precarious near-inability ever to remain upright when driving a cart: the Crofts are the risible yet working invention of an organic Rube Goldberg. Yet it is by means of their somatic mechanics that Austen suggests the costs and strains of marital coupledom.

That Mrs. Croft performs the work of maintaining the Crofts as entity is manifest in her supervision of a potentially unruly husband, managed and "called to order" (68). For every time that Mrs. Croft sounds the nervous alert of the frontseat driver ("that post!—we shall certainly take that post"), she uses a restraining hand that permits them "happily" (as if by chance) to avoid the danger. Driving with the Crofts, Anne imagines "their style of driving . . . no bad representation of the general guidance of their affairs," the directive nature of that familiar indirect marital guidance determined by one partner's habit, habituation, and practice, "coolly giving the reins a better direction herself" (92). As the partner who powers the machine, Mrs. Croft, in a moment that can seem only mildly less comic, reveals Austen's fantasy of the couple's bodily conjugation, a copulation so complete that the health benefits of its exertions extend from one body to the other. Told the gouty admiral needs lively exercise, Mrs. Croft, who would "go shares with him in every thing," is seen in Bath walking "for her life, to do him good" (168). Romantic Anne delights in contemplating their "happy independence," but in her contemplation misses both the generosity and the desperation of a devotion that stakes its life, in dependence, on another's good.

Mrs. Croft comments on her own health:

"The only time that I ever really suffered in body or mind, the only time that I ever fancied myself unwell, or had any ideas of danger, was the winter that I passed by myself at Deal, when the Admiral (*Captain* Croft then) was in the North Seas. I lived in perpetual fright at that time, and had all manner of imaginary complaints from not knowing what to do with myself, or when I should hear from him next; but as long as we could be together, nothing ever ailed me, and I never met with the smallest inconvenience." (71)

The cheerful tone of Mrs. Croft's encomium to togetherness belies the familiar narrative of anxious dependence that has prepared for it: the boredom of the wife-left-behind generates, in hysteria and hypochondria, an imaginative relation between psyche and soma. References to her fancied complaints comprise the slip that reveals the strained efforts by which Mrs. Croft converts hypersensitivity into self-possession. Her case history indicates that Mrs. Croft's evasion of legibility in rough self-possession is no easy achievement and not, then, the product of a characterological insensitivity; beneath a reddened, hardened, and illegible complexion, the sailor's wife might suffer the mortifications of hysterical isolation, material dependence, companionate despair. Or, anxious to avoid the anxious certainty that her complaints can never be imaginary, she might choose to note no inconvenience, "like one who had no distrust of herself, and no doubts of what to do" (48).

In uniting the weather-beaten sign of insensitivity with a history of recognizable sensation, Mrs. Croft dispels the novel's fascinated attendance on the anxious prospect of insensibility and numbness. The centrality to *Persuasion* of such attendance is figured by the novel's memorable seaside tableau: after her injudicious leap from the steps of the Cobb renders Louisa Musgrove senseless and knocks Henrietta Musgrove into a sympathetic swoon, a crowd forms around the mortified sisters, the fallen and the fainted; "many were collected near them, to be useful if wanted, at any rate, to enjoy the sight of a dead young lady, nay, two dead young ladies, for it proved twice as fine as the first report" (III).[25] As answer to the charges of Mr. Elliot and counter to the entertaining vision of some versions of feminine insensibility, Mrs. Croft offers the novel the picture of an appealing and comfortable self-possession, and presents the comforting sight of Austen's recognition that the pleasures and pains she has represented by means of the blush might exist even (as Darwin might say) when the color of the skin does not allow them to be visible.[26]

Liberating herself to imagine feeling beneath the illegible complexion, Austen simultaneously liberates herself to fantasize (if not always entirely to enact) the detachment of dermatological inscription from socially determined and responsible signification of moral character: Austen's blush can do whatever she wants it to do, can mean whatever she wants it to mean. This freeing detachment permits the restoration of Austen's blush to its erotic preeminence, and in *Persuasion* Austen comes to consider mortification and its blush as the felt experience of an eroticized interiority rather than as the resigned productions of surveillance and propriety.

The mortification of Anne Elliot, to which I finally return, is not of course unharnessed from Austenian manners, but it works less in the service of legibility and surveillance than in the service of the marriage plot, and its efficacy is dependent on making Anne's mortification a pleasure, a desire, a desideratum for Anne herself and for *Persuasion*'s readers. The fulfillment of this desire is the miracle of *Persuasion*: the restoration of Anne Elliot's complexion.[27] Austen writes of Anne's first morning alone with her father in Bath:

In the course of the same morning, Anne and her father chancing to be alone together, he began to compliment her on her improved looks; he thought her "less thin in her person, in her cheeks; her skin, her complexion, greatly improved—clearer, fresher. Had she been using anything in particular!" "No, nothing." "Merely Gowland," he supposed. (145–46)

Sir Walter's endorsement of Gowland's lotion includes this claim for it: "Mrs. Clay has been using it at my recommendation, and you see what it has done for her. You see how it has carried away freckles."[28] While love might make a daughter a beauty as flattered attachment immaculates Mrs. Clay's complexion ("it did not appear to Anne that the freckles were at all lessened" [146]), Sir Walter's vision of Anne is troubled by no such fondness. Austen's ingenuity recuperates Anne's father's neglect; his paternal failures make Sir Walter's the most credible testimony to the noticeable change in Anne's complexion. Anne's habitual pallor is seen to have given way to an enlivening and responsive bloom. Refusing to satisfy more than temporarily Anne's famous hope that she had "outlived the age of blushing" (49), *Persuasion* remakes her as a blushing heroine, signaling her youthful delight in attachment by means of an eloquent complexion. Pleasant recollections "animate her features" (192) as her "countenance perfectly informs" the globally alert Mrs. Smith that Anne had been "in company last night with the person, whom you think the most agreeable in the world" (194): "A blush overspread Anne's cheeks. She could say nothing" (194). But Anne's blushes are more often matters of unselfconscious feeling than articles of self-conscious somatic speech: "Her happiness was from within. Her eyes were bright, and her cheeks glowed,—but she knew nothing about it" (185). Anne is, of course, sometimes more conscious of the awakened susceptibility of her countenance and of its speaking potential. Waiting for Lady Russell to notice Wentworth as he passes, Anne refuses to look, Austen writes, "for her own countenance she knew was unfit to be seen" (179). In high heroine style, Anne modestly misunderstands her own effects. What Anne imagines renders her unfit—her blush—is precisely what has restored her to her father's approval, to the realm of attraction, to utility in the marriage plot: to the ranks of those fit to be seen.

In the exactitude with which Austen fulfills it, Austen creates for Anne a nearly heart-breaking if also gratifying fantasy of well-mannered objectification. Austen writes of the tourists' progress at Lyme:

> When they came to the steps, leading upwards from the beach, a gentleman at the same moment preparing to come down, politely drew back, and stopped to give them way. They ascended and passed him; and as they passed, Anne's face caught his eye, and he looked at her with a degree of earnest admiration, which she could not be insensible of. She was looking remarkably well; her very regular, very pretty features, having the bloom and freshness of youth restored by the fine wind which had been blowing on her complexion, and by the animation of eye which it had also produced. It was evident that the gentleman, (completely a gentleman in manner) admired her exceedingly. Captain Wentworth looked round at her instantly in a way which shewed his noticing of it. He gave her a momentary glance,—a glance of brightness, which seemed to say, "That man is struck with you,—and even I, at this moment, see something like Anne Elliot again." (104)

Austen's emphasis on Mr. Elliot's unmistakable gentlemanly quality contains his desire within the bounds of an acceptably excessive admiration;

Anne turns heads, and this is admiration she cannot miss, despite the efforts of a practiced insensibility. That a head swivels toward Anne in the presence of her lost love constitutes a circumstantial revenge which she may be incapable of desiring, but which the narrative is capable of fashioning for her.[29]

The fantastical quality of Anne's miraculous return to complected beauty extends to the nature of her reestablished relationship with Wentworth, who, when declarations have been made, assures Anne that "(so far from being altered for the worse!)—she had *gained* inexpressibly in personal loveliness" (264).[30] Discussing the Musgroves with Anne, and forgetting perhaps the ways in which his flirtations with the sisters must have mortified her, Wentworth responds with confusion of his own to Anne's blush: "A sudden recollection seemed to occur, and to give him some taste of that emotion which was reddening Anne's cheeks and fixing her eyes on the ground" (182). The contagious blush assists at an eroticized bonding; the somatic union always threatened or promised by the confusion of blushing bodies (whose emotion stirs whose blood?) here makes Anne and Wentworth the conjugal couple the Crofts are. And when Anne needs the responses of her body to signal her receptiveness to Wentworth's questioning and evaluative glance, Austen's narrative itself exploits the confusion of their Croftian organic mechanics: "Anne could command herself enough to receive that look, and not repulsively. The cheeks which had been pale now glowed" (239–40). While the second half of the sentence establishes that the attention of Austen's narrative is directed toward Wentworth ("the movements which had hesitated were decided" in walking with Anne), the glowing cheeks of its beginning enact and summarize Anne's dermatological history even as they express Wentworth's desire and joy.

The narrative's momentary and mild disingenuousness about Lyme wind can distract from the question of how Anne's complexion is restored. To accept that "the bloom and freshness of youth" is returned to Anne "by the fine wind which had been blowing on her complexion" (104) is to forget Sir Walter's experienced warnings about the coarsening consequence of sharp winds (142) and to reject the novel's own example of Mrs. Croft, whose complexion—whatever her softened nature—never experiences relief from the hardening effects of a corrosive salt spray.[31] The source of Anne's color, like the source of Anne's pallor, lies in Austen's own restoration to faith in the material work of mortification. Rejuvenating through mortification the heroine who has sought mortification for its numbing and hardening effects, Austen reveals that heroine to have profited by its quickening pains. Austen's homeopathic mortification enlists mortification against itself and dispatches Anne's tired blood to perform its enlivening work.

If, despite its notable attention to appearance, *Persuasion* has most often conceived of Anne's blush as a flush—as, that is, a perceived event of the body—this is because in the limited world of Anne's family Anne and her blush have been invisible. After hearing and speaking collectedly of Wentworth for the first time in the novel, Anne, Austen tells us, "left the room, to seek the comfort of cool air for her flushed cheeks" (25). Austen's interest in soothing Anne's cheeks—the narrative's focus on the painful heat of Anne's flush—conceives of capillary action as a felt thing rather than a registry, as something *for Anne* rather than for the record. Her family's inattentiveness has relieved the obligation of Anne's body to display its fealty to the regime of mannerly legibility: no one is looking, and no worldly mischief encourages Anne to take advantage of that sad fact as lucky circumstance.

Wentworth's return—the return even of an angry former suitor—means that someone is looking, and looking, further, (with the callous sadism of the rejected) to reclaim the right to dismiss, looking to subdue and to mortify. And Anne, adding the conventional regrets of the wiser but sadder jilt to the stepsister-habits and cindery expectations of the underappreciated, is looking to be mortified. Wentworth satisfies. His flirtations with the silly Musgroves double the pleasure with which his apparent inattentions make Anne a mortifying exception to his disposition to please and to be pleased: "He had a heart for either of the Miss Musgroves, if they could catch it; a heart, in short, for any pleasing young woman who came in his way, excepting Anne Elliot" (61). His careless remarks about Anne's altered looks invite Anne's submission "in silent, deep mortification" (60–61). And even those conversations ostensibly not about Anne ("she had heard no evil of herself") but about persuasive or firm natures and the evil of shipboard wives prove to be assaults on her calm ("but she had heard a great deal of very painful import. She saw how her own character was considered by Captain Wentworth" [89]). Still, Anne's "extreme agitation" reminds her that her urgent exceptionalism for Wentworth gives her a vibrant place in his disregard. Anne is encouraged in developing those skills by which to negotiate her position as mortified listener into a heroine's centrality (after all, "thère had been just that degree of feeling and curiosity about her in his manner" [89]). The attention of Wentworth's striking mortifications makes Anne visible. If his overheard query elicits an incorrect response from a Musgrove sister ("Oh! no, never. . . . She had rather play"), it is because that sister has never before seen that Anne is not dancing (72); if her world is suddenly alive to the beauty of Anne's complexion, it is because its variable colors make that complexion visible, and they can do so because, in its ability to alter complexion, mortification has restored complexion to Anne.

The psychic and physical pains of Anne's mortification, that is, restore her complexion, if only sometimes and if only temporarily. Anne's blush of embarrassment and flush of pain come to have a more literal than colloquial relation to the past processes of penitential mortification and the contemporary procedures of cosmetic dermabrasion.[32] Her blushing flesh, like the flagellated flesh of the penitent, experiences mortification at work in its inevitably conflicted mode—diminishment by reminder—and experiences it operating iridescently: deadening and rejuvenating, deadening to rejuvenate, sensitizing to *de*sensitize—but doing so precisely in order to sensitize and desensitize again.

In resolving her problem with mortification's methods—in finding or choosing that the teleology of its pulses may tend toward the quickening as easily as toward the deadened—Austen also reveals that diminishment has always been an alibi for the corporal pleasures of reminder. Stephen Dedalus himself seems to know that his willful inhalations of "a certain stale fishy stink like that of longstanding urine" are as much about exalting his senses' pleasures as about subjecting them. ("To mortify his smell was more difficult as he found in himself no instinctive repugnance to bad odours.")[33] And "the flush of triumph in his face" with which Rev. Mr. Dimmesdale reveals the work of his mortification may suggest to the shocked or the suspicious that his best pleasures have come not only with

Hester Prynne but alone with "the bloody scourge."[34] No less than the penitentially mortified, the socially mortified Anne can find sophisticated pleasure in the reclamation of her body through its pains: "when pain is over, the remembrance of it often becomes a pleasure" (184).

As a pleasure, mortification commands such painful admissions as constitute the narrative of *Persuasion* and the nature of Anne Elliot. Persuaded by mortification of her age or of her faded attractions, persuaded of her exclusion from the marriage plot, persuaded that she needs desire or cosmetics or love, Anne is invariably persuaded into an admission of her mortification. The peculiar intransitivity of Anne's submission ("'Altered beyond his knowledge!' Anne fully submitted in silent, deep mortification") construes her submission to mortification reflexively; submitting to mortification, Anne submits to the experience of her body—reclaiming it from numbness and neglect by that submission—in an act of perverse self-possession.

For mortification is finally a sophisticated pleasure, in Jane Austen, enjoyed by a gifted cadre of the self-possessed. And the cosmetic procedure by which Austen restores Anne's complexion and restores her to somatic pleasure is a difficult and sophisticated process; rejuvenation always is, in being always recognizable as a too-knowing and too-complicated imitation of the juvenility it mimes.

"He enquired after you very particularly," Wentworth tells Anne, speaking of his brother: "asked even if you were personally altered, little suspecting that to my eye you could never alter." In response "Anne smiled, and let it pass. It was too pleasing a blunder for a reproach" (243). I note this moment not to probe with my doubt the narrative's account of Anne Elliot's pleasure in this moment, as I once thought I might. I like Wentworth, and I am convinced by Anne's own argument that the "homage" of Wentworth's assertion is "the result, not the cause of a revival of his warm attachment." But Anne needs reach her conclusion "by comparing [such homage] with former words" (her relation to Wentworth cannot be simple and unvexed); exercising the skills of past practice in mature rejuvenation, the wise heroine converts mortification into a "pleasing blunder," while retaining the ability to delight in "a delicious consciousness" (246).

I am not alone in having discussed *Persuasion*'s restoration of Anne

Elliot's complexion as a given of the novel, a fictional absolute lent credibility by the testimony of father, suitors, and strangers, as well as narrator. And I have done so as part of watching Austen test and reinforce her erotics of mortification, the product of a reinvigorated trust in the power of her own conversion of the sign of manners into the sign of pleasure. But for Austen and her readers—no less than for Anne Elliot—the pleasures of fiction are sophisticated ones, made visible in the pleasing slip or inexplicable blunder that reveals them to be, after all, made up. The narrative's account of Mrs. Smith's visitor as a woman "with every beauty excepting bloom" (153) is surrounded by evidence (Mr. Elliot's and Sir Walter's on one side, the ample testimony of the narrator on the other) that would counter that apparent exception with detailed histories of Anne's responsive complexion. And yet—caught believing—I am mortified by the exposure of my desire for Anne's restoration to youth and bloom, by the exposure of my commitment to Austen's cosmetic fantasies, by my faith in Austen's fictions. Still, the slip (I decide it is a slip) is the body in Austen's writing; like the blush, it is the inscription of involuntarity and—for Anne Elliot, at least—the very index of credibility:

> She prized the frank, the open-hearted, the eager character beyond all others. Warmth and enthusiasm did captivate her still. She felt that she could so much more depend upon the sincerity of those who sometimes looked or said a careless or a hasty thing, than of those whose presence of mind never varied, whose tongue never slipped. (161)

If Anne's characterological preference does not sound like a choice of Jane Austen (a preference for her), it nevertheless helps me see Jane Austen in an exposure that makes her fantasy the more touching and the more compelling.

Austen's difficult perception that blunders—while still blundering—might yet please prepares a solution for problems Elizabeth Gaskell will face in *North and South*. Responding to Austen as predecessor in manners, Gaskell necessarily entertains the blush as a legible signifier of character, but anxious fantasies about class, about the duplicity of women's bodies, and about characters' blushes as written rather than embodied events, interfere with and discredit the reliability of the blush and the body in Gaskell's novel. Trying out substitutions for the blush as register of character and virtue (death, the swoon, the womanly figure), Gaskell explores linguistic error and somatic blunder as unlikely sources of a stability she no longer believes the blush can guarantee.

Chapter Three Gaskell's Blunders:

North and South

Critics of *North and South* have often attempted to account for the peculiarity of its false starts and for its refusal, as industrial novel, directly to approach industrial subjects until its seventh chapter. Martin Dodsworth writes of these false starts as the product of will rather than of error: by their means, Gaskell is able to make clear "first, the sort of novel she is *not* writing, and second, the sort of novel she *is* writing."[1] The novel begins, it might be said, as if written by somebody else. The sort of novel Gaskell *is* writing concerns men and masters in manufacturing Darkshire, strikers, the police, doubting clergy, the intrusions on gentility of "shoppy people" (50) and of workers who feed and die on inhaled cotton fibers. The novel Gaskell seems at first to write—in fact, writes at first—introduces instead the joys and irritations of making wedding plans in London. *North and South*'s early juxtaposition of a silly bride with a more worthy but less appreciated heroine, its immediate introduction of a single man in want of a good fortune, and its initial ironic and epigrammatic omniscience ("her mother had absolutely ordered those extra delicacies of the season which are always supposed to be efficacious against immoderate grief at farewell dinners" [36]) have led readers to determine that the novel Gaskell is not writing is by Jane Austen.[2]

Yet the desire to read Gaskell as rejecting Austen seems a bit like choosing the likeliest side: if Gaskell imitates Austen in order to reject her, the explanation might go, the rejection is Gaskell's loss; anything she can do, readers have tended to think, *she* can do better. But the citation of Jane Austen in the industrial *North and South* argues that Gaskell might be seen more accurately to want to include—perhaps to contain—the novel of manners within the industrial novel. Understood most availably as sincere flattery, such imitation as Gaskell's of Austen is not monolithic but oxymoronic, refusing to choose between repulsion and embrace, but taking relation to entail the taking up of a certain challenge. And Austen's presence in Gaskell's novel does not dissipate with the removal of

the heroine, Margaret Hale, from London; it is perceptible in the mortifications by which—like light- or dark-adapting eyes—Margaret's observations adjust to the conditions of visibility in Darkshire, in the consequent mortified union between Margaret and Mr. Thornton, and in the
sway of a romance that culminates in the glow of a "beautiful shame"
(530).

Since Gaskell's is tribute based on trouble as well as on delight, her
interests involve an instability about class and about the fictional order
that the novel of manners can seem to evade by successfully imagining
itself above. My argument in this chapter makes it possible to see tensions
involved in *North and South*'s capacious and containing gesture toward
the novel of manners as played out in relation to notions of the body's
ability legibly to register character and moral sensibility. Lingering over
her inheritance from Austen—a satisfyingly legible blush—Gaskell will
nevertheless see the legibility of the blush as compromised in its extension
beyond manners to manufactory. In *North and South*, Gaskell raises the
specter of a blush drained of moral content. Her attempts at resolving
problems attendant on that specter lead her further into the realm of
somatic involuntarity in search of a functional substitute for the blush;
dying, swooning, and blundering each take a turn as her provisional
solution. This chapter will consider the workings of Gaskell's attempts,
which are everywhere evident yet everywhere compromised by her weakening faith in the ability of somatic signs to work as natural signs.

Fanny's Blush, Margaret's Blunders

When dinner guest Mrs. Slickson wonders to Fanny Thornton how
Fanny's mill-owner brother finds time to read with a tutor "in the midst
of all his business—and this abominable strike in hand as well" (219),
susceptible Fanny is thrown by the slick ambiguity of the exclamatory
question. Is Thornton to be thought a marvel of efficiency and wide
interest or merely a neglectful dabbler? Unsure how to respond, Fanny
does not puzzle over what to say; instead, she wonders how best to look,
or (to say this more precisely) how Mrs. Slickson might want her to look:

Fanny was not sure, from Mrs. Slickson's manner, whether she ought to be proud or ashamed of her brother's conduct; and, like all people who try and take other people's "ought" for the rule of their feelings, she was inclined to blush for any singularity of action. Her shame was interrupted by the dispersion of the guests. (219)

That readers are supposed to disapprove of Fanny Thornton is made clear throughout *North and South*; that weakness is consequent upon her frivolity is evident to and made evident by even her strong mother, who indulges Fanny but whose endearments and "uneasy tenderness" to her daughter are a way to "hide the poverty of her child in all the grand qualities which she herself possessed unconsciously" (137). Unable to evade consciousness in her visible desire for approval, Fanny is trapped in her moral vacuity by a world of moral choices. The value of her brother's work with Mr. Hale is not, for her, the question, nor is it whether or not she approves of such work; rather, Fanny's concern is whether it is approval or disapproval that would most become her. Moral choices and evaluations are of merely cosmetic utility for Fanny.

The consciousness that makes Fanny blush at any singularity cannot distinguish between singularities and cannot, then, register as singularly virtuous her brother's generosity toward his impoverished tutor or as singularly admirable his efforts at cultivation. The failure of Fanny's will to distinguish (and consequently her ability to distinguish herself) is of course, from the perspective of a moral sensibility, worse than morally vacuous in its moral ambidexterity. Fanny's abjection before the rule of another's "ought" and the subjection of her blush to another's feelings implies the openness of her body to possession. A hint from Mrs. Slickson and Fanny *would* know how to look, surrendering her body with her capacity for judgment in exchange for social approbation.

But whether or not Fanny knows how to look, her look in fact is right, and that's what's wrong with her; Fanny's immersion in sartorial and somatic fashion calls into question her integrity and her consistency as well as her taste. The Oxonian perspective of bachelor Mr. Bell associates not just Fanny's taste *in* but also her taste *for* fabric with a corresponding flimsiness of character. Expressing to Margaret Hale (who seems eager enough to hear it) his disapproval of Fanny's interest in her own wedding clothes (my sympathies with Fanny here), Mr. Bell describes the "perpetual clack" about Fanny's wedding that interrupts his visit to the prenuptial Thornton home: "I was surprised to find the old lady falling into the current, and carried away by her daughter's enthusiasm for orange-blossoms and lace. I thought Mrs. Thornton had been made of sterner stuff" (461). The quality of Fanny's taste is not at issue in isolation; the fact that she *has* a taste for clothing—that fabric for her is fashion and that fashion is pleasure—implies a character in trendy relation to moral "dos" and "don'ts." The currency of Fanny's interest disappoints Mr. Bell and endangers Fanny's mother in his estimation. But Mrs. Thornton's worsted "stuff" is sturdy as well as stern, its moral fabric the stuff of her being rather than of her dress.

Fanny's material joy in "her silks and satins" (442), and Mrs. Thornton's resigned decision humorlessly to humor her in that joy, reflect Gaskell's understanding of their relative places in material culture. Her mother's dismissals of Fanny are a familiar form of generational class conflict: Mrs. Thornton resents Fanny for having become the very daughter she has encouraged her to be, the frivolous possession by which industry would show its accession to gentility but which by its very existence violates industry's utilitarian values. Mrs. Thornton's protectiveness of Fanny, which Margaret metaphorizes into a similar relation to fabric, is her acknowledgment of that product: " 'She would put on any assumption of feeling to veil her daughter's weakness' " (461).

Outlined as they are in Gaskell's novel against essentially the same familial class background, Fanny and her mother look very different against it and understand the family's place in the world very differently. Fanny's experience of the family's acquired riches makes her more comfortable than her mother (if also more fretful) in the world of the *nouveaux,* more appetitive for worldly novelties. Mrs. Thornton makes out of her discomfort a drawing room "twenty times as fine" as Margaret Hale's, but "not one quarter as comfortable" (119).[3] Her attempts at elegant interior design (here is where she would be Fanny's mother) are—in their failures—perverse testimony to her integrity; the upright character cannot create for itself the comfortable space. The room's furniture and chandelier are "bagged up," its carpet covered, its "smartly-bound books" artfully arranged (158). Mrs. Thornton's austere aspirations are remarkable in those sad and sadistic efforts at preservation that render time spent in the room—like time spent on the noisy, sticky, pinching plastic that preserved some 1960s couches—productive of genteel and strenuous silence and concerted immobility: though "talking of what all the world might hear" while calling on the Thorntons, Margaret and her father speak to each other "in low voices," it being the "common effect of such a room as this to make people speak low" (158–59). The "painfully spotted, spangled, speckled look" about the room and its unleisured "evidence of care and labour," misdirected because "not care and labour to produce ease," strike Margaret "unpleasantly"; she "only wondered why people who could afford to live in so good a house, and keep it in such perfect order, did not prefer a much smaller dwelling in the country or even some suburb" (158). While Mrs. Thornton's drawing room enforces good behavior, it also functions as an aesthetic marker of class, and *North and South*'s princess of fallen gentility notes with hardly necessary sensitivity the vulgar pea beneath.

For all that Mrs. Thornton's drawing room is presented by the novel as a defect or an inadequacy, it is nevertheless an inadequacy welcomed by the novel, which it serves as an index by which aesthetics plot a narrative of class. And for all that *North and South* asserts a generous desire (largesse) to read class as unrelated (or even inversely related) to virtue, it nevertheless evinces an anxious desire to separate the descendant gentility of the Hales from the initially ascendant mobility of the Thorntons. It is as register of this distinction that Gaskell has supposed the blush to work—her supposition manifest in her disappointment—and as register of this distinction that she finds the blush wanting.

When Margaret and her father arrive at the dinner party with which Mrs. Thornton appeases the son anxious for her to "like Miss Hale" (193), they find an excess of provision and of ornament that proves "oppressive" (213) and exhausting. Its habitual covers having been removed, the drawing room "blazed forth in yellow silk damask and a brilliantly-flowered carpet" (213). The room's elegant blaze without warmth generates and encloses Fanny's stylish blush without feeling; associated in being fashion's effects, both blaze and blush are no more than refinements of the Thornton family's labor, extravagant purchases of the family's industrial success. Gaskell's textile articulation of Fanny depends on understanding her—understanding, as well, her blush and its vacancy—as the most refined products of Thornton's mill.[4] What's wrong with Fanny's blush is precisely its status as product, its liability to a mechanical and near-voluntary production in response to the vagaries of approval. With the invariably correct instinct of the tastefully fashionable (rather than that of the instinctively moral), Fanny is able to produce the sign of moral virtue because such a sign is suitable, whatever the occasion; wearing the fashionable blush, a woman is always ornamental, always seen to be correct.[5] Fanny's threatened mimicry of apparent legible rectitude disempowers distinction: how might one tell Fanny's stylish blush from Margaret's moral one? how to tell the blush of natural gentility from that which, assumed in calculation, functions as a moral cosmetic?[6]

Alongside the success of Fanny's assumed blush, Margaret's complexion seems insufficiently vivid. Dressing for a dinner, Margaret is found wanting; her coloring needs the supplement of her mother's coral jewelry. The Hales' servant, Dixon, makes "an appeal for admiration": "Miss Hale looks well, ma'am—doesn't she? Mrs. Shaw's coral couldn't have come in better. It just gives the right touch of colour, ma'am. Otherwise, Miss Margaret, you would have been too pale" (212). Her ostensibly loving father, perceptive enough of Margaret's distress, reddens her cheek with a pinch to make over the pale worry he would prefer not to see: "Come; if you look so pale as this, I must rouge you up a little" (190). Dependent on Margaret as a monument of strength, Reverend Hale would rather not see her strength compromised by pallor, would rather rough her up with the classic cosmetic pinch and with an ineluctable insistence that her feelings not obstruct the satisfactions of his view. Margaret's unhealthy working-class admirer, Bessy Higgins—also dependent for sustenance on maintaining an image of Margaret's monumental vitality—responds to her somewhat differently if also somewhat roughly. Evaluating Margaret's looks in anticipation of Margaret's socializing with the manufacturing elite of Milton, Bessy comments bluntly on the flesh of her visiting angel:[7] "I reckon yo're not what folks would ca' pretty;

yo've not red and white enough for that" (200). Bessy's domestication and reduction of Margaret's monumental importance assume, with mistaken familiarity, that she and Margaret have a common perception of Milton's class relations. (Bessy understands Margaret to be an angel, but she knows that angelic status does not overcome class status as she has seen it operate in Milton.) Thinking that she and Margaret alike aspire to the society of Milton's best families, Bessy is surprised to learn that Margaret will dine with the Thorntons ("they visit wi' a' th' first folk in Milton" [199]) and worries about Margaret's ability to create an effect: "'But them ladies dress so grand!' said Bessy, with an anxious look at Margaret's print gown, which her Milton eyes appraised at sevenpence a yard" (200). Told that Margaret will wear the white silk she had worn to a cousin's wedding, Bessy falls back in her chair, relieved that Margaret will not be "looked down upon."

Like Bessy's aspiration for Margaret's social success, Bessy's anxiety about Margaret's reception is not shared by Margaret, whose very ability to call explicit attention to that anxiety ("And you don't think we're quite the first folk in Milton, eh, Bessy?" [199]) bespeaks some assurance of her social superiority. But Margaret's critically notorious aversion to "shoppy people" (her aversion a suggestion that her assurance is maintained at considerable expense) is precisely what *North and South* will demand she relinquish in exchange for marriage to Thornton, or (*more* precisely) what it will demand she display for the pleasing spectacle of its mortifying conversion to attraction. In writing Margaret's moral and erotic lessons, Gaskell negotiates a collapse of class categories that also and nevertheless makes her nervous. If Gaskell is interested in creating characters who cross class boundaries, she seems also to have an interest in suggesting that such boundary crossing entails a confusion under which she does not rest easy.

This unease explains the writing of Fanny's blush as the nearly voluntary fabrication of moral vacancy. So fantasized and so written, the blush suggests that for Gaskell a distressing confusion is generated by the ability of the social manufacturer, Fanny, to ape the cultural signs of gentility. Gaskell's novel expresses a kind of class indignation on Margaret's behalf about fashion's charming alienation of sensibility from morality. Writing the frightening prospect of Fanny's blush, Gaskell writes as if Fanny's own inability to make distinctions makes it similarly impossible for those who see or read her to distinguish her from Margaret. Telling Margaret from Fanny in *North and South* is not at all in fact a problem;[8] Margaret's melancholy generosity in the face of her cousin's neglect identifies her immediately as the heroine (if "in default of a listener, [Margaret] had to brood over the change in her life silently as heretofore," hers was nevertheless "a happy brooding" [36]), while Fanny's petulance ("'Oh! mamma, it's such a long way, and I am so tired'" [137]) as clearly identifies her as something else. But Gaskell's odd insistence on comparison raises persistently a fantasy of indistinction. And Gaskell's comparative treatment of the characters generates around Fanny a certain palpable resentment, based on the fantasy of her access to what the novel imagines ought to be Margaret's by entitlement but what it consistently denies her: control over her own representation.

Among the peculiarities of Margaret Hale as heroine is her tendency to blunder: to do badly what she would do well, to render inadequately her account of a situation or a person, to say wrong what she would most say right, to say before whom she would not hurt precisely what will do injury, to belie her intentions (the novel might say her heart) by some evidently inadvertent error. Eager to rouse Reverend Hale's sympathy for Bessy Higgins's grieving father, for example, Margaret tells her father Higgins's story. Gaskell writes: "Of course, she told it incompletely; and her father was rather 'taken aback' by the idea of the drunken weaver awaiting him in his quiet study, with whom he was expected to drink tea, and on whose behalf Margaret was anxiously pleading" (285).

Margaret's blunders become indeed matters of course in the novel, incidents that, half-unnoticed, determine the direction of the narrative. Happy to reassure his mother that she is not "making any plans on Mr. Thornton's heart," Margaret considers that reassurance as "exonerating" her—as from a charge—and, scarcely warming Mrs. Thornton's maternal heart, "laughed outright at the notion presented to her; laughed so merrily that it grated on Mrs. Thornton's ear" (161). And, explaining to Mrs. Thornton Mrs. Hale's inability to return the Thorntons' call, Margaret, in a kind effort not to alarm her overprotected father (who is listening) about her mother's fragile health, "gave but a bungling account, and left the impression on Mrs. Thornton's mind that Mrs. Hale's was some temporary or fanciful fine-ladyish indisposition" (159).

Among Margaret's mistakes and blunders are responding to Fanny Thornton's expressed pleasure in Margaret's shared dislike of "mills and manufactories, and all those kind of things," by saying "I think I should like to know all about them, if I were you" (141–42); discussing Milton's "vulgarity" before its proud citizen Thornton (Margaret wants to suggest with linguistic largesse that she has acquired Miltonic slang, but seems to Thornton to have dismissed as uncultivated everything about the city) (302); taking a harmless and helpful railway porter for Leonards, the man whose recognition threatens Frederick, Margaret's fugitive brother (333–34); questioning Martha, a servant, in an effort to "set on some work which should take her out of herself," but, having prompted personal revelations, reverting to her own concerns with the result that Martha "quitted the room, with the same wooden face with which she had entered it" (426–27); giving away to Mr. Bell the important secret that Frederick had risked capture and execution by returning to England, on the mistaken assumption that Bell had already been told (462); making clear to Mr. Henry Lennox, a rejected and no longer pressing suitor, her discomfort in his presence by pleading audibly, hastily, and inanely with Mr. Bell not to leave them alone (464). Margaret also bungles her attempts to help out a student stuck for an answer in a grammar lesson (479); to defend, against Fanny's disrespect, Mrs. Thornton's pride in Milton (140–41); and, most significantly in terms of the novel's advancing plot, to protect Thornton's striking workers from their own violent impulses by making a spectacle of her femininity (232–35).

While Gaskell's use of Margaret's blunders suggests that Margaret's good intentions are sacrificed to frequent misunderstanding, the blunders of course suggest as well that Margaret's intentions are themselves sometimes blundering impulses to condescend and to correct: if Margaret is misunderstood to condescend to Mrs. Thornton about her mother's missed visit, she would be correctly understood as condescending to Fanny about the interests appropriate to a woman of her background. When Margaret's intentions stumble, it may be because they have hobbled themselves from the start.

Gaskell's interest in mistakes extends to chapter titles ("Mistakes," "Mistakes Cleared Up," "Mischances," even, by implication, "'The More Haste the Worse Speed,'" "First Impressions," and "Expiation") and to blunders for which Margaret suffers but of which she cannot be seen to have been the cause (the misinformation in a railway timetable; Bell's failure to tell Thornton that Margaret's evening escort was merely her brother; everyone's failure to tell Margaret that Thornton attended her mother's funeral). But, however attributed, the awkward energies of the blunder circulate chiefly around Margaret. Margaret's reputation and self-presentation, as Gaskell writes them, are beyond her control, the consequences of involuntarity and error.

To read *North and South* in a way that is responsive to the narrative's direction of reader identification—to read, that is, with some sympathetic access to Margaret Hale's thoughts and feelings—is to read a story propelled by Margaret's vexations and frustrations in the face of perceived misunderstanding.[9] Margaret understands her blunders as obstacles imposed by a resistant world (which she largely conceives of as the industrial Milton-Northern), obstacles that are themselves resistant to removal and clarification. And Gaskell's use of Margaret's blunders in some way supports that understanding. Margaret's difficulty in making herself clear—in blush or in language—supports a vision of the world as denying her access to expressivity and usurping her right to be read accurately, to be understood. At one moment in the text, Margaret's embrace of this vision will seem to offer all the pleasures afforded by resigned abjection and apocalyptic vindication. When Mr. Bell dies, Margaret thinks about his death as, among other things, a loss of the means by which Thornton might have learned "the simple facts" (505) that would dispel his suspicion of her virtue (a blunder with respect to reader sympathy, that version of Bell's loss): "She must just submit, like many another, to be misunderstood; but, though reasoning herself into the belief that in this hers was no uncommon lot, her heart did not ache the less with longing that some time—years and years hence—before he died at any rate, he might know how much she had been tempted" (506). Margaret's submission to misunderstanding as an existential condition prepares for her the way either brilliantly to be read or felicitously to be misread. Within just seconds or sentences after her offer of a loan, potentially a great blundering offense to Thornton's pride, Thornton warns Margaret (in pre-Harlequin language, "panted out the words"): "Take care.—If you do not speak—I shall claim you as my own in some strange presumptuous way.—Send me away at once, if I must go;—Margaret!—" (529). Margaret assents as rapidly to Thornton's strange and presumptuous yet also simply accurate conflation of financial "proposal" (529) with erotic proposition, and consents to marry him.[10]

The triumphant conversion of this blunder into success is Gaskell's recuperation of the novel she has written as a festival of error. Gaskell's fantasy of characterological legibility fades fast to a recognition that somatic legibility implies the possibility of misreading, and that a system of legibility based in bodily involuntarity and figured by the blush depends upon the illogic of seeking fixity through instability. The blush, ostensibly the source of fixity through legibility, proves itself dramatically the site of misprision and blunder; in a climactic scene from Gaskell's novel, the blush proves sometimes not even reliably to be a blush. When Thornton sees Margaret walking, far from home, in the evening, with a young man Thornton does not know to be her brother, Thornton's reading of Margaret's position as compromised is wrought in part by the effects of light. Standing still, standing together with clasped hands, one (Frederick) reading the other's face "with wistful anxiety" (331), Margaret and Frederick look like lovers, for Thornton, in part because "the setting sun fell in their faces," coloring and coupling them with a tell-tale but not somatic blush. The blush of the setting sun, the product of Gaskell's imaginative manufactory, thus renders Margaret's body and Frederick's liable to the likelihood of precisely what makes Gaskell nervous—semiotic failure and semiotic excess.

Margaret's Figure, Gaskell's Swoon

Troubled by the way she imagines that semiosis may be disrupted or diverted by blush and blunder, Gaskell attempts to establish alternative access (for herself as novelist and for Margaret as a character in a compromised relation to expressivity) to characterological and somatic legibility.

Rather than reject an always potentially unstable body as a ground for meaning and stability, Gaskell seems, in *North and South*, to try out a reconstructed *whole* body; as a figure, rather than as the site of physiology, Margaret Hale's body is employed to stand in for character and to bear the burden of signification. The solid person of Margaret Hale is set the task of answering for the failures of physiology and speech.

Gaskell's physical description of her heroine includes this precis of responses to her physical inheritance: "Sometimes people wondered that parents so handsome should have a daughter who was so far from regularly beautiful; not beautiful at all, was occasionally said" (48). Gaskell recovers a sense of her heroine's beauty (made precarious, of course, only by her own account of it) by balancing each flaw with a virtue: Gaskell construes Margaret's mouth—which she imagines as too wide—as also a "rich red" rosebud mouth that refuses to open except "just enough to let out a 'yes' and 'no,' and 'an't please you, sir,' " and imagines a face she describes as bearing a look "in general, too dignified and reserved for one so young" as also brightened and animated by the presence of Margaret's father. If Margaret's face—evidently at least two steps up from isolation in mother-love—is nevertheless beautiful only to the discriminating or familial, how then to explain the eagerness of the people of Milton to accost her on the streets? The attentions of the girls of Milton might be explained, as Gaskell does explain them, by "a simple reliance on her womanly sympathy with their love of dress" (110) or by a recognition that, like Bessy's, their "Milton eyes" betray a professional rather than necessarily gendered interest in fabric. The men of Milton, however, are equally attentive to Margaret, though they seem more unsettling to her because they are less interested in her clothing, more interested in her person:

She alternately dreaded and fired up against the workmen, who commented not on her dress, but on her looks, in the same open, fearless manner. She, who had hitherto felt that even the most refined remark on her personal appearance was an impertinence, had to endure undisguised admiration from those out-spoken men. But the very outspokenness marked their innocence of any intention to hurt her delicacy, as she would have perceived if she had been less frightened by the disorderly tumult. (110)

The habitual "undisguised admiration" with which Gaskell imagines the men of Milton regularly look on Margaret (110, 332) seems of a piece with the textual energy Gaskell devotes to Margaret's figure, which is itself repeatedly noticed by characters *in* the text (her father tells Margaret that, in suitor Henry Lennox's sketch of it, her "figure and way of holding [herself] is capital" [58]) and the stature of which is repeatedly noted *by* the text. Margaret—the knowledge is inescapable in reading *North and South*—is tall, stately, dignified, in possession of a "finely made figure" (39), queenly of stature and bearing. ("What a queen she is!" in the exclamatory thinking of her mother's doctor; "with her head thrown back at first, to force me into speaking the truth; and then bent so eagerly forward to listen" [174]). Margaret's commanding figure *means* and tells something about her, and its characterological consequences include "stately simplicity" (42) and a "high maidenly dignity" (61).

The attention paid to Margaret's figure suggests something beyond respect or, rather, something akin to the nearly comic respect that (now become a contemporary film or television cliché) seems commanded by the womanly figure or the good body.[11] "Stately" seems, in Gaskell's usage, the nineteenth-century equivalent of "stacked," and the effect of Margaret's powerful body (whether on the passing workmen who comment or on the professionals who exclaim to themselves) creates improbable congruences between the uprightness of her carriage, the erections that mark some sexual desires, and the moral-seeming rectitude that converts good posture and full figure into personal dignity and national symbolics ("What a queen she is!").

Margaret's relation to the power of her body is visible in the ease with which, as if unconsciously, she strikes a pose. Her introduction in the novel rapidly devolves into her standing "as a sort of lay figure on which to display" the Indian shawls in Edith's trousseau (39). Later, her father finds her curled up in a window-seat, thinking about the consequences of his religious crisis: "The moonlight was strong enough to let him see his daughter in her unusual place and attitude." Prompted by her posture (attitude) to consider her emotional state (attitude), the Reverend Hale approaches and—like father, like daughter—they kneel together in prayer or tableau, "he looking up, she bowed down in humble shame" (77). Angered by the freedom with which the family servant comments on her father's decision to resign his parish, Margaret employs the power of her stance to acquire Dixon's obedience and admiration: "She stood upright and firm on her feet now, confronting the waiting-maid, and fixing her with her steady discerning eye" (83). Another night, awaiting the descent of her discouraged father, Margaret prepares her look for his appearance: "She was ready to look up brightly when her father came down-stairs" (86).

Gaskell rejects the epistemological advantage over Margaret that she enjoys as author, claiming a certain distance from Margaret's body and imagining that the novel's narrator, like its characters, is in a position only to read and not to determine Margaret's posture and attitude:

Margaret sat down on the rug, partly to warm herself, for the dampness of the evening hung about her dress, and overfatigue had made her chilly. She kept herself balanced by clasping her hands together round her knees; her head drooped a little towards her chest; the attitude was one of despondency, whatever her frame of mind might be.

In refusing to assert the omniscience of the narrative and in refusing to acknowledge here her own authority over the relation between Margaret's body and her emotions, Gaskell considers the disparity between attitude and attitude that the passage will suggest Margaret exploits for the benefit of her father. Gaskell goes on: "But when she heard her father's step on the gravel outside, she started up, and hastily shaking her heavy black hair back, and wiping a few tears away that had come on her cheeks she knew not how, she went out to open the door for him" (91).

The monumental effects of Margaret's person are more and less successful in the novel. Margaret exploits her body to calming effect for Nicholas Higgins, relying precisely on her stillness, on her ability to become statuesque. When Higgins, grief-stricken over Bessy's death, seems about to go out to drink, Margaret joins Higgins's other daughter, Mary, in trying to stop him. Mary tries actively to restrain him, "but Margaret stood in the doorway, silent yet commanding" (282). Gaskell writes:

He had shaken off Mary with violence; he looked ready to strike Margaret. But she never moved a feature—never took her deep, serious eyes off him. He stared back on her with gloomy fierceness. If she had stirred hand or foot, he would have thrust her aside with even more violence than he had used to his own daughter, whose face was bleeding from her fall against a chair. (282)

Margaret's Medusan stare seems dependent, for Higgins, on her ability to keep still—to make herself a monument—and her success with him satisfies her: "Margaret felt that he acknowledged her power." "Softening" in her fixity and toward Higgins, Margaret diverts his attention toward his dead daughter as sepulchral monument. If, as corpse, Bessy is merely a "poor dumb form" (283), she will remain useful to Higgins in his memory purely as a form, never subject to the strain of monumentality as Margaret is subject to it and never (never again?) the object of the violence that has knocked her sister down. Gaskell wonders for Margaret, "What could she do next?" Margaret's predicament as living monument is how to resolve the tension generated by her responsibility to maintain stillness, given the inevitability of her need to *do* at all, her ineluctable liability to movement and her subsequent vulnerability to the potential violence of "half-conquered, half-resenting" spectatorship.

Margaret deliberately assumes monumental status when she tries to stop with the spectacle of her body the raging violence of Thornton's striking workers. She thinks that her presentation of what she will call woman's "reverenced helplessness" (253) will be sufficient to arrest the workers and protect Thornton, not as himself (an important distinction for her) but as any man "in danger from the violence of numbers." In the first and last moments, Margaret accurately assesses the extent to which she can rely thus on her body actively to signify, even if—in order to invoke her "reverenced helplessness" as a woman—she can use it only to signify passivity; seeing her, the men come to look "irresolute, and as if asking what this meant" (234). As a figure on the barricades, Margaret is a passive and pacifist Marianne, hoping to quell action and ending as its object. But, forgetting that she has embraced Dissenter John Oldfield's lesson on silence ("He can do it by thy silence as well as by thy preaching" [68]) and dissatisfied with the helplessness of reverenced silence, Margaret blunders into speech, promising what is not hers to promise, "relief from your complaints, whatever they are" (234).

Margaret's reliance on her body's monumentality depends on its ability to signify at once its sexuality and its rectitude. The supposed ability of her sex to offer protection (to her or to Thornton, for whom she makes "her body into a shield" [234]) is disrupted by her speech and diverted by the crowd's response to her, the "reckless passion" of the "savage lads, with their love of cruel excitement" who "always . . . head the riot" and who strike her with a flung stone. But the ability of her sex to offer protection is as much *dependent on* as *disrupted by* the sexuality of the crowd, which quiets itself on seeing her "lay like one dead on Mr. Thornton's shoulder" and on seeing "the thread of dark-red blood which wakened them up from their trance of passion" (235).[12]

Margaret's poses, part of Gaskell's scheme to register legibly and with the whole body (with her womanly figure) Margaret's character and moral sensibility, disrupt that scheme not only by their apparent sexuality but also by their apparent self-consciousness. Writing of *North and South*, P. N. Furbank accuses Gaskell of declining to "play fair" in her treatment of Margaret.[13] He understands Margaret as "not a straight girl at all," despite Gaskell's references to Margaret's "straight looks," and imagines Gaskell might have kept better faith with readers by discussing Margaret's straightness only in "inverted commas" (her "straight" looks). Commenting on Gaskell's indication that Margaret retains her shawled pose when Henry Lennox interrupts her modeling "thinking she might yet be wanted as a sort of block for the shawls" (40), Furbank writes that "here we really cannot take Mrs. Gaskell literally, and must be meant to realise that she is telling a fib. Margaret's reason for standing perfectly still is clearly not just what we are told it is." Linking Margaret's mendacity to Gaskell's bad faith, Furbank sees Gaskell as getting into "a muddle" that leads to her duplicity. However "cunning, devious, and deceitful" Gaskell herself may be, the extension of such a characterization by readers to a heroine she seems to want to portray as, in honor and in physicality, "straight" surely *is* a muddle. What, as Gaskell might write of herself, could she do next?

Gaskell's resort to the swoon imagines that the problem of a self-conscious relation to the body is not answerable with mere unselfconsciousness (which is even unimaginable, perhaps) but only with physical unconsciousness. Margaret's effective swoon before the strikers echoes (in the story) but anticipates (in the telling of it) the swoon of a young Mrs. Thornton. Her swoon enables the body of young Mrs. Thornton to complete the task assigned its weakness; but her body fails her in its ability to accomplish the task she sets its strength. Like Margaret in this, Mrs. Thornton risked herself to save a mill owner from the anger of his striking workers, though Mrs. Thornton acts from sympathies unlike those Margaret acknowledges. The workers, Mrs. Thornton reports, had threatened to kill the owner the moment he appeared. She tells Margaret of her venture, with some pride:

"Some one had to go and tell him, or he was a dead man; and it needed to be a woman,—so I went. . . . So I went up to the roof, where there were stones piled ready to drop on the heads of the crowd, if they tried to force the factory doors. And I would have lifted those heavy stones, and dropped them with as good an aim as the best man there, but that I fainted with the heat I had gone through." (163)

Mrs. Thornton is saved from being the best of men by proving herself the best of women, doing so the more effectively because unhampered by a self-conscious understanding that she has displayed woman's "reverenced helplessness." To the extent that Margaret, similarly circumstanced, makes a spectacle of her capacity to be reverenced, she undercuts her own desire to perform a spectacle of helplessness.

As part of its recurrent interest in death, *North and South* fetishizes the display of bodies helpless and insensible—yet significant (yielding signification)—because dead. A letter in which Gaskell discusses her work on *North and South* reveals the importance of death to the novel: "I think a better title than N. & S. would have been 'Death and Variations.' There are 5 deaths, each beautifully suited to the character of the individual."[14] In fact, the novel includes seven deaths (those of Bessy Higgins, Mrs. Hale, Leonards, Boucher, Mrs. Boucher, Mr. Hale, Mr. Bell); one wonders which deaths do not count for Gaskell, and whether, neglected, they do not count because they seem to her not beautiful or not suited. Mr. Bell exhibits something of Gaskell's interest in styles of dying and in death's capacity to render distinctly the nature of the dead person, when he compares the particularity of deaths with eating's democratic refusal to differentiate by type: "Nothing like the act of eating for equalising men. Dying is nothing to it. The philosopher dies sententiously—the pharisee ostentatiously—the simple-hearted humbly—the poor idiot blindly, as the sparrow falls to the ground" (446). Gaskell's inclusion of so many deaths in *North and South* makes the style of dying a way for the body to be lastly testamentary in the delineation of character; the problem of course is that testimony comes only after the fact of character. But death's finality makes it hardly useful for the heroine in the marriage plot, whose death as heroine is more conveniently managed by a change of name. Nevertheless, death's appeal for Gaskell as novelist—its uses in making distinctions, in generating didactic spectacle, in preempting the charge of self-consciousness—makes it a narrative fantasy hard to give up.

Gaskell's startling conception of death as susceptible to variation effects a novelistic conversion of death into the swoon.[15] Though Margaret is "taught by death what life should be" (502), it is not so clear what in *North and South* death's lesson is, if not a matter of how the body is arranged to best (moral and aesthetic) effect. Gaskell's dealings with the body in the novel depend upon conceiving of the swoon as a kind of death—insofar as it serves the text as an index of character—and as a kind of blush—insofar as it partakes of involuntarity to display the workings of a moral sensibility.

The strain with which Margaret maintains her poses (her "bearing up better than likely" after her mother's death [341]) is released when she collapses subsequent to her questioning by the police. Margaret lies to the police about her presence at the railway station on the evening of Leonards's death in order to keep the police from knowing that her mutinous (and therefore "wanted") brother was present with her and that his tripping Leonards is what made Leonards fall. Margaret's pose impresses the inspector ("she never blenched or trembled"), who is "almost daunted by the haughtiness of her manner" (342) but more attracted than daunted by her "superb air of disdain" (343). The erotics of Margaret's poses are nowhere so apparent as in the "enforced tension of the muscles" which swell her lips "into a richer curve than ordinary," in her "unwonted sullen defiance," and in the inspector's registration that in her immobility at least her "large dark eyes . . . dilated a little." Despite his doubts and despite the testimony of the grocer's assistant who recognized her (Margaret is betrayed, in small textual revenge, by the "shoppy people" she had disdained), the inspector believes Margaret because of her "unflinching, calm denial," given with "a composure that appeared supreme" (344). Repeating the words of her denial—unable to improvise within her lie— Margaret controls the involuntary wink, not ever closing her eyes, and shows "no change of colour, or darker shadow of guilt, on her proud face." Looking away and then back, as if to catch her moving would be to catch her in a lie, the inspector seems to note that "she had not moved any more than if she had been some great Egyptian statue" (345).

For the police inspector, Margaret's immobility validates her credibility. But readers of *North and South* have learned from Gaskell to mistrust self-conscious control of the ostensibly involuntary. Margaret's response upon the inspector's departure is the only right one in terms of the novel. Having locked the door to keep the police from surveying her exercise of "some passionate impulse" (346), Margaret staggers, the novel indulging almost cinematically its description of her lack of control: "Then she went into the study, paused—tottered forward—paused again—swayed for an instant where she stood, and fell prone on the floor in a dead swoon" (346). Margaret's swoon recovers for Gaskell the function of the blush: as she faints, Margaret is rescued from the dishonor of the lie by her truth-telling body. Margaret's virtuous body, systemically overwhelmed by the determined lie, shuts down its circulation; and, as a display of moral character, Margaret's surrender to her swoon is symbolically a little death. The text indicates that for some time "Margaret lay as still and white as death on the study floor" (348), and Dixon, with rough concern, later comments on Margaret's consequent looks and on her health: "You are more dead than alive" (353).[16] The swoon assumes the virtues of death in offering textual reassurance of Margaret's good character: her naive body's efforts at the sophistications of control finally overwhelm it, and Margaret's body succumbs to a sensibility so excessive as to render her insensible and to unselfconsciousness so complete as to mean she is unconscious.

When she is hit by the striker's stone, Margaret passes out and is brought into the Thornton's home to recover consciousness. The Thorntons' servant comments on Margaret's appearance: "She looks like a corpse now" (239). Fanny Thornton's petulant response—her wish that someone would come relieve her in caring for Margaret—escalates her estimation of Margaret's unconsciousness: "I never was in the room with a dead person before." Fanny's half-belief in her inaccurate assessment of Margaret's condition permits her to gossip freely with the servant while standing over Margaret's body; Fanny believes in the unconsciousness of the unconscious. But Gaskell imagines the unconscious as perceptive and sensible in their insensibility. She writes of Margaret:

> She was conscious of movement around her, and of refreshments from the eau de Cologne, and a craving for the bathing to go on without intermission; but when they stopped to talk, she could no more have opened her eyes, or spoken to ask for more bathing, than the people who lie in death-like trance can move, or utter sound, to arrest the awful preparations for their burial, while they are yet fully aware, not merely of the actions of those around them, but of the idea that is the motive for such actions. (238)

Gaskell's fantasy of the swoon endows it with the pathos of a death in life. As self-consciousness has sometimes seemed to her to imply a distance from feeling, unconsciousness—counter to intuition and definition—is valuable precisely in that, while seeming to deprive bodies of sense, it in fact affords an oddly greater and more immediate access to feeling.

The swoon's sensible insensibility works for the subject of the swoon, even to permitting an indulgence impermissible in consciousness (something decadent about that longing for the bathing to go on). But the swoon will not successfully and comprehensively replace the blush for Gaskell because it proves to bring with it to narrative the same problems as the blush. Like the blush, it is subject to perception, liable to misunderstanding and to incredulity. Nothing literarily more suspect than the woman's faint;[17] nothing culturally more suspect than that sexual honor for which it declines to stand.[18] The swoon is indicted by the fact that Fanny Thornton faints, too, and Gaskell is at some pains to suggest that Margaret's most private swoon is not the fainting of the fashionably hysterical woman. With admiration and praise, her mother's doctor considers Margaret's response to the severity of Mrs. Hale's illness: "It's astonishing how much those thorough-bred creatures can and do suffer. That girl's game to the backbone. Another, who had gone that deadly colour, could never have come round without either fainting or hysterics. But she wouldn't do either—not she!" (174–75). Later, when Gaskell exploits the swoon to suggest the honor of Margaret's body, that use is available to her only because she has here tried to save Margaret from the taint of seeming to swoon as a hysterical recourse to unconsciousness: fainting imagined as an act of evasion or a performance of demand. But Gaskell's effort to make this distinction betrays a lasting anxiety, and her worries about fainting and swooning parallel her concerns about blushing; the extremity of the faint, the obviousness with which it connects psyche and soma, attaches to vulgarity and seems thus unbelievable and unworthy of trust.

In seeming as susceptible as the blush to production by fashion or art, the swoon fails Gaskell as a stable register of character, or, more precisely, Gaskell fails to trust the swoon as stable register. If, as she thinks about it, the body is liable to use, it is liable to *her* use in the novel as much as to the use of Margaret or Fanny in faint or in blush. Gaskell's mistrust of the arts with which the body's involuntarity can seem—like any product of Thornton's mill—manufactured, made to order, seems finally a mistrust of art. If the blush and swoon in *North and South* are subject to control, they are subjected because written, subjected by Gaskell's writing.

Margaret's Blunders, Gaskell's "As if"

Midway through *North and South,* Mrs. Hale, aware that she is dying, longs to see her exiled son, and cries to Margaret in despair. Gaskell writes that, in response, "Margaret sat down by her mother's sofa on a little stool, and softly took hold of her hand, caressing it and kissing it, as if to comfort" (262). Gaskell's "as if" would seem to suggest some equivocation about Margaret's urge to comfort her mother, not wholly incredible, given that Mrs. Hale has just recalled thinking Frederick a beautiful child, whereas at the first sight of Margaret Mrs. Hale says she exclaimed, "Dear, what an ugly little thing!" (262). And yet the "as if" does not make precise enough sense. If Margaret's hand-holding only pretends to provide comfort, it is still hard to know what else (what more insidious) it might really do: however equivocal are her mother's feelings for Margaret, Gaskell does not suggest other than by a logic of reciprocation that Margaret's feelings are particularly mixed. Readers of *North and South* might know by this point in the novel, though, not to take *too* seriously Gaskell's "as if," which comes to seem a curious tic of her writing.[19]

Gaskell's as ifs, not always of much local significance, signify more largely a refusal of conviction, a resistance to fiction, the habituation of a crisis of signification. Writing endlessly "as if," Gaskell is always a little withholding, a little self-conscious, a little uncommitted, a little anxious always to be seen to call a sign a sign. If fiction is discursively dependent on an unspoken as if, that dependence itself rests on a reliance that the as if remain unspoken. Gaskell's self-conscious "as ifs" tend to congregate around the body (hands held as if in comfort, ladies starting as if ashamed, mouths opening as if to speak), and her anxieties tend to revolve around the place of the body in writing, the use of the body as sign. Gaskell's desire for the body in writing—like that of many other nineteenth-century novelists—is that it occupy the space of the natural, that it offer the support of the contingent, that its involuntarity yield unwilling legibility. This is what, gesturing toward Jane Austen, she wants to evoke and to contain. But using the body as sign involves seeing it as sign; writing the blush means making the blush over with artful linguistic cosmetic and sacrificing to control its promise of contingent and powerful support.

When Frederick Hale sneaks back from Spain to his mother's deathbed, he provides, among other things, an account of Margaret's blunders that is different from her own. Where Margaret has seen herself as stumbling against the obstacles of the world, Frederick sees her as blundering congenitally. "What a bungler you are!" he tells Margaret, as she tries to build a fire. "I never saw such a little awkward, good-for-nothing pair of hands" (312). With all the assured charm of one who never will own his own missteps, Frederick makes clear that Margaret's tendency to bungle projects and to blunder with language is a failing born, not made, and, further, inevitably correspondent to a certain kind of body. To perceive Margaret's blunders as inherent or essential is to imagine them as an eruption of the natural and contingent. Recuperating Margaret's blunders in this way (as if Gaskell had just been using them to test reader attention or devotion) restores to her an access to sincerity and gentility that the more fashionable Fanny Thornton, for example, is denied. When Eliza Doolittle is declared a fraud in *My Fair Lady* by linguist Zoltan Karpathy, it is because she is too schooled in English aesthetics and manners, too good at the English language. The great class comfort of imperfection rewrites flaw as virtue, compensates for imperfection by declaring perfection fraudulent. The fear that art exceeds the natural (in class terms, that manor and manners born fall to their rival "as if") produces the compensatory sense that the natural succeeds precisely insofar as it is seen to fail.

By this logic, Gaskell's failures with blush and swoon turn into success with blunder and tic. The blunder, even when it involves saying the wrong thing (the foot in the mouth), seems physical, and Gaskell imagines Margaret's blunders in speech as an action of her large body. A gesture made in language as if by a certain type of body, the blunder is an intrusion, an awkwardness, a clumsiness, its disruption precisely dependent on its ability—getting something wrong—nevertheless to get it right.

Why all this might be felt crucially as an issue—why legibility might matter to the legible subject as well as to that subject's monitor—is expressed in *North and South* only as a loss generated by a willful deprivation. Nicholas Higgins describes for Margaret what it might be like to live under his trade union's "ways and means" of effecting mandatory membership:

"Yo' try that, miss; try living a year or two among them as looks away if yo' look at 'em; try working within two yards o' crowds o' men, who, yo' know, have a grinding grudge at yo' in their hearts—to whom if yo' say yo're glad, not an eye brightens, nor a lip moves,—to whom if your heart's heavy, yo' can never say nought, because they'll ne'er take notice on your sighs or sad looks (and a man's no man who'll groan out loud 'bout folk asking him what's the matter?)—just yo' try that, miss—ten hours for three hundred days, and yo'll know a bit what th' Union is." (295–96)

The isolation and ostracism imposed by the union is imagined in bodily terms as a refusal of signs ("not an eye brightens, nor a lip moves") and a refusal to read signs ("they'll ne'er take notice on your sighs or sad looks"). Gaskell's conception of punishment as being denied legibility bespeaks the longing of novelist and of person to be read, and understands that longing as so essential as to be somatic. As an interpretation of capillary action, the blush is an attribution of desire to the body, a fantasy of the body that conceives of the body as writing its desire on itself, as if—blushing—the body is asking to be read.

Chapter Four Dickens's Scar: Rosa Dartle and *David Copperfield*

*J*ane Austen's blush negotiates with considerable delicacy (if also with ostentatious success) the demands of legibility and the energies of somatic signification. Elizabeth Gaskell's response to the force of Austen's blush involves her in a crisis about the status of the body in fiction; the involuntarity of the blush is crucial to its work as a sign of character, and her own writing of the body and the blush in *North and South* makes it impossible for Gaskell to believe in the blush as sign. Gaskell's half-resolution to her problem (the substitution of the blunder for the blush) enables her to half-appreciate what her own crisis reveals: a fantasy of legible physiology as the product of the body's authority and intention. Charles Dickens has no such crisis of faith, and his management of the blush suggests that Dickens believes so powerfully in his fictions that they seem to threaten him with action and meaning (with signification) in excess of Dickensian authority. The blush is a site of anxiety for Dickens (about class, about women, about the body, and about significatory excess), and his substitution of the scar for the blush is an attempt to substitute fixity for instability. Dickens's physical graphics of mortification is a scarring of his text: a response to exasperation and a display of control. Moving from manners to melodrama, Dickens reads mortification as violence and makes the blush-as-scar a mark of lurid signification.

Visibility and Its Discontents

Preparing to write about blushing in *The Expression of the Emotions in Man and Animals,* Charles Darwin circulated queries about blushing (and other somatic expressions) among various observers of "all the races of mankind."[1] Darwin's project uses the people encountered by British and Continental travelers as control and background against which generalizable observations that are important insofar as they tell about white Englishmen may be formulated and foregrounded. Anxious to discover whether certain expressions are "true ones,—that is, are innate or instinctive," Darwin wants to know whether shame is able to "excite a blush when the colour of the skin allows it to be visible" (15), but the qualification in his question—"when the skin allows it to be visible"—indicates the presence of an edgier concern. Darwin's original question excites a corollary wonder about whether shame excites a blush when the color of the skin does *not* allow it to be visible. The inclusiveness of Darwin's category—"all the races of mankind"—veils the exclusivity of the group (he will call it simply "us") whose responses set his norm. Interest in true expressions among "all the races of mankind" generates a real question only with respect to all the *other* races of mankind, and Darwin incites observers to wonder whether people with black or brown skin blush "under such circumstances as would raise a blush in us" (317). But the dominance of Darwin's "us" as the group whose blushes and whose circumstances are the full measure of sufficiency fades into a kind of anxious insistence on the primacy of that us. The respondents to Darwin's questions ("how low down the body does the blush extend?" [15]) are permitted to answer for the truth of blushes "in us" only by means of what they are able to read on the skins of "savages."[2] Darwin's science licenses the amateur scientific inquisitor to conduct an inquiry that enacts the inquisitor's dependence on legibility; that inquisitor will, in the oscillations of ambivalent searching, now see nothing on the skin of the other, now see its ability to blush "brown" (318).

In raising on behalf of his insistent "us" questions of self-examination that prove answerable only in terms of a potentially unblushing "them," Darwin disrupts the fantasy of legibility maintained by mannerly blushes, articulating for "us" the always-present possibility of such disruption. Darwin's questions about "them," understandable as products of his wondering "*do* they blush?" or "have they our moral sense?," modulate into questions about what is to be done by "us" in the face of blushes seen as an intensification of blackness (318). The apparent self-sufficiency of Darwin's "us" is challenged not only by its dependence on its perceived other for the answers to its questions, but by the questions themselves. Darwin's queries probe the social and novelistic premise of the blush: that blushes exist to be read, and, further, that they exist to be read by "us." Perceived or imagined as blushing, reddening cheeks are imagined to announce their vulnerability and to offer themselves to the observer for reading; the prospect of the other's somatic legibility enables a fantasy of possession. (Your blushes are for me.) But to ask whether the cheek blushes when the darknesses of night or skin or supposed ill manners render it invisible is to invert legibility's fantasy of the observer's primacy by considering the blush as an event felt rather than as a thing seen; invisible, the pink blush loses its interpretive dominance over the warm flush and raises phantasmatically the possibility that the blushes of the other might be not one's own but the other's. Averting their eyes suspiciously, those who are blushing might be imagined by those who observe them to claim a kind of public isolation and self-possession. Avoiding other eyes conspicuously, those of us who blush might be seen to make—by means of our coloring—a space in which undistractedly to indulge blushing's solitary pleasures. The prospect of blushing's possessive privacy creates for manners a renewed desire for legibility, and a new demand that legibility be fixed, permanent, tangible.

With other anecdotal evidence in the chapter on blushing, Darwin includes for consideration a story from Dr. Burgess's treatise on blushing. Burgess, Darwin indicates with a vagueness or discretion he has borrowed from the doctor himself, "had frequent opportunities of observing a scar . . . on the face of a negress."[3] Seizing his opportunities to observe the scar and to watch the woman, Burgess, Darwin reports, "saw that [the scar] 'invariably became red whenever she was abruptly spoken to or charged with any trivial offense.'" The frequently scrutinized scar on the frequently flushed face of the invariably accused black woman is one of those that, Burgess and Darwin notice, "remain for a long time white in the negro." The scar—now imagined as the white part of the black woman—provisionally satisfies Darwin in enforcing the fulfillment of blood's promise to tell.[4] And telling, as it seems, the woman's embarrassment or shame (one wonders if it might not also have told her anger), the scar offers Darwin the fantasy of a corrigible black body, "white" like "us" in its ability to show red, and corrected, at least in unpleasant Darwinian fantasy, by the imagined assault that could have made the scar. Yet, recorded by Burgess and Darwin, the implications of what is told—who is told on—extend beyond the scarred and flushing woman. There is something that, if it is unsurprising, is nevertheless also breathtaking about the ease of Darwin's simple registry of the blithe unconsciousness and active disregard with which traders, missionaries, and doctors have noted the instances of painful self-consciousness they have provoked and exploited.[5] Those Darwin has incited to observation, along with Burgess and the other predecessors in observation who have so incited him, make of Darwin's record of blushes "among all the races of mankind" a record also of vigilance and of accusation. Whatever provenance it remarks, the woman's scar, in its ability to make her blush legible, makes itself desirable; or, rather, the ability to see the scar as able to make the blush—or the blackness—visible is both generative of and generated by a kind of desire for the scar.

Even as Darwin bespeaks it, the Victorian novel is fulfilling this desire, answering this need, supplying this demand in its discovery and production of the scar. Darwin's articulation of cultural fantasy helps make intelligible for me the prevalence in the Victorian novel and in other Victorian fiction of characters who are scarred or marked. Its marked men and women offer evidence of Victorian fiction's fascination with legibility, but they also offer evidence of its fascination with the way writing about bodies can entail a particular response to them: writing about bodies resembles and generates a desire to write on them. A partial list of characters in Victorian fiction who are scarred or marked in other ways includes Trollope's George Vavasour (*Can You Forgive Her?*); Esther Summerson (*Bleak House*); Isabel Vane in Ellen Wood's *East Lynne;* Sir Percival Glyde in Wilkie Collins's *The Woman in White* and Mannion in Collins's *Basil;* Rochester in *Jane Eyre;* Margaret Hale in Gaskell's *North and South* and Jem Wilson in *Mary Barton;* both Mina Harker and the Count himself in Stoker's *Dracula;* Magdalen in Collins's *No Name,* identifiable, when it is necessary for her to be so, by a mole; Caddy Jellyby in *Bleak House* (ink-stained); and Oscar in Collins's *Poor Miss Finch* (colored blue by medicinal silver nitrate); Boucher in *North and South,* his skin stained by the dye-polluted water in which he drowns; and, in shorter fiction, Doyle's man who, using makeup, twists his lip, and Lord Arthur Saville, whose crime or inclination might be written in his hand.

Where the blush fails in its promise to render character legible, the scar speaks to a fantasy of violent corrigibility and promises to ensure legible permanence. For Dickens, as for Darwin, the scar offers a calming fixity to ease the frustrations that ensue when fantasies of legibility are metamorphosed into fantasies of illegibility; as its substitute, the scar might seem to improve upon the blush in bringing stability to that site where the vagaries of complexion and the temporal nature of physiology tease efforts to find—or, not finding, to construct—legibility of character and of the body. But Rosa Dartle's scar in *David Copperfield* works in a way that violates these suppositions about the blush and the scar. Taking the place of the blush, the scar takes up, as well, its occupation as an indicator of the cultural lessons that have been learned through and displayed with self-consciousness and mortification; making the blush visible against itself as background, the scar comes to assume the blush's own reputation for a merely intermittent commitment to legibility.

Fierce Little Pieces

"Why, there's a pretty wide separation between them and us," said Steerforth, with indifference. "They are not to be expected to be as sensitive as we are. Their delicacy is not to be shocked, or hurt very easily. They are wonderfully virtuous, I dare say—some people contend for that, at least; and I am sure I don't want to contradict them—but they have not very fine natures, and they may be thankful that, like their coarse rough skins, they are not easily wounded."[6]

Envying from a genteel distance the exemption from socially obliged sensitivity he imagines the Peggottys enjoy, and lamenting the pains he fantasizes he would have to take in the wounding of their rough skin, *David Copperfield*'s James Steerforth describes that skin as coarse. Doing so, failing to read in the coarse the story of its coarsening, Steerforth at once coarsely celebrates and callously forgets the susceptibility with which Rosa Dartle must hear him. That she is "the motherless child of a sort of cousin" of his father (240) is, Steerforth claims, Rosa Dartle's history, with the addition that her "remarkable scar" (240) is the mark of his exasperation and of his hammer.

Rosa Dartle's is a memorable scar. A seam, David Copperfield would "rather call it," when she is calm, "for it was not discolored" (238). Dickens's novel will not accede to David's preference, however, for a scar that has healed, pulled together. The colors of Rosa Dartle's passion undo with violence the scar's therapeutic work, as David cannot keep from noticing with a "painful interest" of his own (241): "As she looked full at me, I saw her face grow sharper and paler, and the marks of the old wound lengthen out until it cut through the disfigured lip, and deep into the nether lip, and slanted down the face" (351–52). David's fascination is surely not culturally inexplicable: the woman "not agreeable to look at, but with some appearance of good looks too" who has been "so long to let" (238) promises and threatens her availability for occupation, and Rosa Dartle's transfixing wound is, among many other things, vaginal and Medusan. David's fascination and that of the novel's readers (perhaps no more inexplicable than his) highlight the means by which a mark made in cruelty is linguistically and cognitively metamorphosed into what David calls it, a "cruel mark" (352). Having absorbed the agency with which Steerforth flung the hammer, the mark now seems to David itself capable of inflicting pain. Yet David's inability to "dissociate" from the scar "the idea of pain" (352), curiously also a reluctance to identify the pain as someone else's, keeps him in a relation to Rosa Dartle that is both sympathetic and aggressive: watching her portrait as it seems to watch him, David Copperfield makes for himself the scar the painter has blandly omitted. "There it was, coming and going: now confined to the upper lip as I had seen it at dinner, and now showing the whole extent of the wound inflicted by the hammer, as I had seen it when she was passionate" (243).

Like her scar, Rosa Dartle, too, seems to have absorbed with Steerforth's blow something of the fierce energy with which the novel encourages readers to imagine it must have been struck. The woman who has "worn herself away by constant sharpening," who is "all edge" (240), has been made a kind of weapon. Aptly signifying the "second nature" Mrs. Steerforth tells Rosa Dartle she has acquired in the years since "her manner was different" (353), the scar performs its work in the novel by erasing, in all but outline, the narrative of its making. Written as Dickens has written her—not, that is, as the barely evoked Rosa whose uncut blushes might perhaps have been more appropriate to her now touchingly inappropriate first name—Rosa Dartle bears what serves as a mark not only of the lesson by which she might seem to have acquired character but of a character that might seem to render such marking suitable, such a lesson well taught. Like the novelist of manners who—making over the blush—works at making it legible, Dickens—making the scar—works at disguising its status as product, transforming it from thing made to natural sign.[7] In the slippages (her name, her pain) by which some prior Rosa *is* evoked, Steerforth's hand—however well it has seemed to mimic nature's in forming Rosa Dartle's character—reveals itself in the discomfort with which Rosa Dartle assumes, as one does, a manner that, if become a kind of nature, is yet second.

Merely following nature, Steerforth does the work of an angry sculptor ("the scar made by the hammer"), and, like Balzac's Sarrasine, he might seem to throw his hammer with "such extraordinary force" that it misses.[8] Though Steerforth's hammer has of course not missed Rosa Dartle as Sarrasine's has missed his statue of La Zambinella, the two uses to which these hammers have been put (sculpting, throwing) are alike processes of formation (of figure, of a second nature). But, as "Sarrasine" does for Sarrasine, *David Copperfield* plots for Steerforth the trajectory by which even the blow struck also misses (fails to satisfy) in striking back. As "she brings everything to a grindstone" (240), Rosa Dartle, herself "all edge," exasperates (roughens, irritates—as of skin); recalcitrant (kicking back), she returns Steerforth's blow, anticipating and answering its direction.[9] In refusing us the whole story of the incident in which Steerforth scarred Rosa Dartle, Dickens might seem to protect her from charges of provocation, and yet, characterizing Steerforth as "exasperated" (240), he permits, even enlists, a reciprocal characterization of Rosa Dartle as exasperating.[10] Impenetrable, then, hard to read in some way, "a fierce little piece of incomprehensibility" (355), Rosa Dartle, her thin skin broken by violence, ought to have been made legible by the leavings of Steerforth's exertions, which, David Copperfield tells us, would "start forth" on her face "like the old writing on the wall" (241).[11]

But, when the evidently exasperating Rosa Dartle responds with exclamatory wonder to Mrs. Steerforth's injunction to recall and to reproduce her former self—a self "less guarded and more trustful"—she recalls instead the narrative by which her scar was produced: "How can I, imperceptibly, have changed, I wonder!" (353). Seeming to wonder at herself, Rosa wonders, instead, at the way her altered manner is wondered *at* by those who have wrought the mark that makes her alteration start perceptibly forth; scarred, she *cannot* imperceptibly have changed. The peculiar brand of Rosa's self-consciousness has its utility for her and for Dickens: the identity of Rosa Dartle seems to lie precisely in insinuation, in a kind of flirtation with legibility that wants, finally, to refuse legibility.[12] (In this sense, Steerforth's blow "misses" by not making Rosa easier to read.) "It appeared to me," writes Dickens for David Copperfield, "that she never said anything she wanted to say, outright; but hinted it, and made a great deal more of it by this practice" (239). In her speech, Rosa Dartle practices a kind of self-conscious self-qualification that, saying nearly nothing, nearly says what it wants said.

Of the physical mortification with which Steerforth has tried to make her readable, Rosa Dartle has fashioned a mode of behavior. Covering with her hand the twitching and throbbing of her scar as they threaten David with the advances that, for a moment, exceed her retreats, she grotesquely accepts—for that moment—socialization, legibility, manners. In concealment and in revelation, her gesture parodies Dora Spenlow's shaking out of the curls that hide and display her blushes: the covering is a gesture of embarrassment. But it is the practices of mortification, rather than manners, that have become to Rosa Dartle "second nature." Her face "darkened" by rage, as David recalls it, "the scar made by the hammer was, as usual in this excited state of her features, strongly marked. When the throbbing I had seen before, came into it as I looked at her, she absolutely lifted up her hand, and struck it" (384–85). The excesses of Rosa's complicity with the demands of mortification decline support to a system of legibility; Rosa Dartle will not yield. Turning herself on herself, she sets edge on edge. Taking her body as object, she remakes—and claims by remaking—the scar Steerforth had made of that body ("a fierce little piece of incomprehensibility"). Rosa's mortification of this "most susceptible part of her face" (241) makes of the material of her self-consciousness a kind of difficult self-possession. In its physical obduracy ("a fierce little piece"), the scar, an objectification of Rosa's pain and a function of her self-consciousness, produces a behavioral obduracy that correspondingly protects and indulges the self. The tangibility of self-consciousness in the scar makes of self-consciousness the manipulable possession of what seems a toughened self. Exercising this self-possession, Rosa Dartle responds to Steerforth's disquisition on the wounding of rough skin: "I don't know when I have been better pleased than to hear that" (240).

What Rosa has heard—Steerforth's claim about the roughness of Peggotty skin—is a claim made repeatedly in the language of *David Copperfield*. Recounting as narrator his childhood observations of Peggotty, David Copperfield notes "cheeks and arms so hard and red that I wondered the birds didn't peck her in preference to apples" (10), displacing onto "the birds" his own temptation to try Peggotty's insensitivity. Peggotty yields herself more completely to the temptation; pensive, she is to be found "sticking her needle into various parts of her face and arms, all the time" (14), as if searching them, with thoughtful or with absent mind, for such feeling (such pain) as is there to be found. Skin so roughened, to whatever degree also reddened, is skin that is both illegible and inexpressive of sensation without trial in physical mortification; a complexion habitually the color of the "red velvet footstool in the best parlor" (13), demonstrably educated at a "school of beauty" different from that which produced the socially responsive complexion of Clara Copperfield, will not reveal embarrassment with a delicate blush and—in declining so to reveal it—will meet with a toughened resistance the demand for revelation. David learns the language of sensible embarrassment with which to contrast insensate silence when his mother blushes at a compliment from her suitor Mr. Murdstone: "I never saw such a beautiful color on my mother's face before" (15). Clara Copperfield's complexion responds to the pressure of circumstance by assuming (for just a moment) the color that is always the color of Peggotty's complexion. For the young David, the novel has already made clear, "such a beautiful color" is the red shared by Peggotty's rough skin and the smooth groundwork of that favorite footstool.[13] Clara Copperfield's skin will sometimes be as beautiful as red velvet. Clara Peggotty's, ostensibly always so beautiful, can never really be so, since it cannot signal intermittently—for David or for the novel—the charms of attraction, self-consciousness, embarrassment. David's fantasy of pecking belies his claim to appreciate Peggotty's beauty: pecking, he or the absent Blunderstone rooks would write on her skin, scattering over its blank redness corrective diacritics. Unblushing or always blushing, Peggotty's classed body fails her in declining to extend the lure of legibility; unattractive to the bride and groom, she will have to watch the wedding from the gallery (516).

Dan'l Peggotty, too, is hardened and darkened by labor. The uses of the textured complexion in the world of gentility need explanation, he seems to know ("You'll find us rough, sir, but you'll find us ready" [25]), and the "muck" of his business needs not a mere cleansing but in fact a scalding such as is usually reserved for cooking the creatures that pass through his hands. David writes of his first encounter with Mr. Peggotty: "He soon returned, greatly improved in appearance; but so rubicund, that I couldn't help thinking his face had this in common with the lobsters, crabs, and crawfish,—that it went into the hot water very black, and came out very red" (25). Improved, the dirt and blackness of work cleansed by the pains he has taken, Mr. Peggotty is still not good enough. The redness produced and revealed by immersion in the boiling water remains constant and entire, and it thus retains an association with labor that—of course—interferes with blushing's telegraphy of ethic or of sentiment.[14] David's identification of Mr. Peggotty with crustaceans and mollusks is no stronger than Mr. Peggotty's own. Using as a kind of shorthand the names of the creatures in which he deals, Mr. Peggotty forges a kind of self-expression: " 'I'm a reg'lar Dodman, I am,' said Mr. Peggotty; by which he meant snail, and this was in allusion to his being slow to go" (83).[15] For the mannerly, the toughening and resistance of roughened skin alternatively reinforce class distinction and threaten it by suggesting the development of an obdurate privacy. But felt from within, Dickens's use of Mr. Peggotty suggests, toughening might occasion regret; like Gaskell's Higgins, Mr. Peggotty appreciates the force of his desire to be read. Imagined as involuntary, blushing would seem to afford opportunities for expressivity as well as for the pleasures of display and revelation lost to those whose blood's responses are rendered invisible by their labors. Imagined as the indicator of gentility, blushing might seem, too, fit aspiration for those outside the mannered classes.

"'If this ain't,' said Mr. Peggotty, sitting down among us by the fire, 'the brightest night o' my life, I'm a shellfish—biled too—and more I can't say'" (255). Evoking what is shelled to represent his state of being, Mr. Peggotty ("shellfish—biled") says he is tickled pink. When he announces to David and to the gentlemanly Steerforth the engagement of Little Em'ly to Ham, Mr. Peggotty is especially eager to point out to Steerforth the appropriately coloring complexion of the engaged girl; he indicates her, "'This here little Em'ly, sir,' in a low voice to Steerforth, 'her as you see a blushing here just now—'" (255). In the presence of all that the novel calls James Steerforth, and in some way aware of his skin's inadequacies in the realm of social expression ("more I can't say"), Mr. Peggotty displays with delight the family's best product, a body able to record on itself the family's sensitivity. Rough labor has not been without aesthetic issue: far from reproducing its ostensible insentience, the laboring family has yielded a semblance of the genteel, in Emily, that is conspicuously the source of its complected pride. Blushing for Steerforth, Emily functions in and for the family as she is supposed to: as its blush. Beside Mr. Peggotty, she makes visible for and about him what more it is he cannot say: wanting his pleasure read, Mr. Peggotty achieves some satisfaction with the complement of Emily's blush.

Where Steerforth expects to find "coarse rough skins . . . not easily wounded" (240), he encounters instead the blushes of little Emily. That Emily serves as invitation to Steerforth is both the logical consequence of the Peggottys' desires and, of course, the overturning of these desires in their collision with Steerforth's fantasies.[16] Little Emily's disruption of his fantasies of the Peggottys' insensitivity suggests for Steerforth the possibilities for dalliance in the space created by the "pretty wide separation between them and us" (240). The undifferentiated redness of the

Peggottys has seemed to make them—like Austen's sailors in the estimation of Sir Walter Elliot—legible in just one way. The Peggottys are readable solely in class terms, as those who labor. But Emily's blushes bespeak the laboring family's capacity for the intermittent redness constitutive of the body in manners. Steerforth will not read Emily's blushes in quite the way the Peggottys might wish. For him, her pink and genteel delicacy cannot simply substitute for rubicund Peggotty labor. Her blushing indicates that her family has made an acquisition of genteel semiosis, and, in doing so, it will fascinate Steerforth, as it surprises him into the discovery that reading labor is potentially as complex as reading manners. Yet even as the exhibition of verisimilar gentility by one among them makes members of the working class seem to demand close reading, the redness and roughness consequent upon their very utility keeps them, while legible in labor, illegible in manners.

Little Emily, knowing to blush, vexes the facial semiotics of class, even as, knowing to blush, she permits her family to enter the realm of mannerly signification. Emily's blushing, which raises for Steerforth the problem of the laboring family's place in mannerly legibility, also represents the possibility of a solution to that problem. Her ability to show color, promising and threatening her escape from the system of utility, ultimately recuperates her for inclusion within it. If she cannot actually solve the problem for Steerforth—cannot unmake it—she can offer the fascination of its continual reproduction. Steerforth's desire for Emily keeps her productive of the signs of legibility; so keeping her, Steerforth effectively keeps her in her place, keeps the Peggottys in theirs. To use Emily is to put her to work.[17] The sexual and psychological labor she performs for Steerforth gives content to the structurally significant fact of work itself: the resumption of appropriate class positions is achieved, for Steerforth and Emily, by their occupation of gendered sexual positions within the familiar plot of heterosexual seduction. And the way to maintain Emily's usefulness is to enlist her body in the generation of the signs by which her laboring family might be rendered legible. Steerforth does this—keeps Emily blushing—by taking advantage of the erythristic properties of scandal.[18] Involving her in scandal, he satisfies, in one way (the way of seduction) or in a way very much another (the way of shame), his desires—and, most perversely, those of her family—for the appearances of Emily's blush.

"I would have her branded on the face"

While Emily's blush functions within *David Copperfield* by trying to quell for Steerforth the very anxiety it creates about labor's intelligibility, it has had also to function for *David Copperfield* by participating in the novel's exploration of the uses for the self of the marking of the other: the novel's exploration of those needs that produce the desire for the other's legibility. The redness of those who labor offers a negative definition of mannerly identity; if Emily complicates the ease of that definition, she also offers a ground on which that definition may be written repeatedly by Steerforth in his scandalous production of her blush. For Steerforth, Emily's blush deciphered—like Rosa Dartle's scar—is meant to "read" (to name, say, see) James Steerforth as certainly as is the name "cut . . . very deep and very often" among the boyish inscriptions on the old door at Salem House (63). While the expressivity of his blush—could anyone see it—might constitute identity for Mr. Peggotty, and while the obdurate yet insinuative work of her scar constitutes identity for Rosa Dartle, for James Steerforth, identity is constituted by and rehearsable in the blushes he provokes and the scars his cuttings leave behind. Unlike carved initials, the other's visible blush, like the need it satisfies, is characteristically intermittent, enacting the disappearance of identity, even as blush and identity reassuringly reappear to answer provocation: just checking, I hope to find I am still there; there, again.[19] But the evident frequency and depth of Steerforth's cuttings (his carved surname, his graphic mortifications of women) suggest that he loses himself in the blush and the scar as often as he finds himself there.

Surely not isolated in these discoveries and these losses, Steerforth is just one of the characters in *David Copperfield* interested in the self's desire to mark the other for the sake of reading itself. David Copperfield, for example—when biting or striking others—is inevitably enabled by the impression he makes to perceive that impression as made on himself. For

David as he writes, even the memory of biting Mr. Murdstone "sets his teeth on edge," and, if the instant when, as a child, he bites is "the same instant" that he is struck, the "stripes . . . sore and stiff" that he sees on his "face in the glass, so swollen, red, and ugly" seem self-inflicted, the consequence of his gesture rather than Murdstone's (46).

But reading the self by the other fails, more often than not, to yield a distinct sense of self; rather it engenders a confusion that pleases or disturbs. When, returned from Salem House, David first encounters his stepfather, Mr. Murdstone (David tells us) "looked at me steadily as I entered, but made no sign of recognition whatever" (92). David approaches Murdstone to beg his pardon for the bite, but only after "confusion" that the narrative chooses to attribute neither to boy nor to man but to "a moment" both endure.[20] Murdstone's powerful if ostensible (powerful *because* ostensible) inability to recognize David becomes a confusion of David's own: "The hand he gave me was the hand I had bitten. I could not restrain my eye from resting for an instant on a red spot upon it; but it was not so red as I turned, when I met that sinister expression in his face" (92). David's desire for Murdstone's recognition (his fantasy that he is recognizable to Murdstone) is a desire to have made on his stepfather a lasting impression. David's desire eroticizes their relation and re-creates the "instant" in which David and Murdstone, indistinct, were blurred in simultaneous and circulating gestures of aggression, bound in a single exertion. The confusion embarrasses David, as Murdstone's "red spot" impresses itself on him as a blush; here, as in the customary usage of the novel of manners, confusion comes complexly to *mean* embarrassment.[21] When, hearing the sounds of David Copperfield's birth, Aunt Betsey stuffs Ham's ears with cotton "as if she confounded them with her own," it is he who reddens (9); from the earliest pages of the novel, embarrassment is consequent upon the confounding of bodies.

In figuring for David the confusion that is their potential resemblance (in circumstance if not in person), Uriah Heep, David thinks, invites with his "lank cheek" the blow David strikes "with open hand." David writes of the physical bonding with Uriah facilitated by David's acceptance of that apparent invitation: "He caught the hand in his, and we stood, in that connexion, looking at each other. We stood so, a long time; long

enough for me to see the white marks of my fingers die out of the deep
red of his cheek, and leave it a deeper red" (506). The finger marks David
leaves on Uriah, and the blush that succeeds them, are matched for David
by the tingling of his own fingers, burnt by the heat of Uriah's cheek; the
accuracy of Uriah's estimation of David's "quite . . . wrong position,"
writes David, "made me chafe the more" (507). In keeping David's hand,
Uriah articulates their connection and reproduces the conditions of his
first threat to impress himself upon David. Writing, David recalls the
indiscriminate largesse with which, "feeling friendly towards everybody,"
he gave the young Uriah his hand: "But oh, what a clammy hand his was!
as ghostly to the touch as to the sight! I rubbed mine afterwards, to warm
it, *and to rub his off* " (183). David's subsequent fantasy that it is his hand
that has been impressive ("I remembered the mark of my hand upon his
cheek" [612]) answers his evident inability to rub Uriah off (his "uncomfortable hand . . . was still cold and wet upon my memory" [183]).

The "pervading red" (610) of Uriah Heep suffuses *David Copperfield*:
"in the grain" of his face "there was that tinge of red which is sometimes
to be observed in the skins of red-haired people" (178); "every now and
then, his sleepless eyes would come below the writing, like two red suns,
and stealthily stare at me" (180); "his shadowless red eyes . . . looked as if
they had scorched his lashes off" (308); his habitual scraping of "his lank
jaw" (310) must leave streaks that are first white, then red. The association of Uriah's color with his lank- and limpness connects it with his
transgressive and chastised hand ("it felt like a fish, in the dark" [192–93],
"like a frog in mine" [307])[22] and with the pendant sexuality whose
"odious passions" (612) are nevertheless uniquely perceptive of the body
of Agnes, who is most often disembodied by the novel as an "appealing
monitor" (615). David responds to the sexuality of that redness with a
desire for a still more intense red: facing Uriah's feelings for Agnes and
for David himself ("I have always overflowed towards you since the first
moment I had the pleasure of beholding you in a poney-shay" [311]),
David wants to run through "the red fox" (423) or "red-headed animal"
with a "red-hot poker out of the fire" (311). The faintly visible theatricality of Uriah's memorable humility powerfully embarrasses those
who, like David, have accepted its conspicuous tributes. Professing "so
much emotion, that I could joyfully have scalded him" (308), Uriah

terrorizes David with his asseveration of excess and overflow in the system of their connection. "The detestable Rufus with the mulberry-colored greatcoat" (314) almost becomes, for the narrative, the marks David fantasizes leaving on them both; Uriah figures, rufous, the confusion (embarrassment) he generates and the confusion (subject and object) of those marks. Since David's fantasies (poking, scalding, or slapping) turn on himself, he notes with discomfort the way, in contact with Uriah, he becomes all too legible. As Uriah challenges David and, *knowing* him, demands public assent to the confused mutuality of that knowledge ("You know you knew what I meant, Copperfield"), David feels "the confession of my old misgivings and remembrances . . . too plainly written in my face to be overlooked" (504).

As she recounts David's story for Mr. Dick, Betsey Trotwood identifies the wandering child who has appeared on her doorstep as an undeveloped Cain: "He's as like Cain before he was grown up, as he can be" (161). The explicit sense she makes of her allusion—like Cain, David "prowls and wanders"—masks her implicit fusion of David with the "murderer" his mother has married; David seems to his aunt to have killed, by arriving in her stead, the sister she personifies and names. As with Cain in his maturity, David's fantasies make him bearer of the marks he makes: physical impressions in *David Copperfield* operate reflexively.

Rosa Dartle's desires for Emily are desires for reflection of the scar Rosa already bears, its physical graphics a painful citation of her previous occupation of the imaginative space both women, in fact, have occupied; what she calls Emily names that space—"James Steerforth's fancy" (585). Both women are James Steerforth's fancy, united in a confusion that Rosa's strong will would mark with matching graphics. Rosa passionately describes to Mr. Peggotty and to David her will for Emily: "I would have her branded on the face" (385).[23] The horror of that will is suborned by the complexity of her scar's function for Rosa Dartle. In its physical obduracy, the scar can seem to stand for a corresponding personal and behavioral obduracy that, for Rosa, has served sometimes to protect her, to protect her self, from the further incursions of James Steerforth's forceful charm and from the invasions of his pointed disregard. Imagined as material for the formation of a toughened, calloused, protected self, the marking Rosa wants to share with Emily becomes a perverse gift, though one she proves finally—happily—incapable of giving precisely because she is and has been "so darkened and disfigured by passion" (587). When she strikes at Emily, "the blow, which had no aim, fell upon the air." Rosa Dartle's real cruelty toward Emily involves, despite itself, the mottled generosity of throwing a fit rather than a hammer, making a scene rather than a scar.

Makeovers

Phiz includes in his illustration of Mr. Peggotty's reunion with his niece a peculiar literalization of Rosa Dartle's prescription for Emily (fig. 1). Striking among the objects strewn about the room Emily shares with Martha is a dropped half-mask, an accessory to flirtation—paraphernalia of "delicate mock-modesty" (585) from Emily's tour with Steerforth, it seems possible to imagine, or palpable residuum of Martha's shame. Seeming fancifully to follow Rosa's directive (Emily had best "drop" her "pretty mask" [591]), Phiz omits the sentimental prop with which Dickens has equipped Mr. Peggotty: "He gazed for a few seconds in the face, then stooped to kiss it—oh, how tenderly!—and drew a handkerchief before it." Phiz's reading of the scene displaces with the figurative mask the dramatically substantive handkerchief and exposes as alike protective and alike violent the gestures toward Emily made by Mr. Peggotty and by Rosa. The color once described as "mantling" Emily's cheeks (114) materializes as a handkerchief, drawn ostensibly in decency across that which Rosa would, with fancied indecency, expose. Yet, produced by the desire to mask a blush seen or perhaps to mime a blush unseen, Mr. Peggotty's gesture makes over Emily's complexion and renders her body subject to his correction.

In this rendering, Mr. Peggotty's project resembles Dickens's project in *David Copperfield*, which novel becomes for Dickens a ground on which to display and to correct flawed textual bodies (bodies flawed because written that way, flawed because written, but also flawed because bodies) in order to rewrite a larger understanding of the physical body. (Not just in themselves do women, or those roughened by labor, or

Figure 1. Mr. Peggotty's Dream comes true
Drawing by Phiz for *David Copperfield* (Oxford: Oxford University Press, 1987).

reddened by the strains of desire or humility prove troubling for Dickens; they also trouble as alike habitants and dependents of the body, members of its company.) The visible alterations physiology works on the body (the alternations of color wrought by the blush) offer themselves for interpretation, but—in this like Rosa Dartle—refuse to put themselves out to intelligible service. The body's characters, like those of Words-worth's great Apocalypse, are readable as promises and refusals of legi-bility, intimations of an author where one is at best absent.

In its makeover of the blush, Austen's novel of manners proposes to resolve the tension between these promises and refusals, and in places its negotiations are so successful as to dazzle. But the strains of Austen's struggle with the physiology of the blush, visible in *Persuasion* (what if mortification mortifies?), derive in part from the self-contained super-adequacy of the blush's ostensible self-evidence. As with apparent spades, calling a blush a blush precludes calling it something more or less useful. Calling a capillary action a blush limits its suffusion, contains its contagion, locates it immediately and firmly within a sphere of particular significance: the moral realm of modesty, embarrassment, shame. These particular accounts of the blush's social life might as well yield to other social phenomena (arousal, anger, intoxication) or to the physical (fever, chill, the skin's response to the touch of sun or ice). But the way to read the blush in the system of manners, as Dickens and Darwin play it out, is rendered problematic by texture, pigment, the colors of artifice, by an interest in finding that unreadable bodies are not one's own but belong to the rough or the brown or the female. To read the blush in manners is to try to establish something fixed and stable about the body: I can read you—I know you—because your body tells your truth and, perhaps but only incidentally, mine. But, based as it is on a notion of somatic involuntarity, this effort is doomed not to produce the desired stability. Not only particular bodies but a notion of the body itself resists what legibility would determine: not only fantasies of particular bodies but a phantasmatics of the body demands escalation from blush to scar and, finally, collapses scar and blush.

The manifestation of this collapse in *David Copperfield* is Rosa Dartle's scar. Trying to render Rosa legible (and trying by means of the novel to render the body corrigible), Dickens inescapably links his corrective markings of bodies with a resistance to legibility, to what flirts with legibility but eludes it. The particularity of Rosa Dartle's scar lies in its capacity to highlight, by exceeding it, what makes necessary and functional the markings on characters in Victorian fiction. A certain response to Rosa Dartle—the one I remember having as a child to her incarnation in the Classics Illustrated comic book *David Copperfield*—would read her scar as indicating uncomplicatedly that villainy of her character that leads to an unmotivated tormenting of Emily. Perhaps only a child would miss the softening motivations and fail to recognize as complicated her own fascination with the tantrums of a comic-book diva. But soap opera and the contemporary mystery novel have adopted for their use the scar that functions as made-up and made-over scars seem supposed to in uncomplicatedly indicating villainy of character. Scarred, the villain is identified as villainous; scarred, always a villain and always recognizable as such.[24] The scar so imagined answers legibility's need to establish and fix character. Unsupple and unresponsive, this scar is detached from the vagaries of physiology. If the scarred villain is incorrigible, his discursive body is reassuringly not so and it bears the mark of correction by identification. So marked, the villain's written body answers temporarily and phantasmatically an anxiety about the corrigibility of the physical body.

Not finally able in this way to subject his anxieties about the body to his authority as novelist, Dickens writes for Rosa Dartle another kind of scar, one which, endowed with the signifying properties of the blush, is also endowed with what makes the blush troublesome: the intermittence (now you see it/ now you don't) that means its language is syntactic rather than symbolic. Losing its imagined fixity, Rosa Dartle's scar comes to resemble the unstable blush it has replaced. Dickens's work in *David Copperfield* of writing *on* those bodies that he has written out of anxieties about class, about a potentially incomprehensible femininity, about confounded masculinities—Peggotty's body, Emily's, Rosa Dartle's, Heep's, Murdstone's, David's own—generates a familiar oscillation between anxiety and reassurance.

Dickens wants the scar to exceed the blush in escaping the flirtatious semiosis of bodily involuntarity to achieve clarity in fixity. To imagine the scar performing the work of the blush is to imagine it not as the body but as something some body has—as some body's possession. So imagined, the scar would be subject to controlling circumstance rather than to uncontrolled physiology. But in imagining the scar as some body's possession, Dickens inevitably also imagines that body as enriched and empowered by its possession. Writing Rosa Dartle as marked legibly with her scar, Dickens also writes her as escaping legibility by manipulating her scar physically, linguistically, and behaviorally. If Dickens writes Rosa Dartle's scar in authoritative response to his own exasperation with the body, he also imagines in Rosa's manipulation of her scar a way for the body to speak back. Having it both ways, Rosa Dartle converts the fixity of her scar into self-possession, its intermittence into insinuation.

Copperfield's Insinuations

The speech of all the marked characters in *David Copperfield* is itself marked, like Rosa Dartle's, by more or less successful strategies of indirection. The tinker woman, for example, who warns young David away from the tinker who would steal from him, mouths her warning ("she made the word 'go' with her lips" [151]), but she is, despite or because of that caution, knocked down and bloodied by the man she knows enough to warn only David (not herself) away from. And Clara Copperfield mouths to David the lessons he is too terrified to recall in the presence of Murdstone. The structure of her relation to Murdstone suggests that, like the tinker woman, David's mother is rewarded for her efforts with the "great pains" (91) that, she tells Peggotty, Murdstone is good enough to take with her. I wonder about those pains, of course; that is to say, I wonder who is taking them, because mouthing seems here and elsewhere in Dickens the proximate speech of the abused. When Clara Copperfield provides clues "by the motion of her lips" (43) and the tinker woman by the shape of hers, their mouthed words lodge, half-protected, within the body, shaped as well as named by a body part. When recognizable, mouthed speech is pure form, as well as pure defense. "Don't mind me," or even "don't hit me," it seems to say in Dickens, "and don't let yourself get hit." The abused women in *David Copperfield* act out a self-forgetfulness born of concern for David, braving discovery by means of a common mistake: mouthers must be seen if not heard, and David's mother gives him hints, he writes, "thinking nobody is observing her" (43).[25] It is with mouthing, too, that David Copperfield informs Rosa Dartle of Steerforth's death, protecting Mrs. Steerforth and perhaps himself from the emotional display he expects will be the consequence of what he has to say. Death in *David Copperfield,* however suddenly it might come to the dying, takes in its narration to their survivors the place of a natural, nearly goes-without-saying conclusion of a progress (" 'My son is ill.' 'Very ill.' " [652] or " ' . . . your mama is very ill'. . . . 'She is very dangerously ill,'. . . . I knew all now. 'She is dead.' " [98]). If mouthing suggests one is, as culture says of a certain type, afraid of the sound of one's own voice, one's voice unsounded can nevertheless have consequence. When David tells Rosa Dartle in the way he does that Steerforth is not just ill but "dead," the word formed by his mouth seems to write itself on Rosa's already-marked face; David tries to keep Mrs. Steerforth from looking to her companion, that she might not "read, plainly written, what she was not yet prepared to know" (652).

Indirection of address seems sometimes to be a penalty imposed on characters, most often on the morally suspect by those who find them so and who find themselves, by happy comparison, upright. Rosa Dartle does not permit Littimer, for example, to address her directly when he reports his news of Emily and Steerforth ("'Don't address yourself to me!' she interrupted with a frown"), and David follows her strong lead ("'Nor to me, if you please,' said I" [545]). David, though, is finally not proof against Littimer's assertion of "infinite respectability": while Littimer accepts Rosa's right to refuse his address ("Mr. Copperfield and you, miss, are different people"), if David would know of Littimer what he wants to know, David must speak *to* Littimer and hear *from* him what he has to tell. "I have," indicates Littimer in announcement of his Dickensian obligation, "a character to maintain." Maintaining that character by refusing imposed indirection, he breaks down the character of David, who reports a "momentary struggle with myself," mimicked in Littimer's gesture—"an occasional separation and reunion" of his fingers' "delicate tips" (548).

Later, however, as model prisoner Twenty-Eight, Littimer adopts for its strategic value a rhetoric of indirect address. Seeming not to speak to David, Littimer addresses him all the more effectively by speaking *about* him:

"Sir," said Mr. Littimer, without looking up, "if my eyes have not deceived me, there is a gentleman present who was acquainted with me in my former life. It may be profitable to that gentleman to know, sir, that I attribute my past follies, entirely to having lived a thoughtless life, sir, in the service of young men; and to having allowed myself to be led by them into weaknesses, which I had not the strength to resist. I hope that gentleman will take warning, sir, and will not be offended at my freedom. It is for his good. I am conscious of my own past follies. I hope he may repent of all the wickedness and sin, to which he has been a party." (698)

For those listening to him with David, Littimer's indirection resembles a saintly delicacy, and it might be thought at least to save David the trouble of reply; Littimer's patron assures his protégé of David's sensibility to his remarks. But language is the weapon this model prisoner gets to keep; more accurately, perhaps, his retention and deft use of this particular weapon is what makes this prisoner the model. Littimer's refusal to address David directly—ostensibly in respectful consciousness of "his past follies"—is the resentful reproduction of his not being allowed to do so, but his refusal's power as resentment derives precisely from Littimer's assumption of a deferential masquerade.

The rhetorical indirections taken by characters in *David Copperfield* do not go unnoticed in the text. Rosa Dartle, Uriah Heep, and Peggotty are all identified by the text and by characters within it as practicing an insinuative discourse, and their insinuative discursive practices have guilty association with their own illegibility. When Peggotty mutters against Mr. Murdstone, Clara Copperfield Murdstone expects at least the respectful and respectable consolation of Peggotty's being visibly ashamed of herself: "I wonder you don't color up like fire" (90). Peggotty's subsequent disgruntled mutterings about Miss Murdstone's failures of devotion to the household produce, against her denial, an accusation that she insinuates:

> "I don't insinuate at all," said Peggotty.
>
> "You do, Peggotty," returned my mother. "You never do anything else, except your work. You are always insinuating. You revel in it. And when you talk of Mr. Murdstone's good intentions—"
>
> "I never talked of 'em," said Peggotty.
>
> "No, Peggotty," returned my mother, "but you insinuated. That's what I told you just now. That's the worst of you. You *will* insinuate." (91)

Mrs. Murdstone's critique of Peggotty robs insinuation of its predicate; her anger at Peggotty expands beyond the specifics of Peggotty's mistrust of Murdstone brother and sister to a critique of a habitual mode of speech, and understands that mode as among the guilty pleasures that might be taken by a maid at liberty. Peggotty's genuine insinuation (indeed she never talks of Mr. Murdstone's good intentions) seems, whenever it occurs, to constitute time off; she never does anything else, except her work. Peggotty's unblushing body and the indirections taken by her speech are troubling to her employer in lying beyond the regulable realm of Peggotty's domestic duties.

Peggotty's insinuation lets her say something impermissible to her in the realm of frankness. Insinuation can work this way for Rosa Dartle, too, who wants sometimes to suggest that Steerforth lives a wild life, say, or to point the way to the collision course on which he and his mother are bound to embark.[26] But at other moments, Rosa wants information or wants the secure pain that accompanies information confirmed, and insinuation is useful to her here as well. Of his conversation with Rosa about having visited the Peggottys with Steerforth, David writes:

Miss Dartle was full of hints and mysterious questions, but took a great interest in all our proceedings there, and said, "Was it really, though?" and so forth, so often, that she got everything out of me she wanted to know. Her appearance was exactly what I have described it, when I first saw her; but the society of the two ladies was so agreeable, and came so natural to me, that I felt myself falling a little in love with her. (291)

David's attraction to Rosa Dartle—an attraction acknowledged, with palpable largesse, in despite of her appearance—indicates a certain pleasure in her extractions. The hints and guesses that comprise these extractions recall the terms with which David has written about his less pleasurable but no less insinuative childhood encounters with Uriah Heep and his mother: "A tender young cork, however, would have had no more chance against a pair of corkscrews, or a tender young tooth against a pair of dentists, or a little shuttlecock against two battledores, than I had against Uriah and Mrs. Heep" (208).[27] The corkscrew as figure for insinuation is a favorite in *David Copperfield*. Having warned Uriah Heep not to be "galvanic" in his movements, Aunt Betsey tells him he can be a man or an eel: "If you're an eel, sir, conduct yourself like one. If you're a man, controul your limbs sir! . . . I am not going to be serpentined and corkscrewed out of my senses" (422). Made into a verb, "corkscrew" describes an action that pushes and twists—insinuates—in order to extract. To describe insinuation in terms of the work of the corkscrew makes clear insinuation's status as action, while revealing its perceived physical character. Operated upon by Heep's insinuations, David and his aunt might feel their effects as bodily; forcing you to say what you know but do not want always to know you know—forcing its admission as it performs its extraction—insinuation, like the pulling of a cork, might leave outer shape unaltered while effecting internal compression.

When David wonders what will become of Uriah Heep after Heep's manipulations of Wickfield have been discovered, Traddles explains that, even moneyed, Uriah would tend to find his way into trouble:

"He is such an incarnate hypocrite, that whatever object he pursues, he must pursue crookedly. It's his only compensation for the outward restraints he puts upon himself. Always creeping along the ground to some small end or other, he will always magnify every object in the way; and consequently hate and suspect everybody that comes, in the most innocent manner, between him and it. So, the crooked course will become crookeder, at any moment, for the least reason, or for none." (636)

Traddles's *de rigueur* disapproval of Uriah cannot quite overshadow a sympathetic account of Uriah's movements in the world. The surprise of Traddles's perspicacity here is liable to a similarly sympathetic construction. When David claims that Uriah is a "monster of meanness," Traddles—despite his domestic contentment, in some position to know—replies that "many people can be mean, when they put their minds to it." Traddles's recognition of Uriah's serpentine creeping as compensatory for restraints not so necessarily self-imposed indicates the extent to which his own cheer is purchased at the cost of some strain, still barely visible in his almost involuntary sketching of skeletons, as in this moment of qualified understanding.

In Traddles's account of Uriah, Heep's notorious crookedness in speech and in moral matters is less a choice than a condition of satanic mobility. Traddles merely follows the course of Dickens's own characteristic conflation of body and language in using "insinuate" and "corkscrew" interchangeably to designate both speech and physical movement. Peggotty insinuates that Murdstone is not to be trusted and Heep corkscrews information from David; Canterbury's market day gives Betsey Trotwood opportunity for "insinuating the grey pony among carts" (177–78), while, in *Pickwick,* making the same movement, "Mr Bantam corkscrewed his way through the crowd."[28] (The language of "pulling punches" gets at a similar thing—gets at, that is, the conflation of body and language but also at the way in which that conflation is about defending the body.) Whether somatic or linguistic actions, corkscrewing and insinuating are defensive as well as compensatory in managing to suggest movement toward at the same time as movement away from. The insinuator incorporates insinuation's correspondent posture as an S-shaped body, Uriah's as he writhes. Operating upon Betsey Trotwood or David Copperfield, Uriah Heep or Rosa Dartle might use language in a way that protects as it progresses, moving toward as simultaneously it moves away from; abstracting from insinuation this understanding of the structure of its movement makes it possible to see insinuation's ambivalent support of and utility for both flirtation and aggression.

The vulgarity of Miss Mowcher's wink is able to reveal the extent to which insinuation's exploitation of complicity derives from its ability to generate a sense of inclusiveness; her wink makes Miss Mowcher's insinuations discomfittingly companionable.[29] Dickens describes Miss Mowcher as herself a "morsel of a woman" (268); even in its entirety, her body cannot be seen as more than a piece, suggestive of the capacity of the *corps* to be *morcelé*. Miss Mowcher is further seen as attempting to supplement her small body, as well as her income as cosmetician, by means of an "extensive connection" (272): taking from her purse the body bits she shores against challenge to that connection ("Look here! . . . Scraps of the Russian Prince's nails!" [268]),[30] her "pursy" self suggests, as well as its hoarding (of fat, of air, of things), its own distribution ("Bless you, man alive, I'm everywhere. I'm here and there, and where not, like the conjuror's half-crown in the lady's handkercher" [266]).

Miss Mowcher's body is inevitably her issue, and when Dickens—his attention having been called to his insensitivity[31]—imagines her explaining herself, that explanation seems to involve the conversion of her body into language: "If there are people so unreflecting or so cruel, as to make a jest of me, what is left for me to do but to make a jest of myself, them and everything?" (377). The self-conscious self-deprecation that this explanation evokes involves indeed a second Miss Mowcher, altered by earnestness into the jest that, pursy and volatile, she might have been seen to defend against:[32] rewritten, she has to ask David to see her with the pity her wink would never permit, as the very image of "a very helpless and defenceless little thing" (380). The condescension with which Dickens does his impression of a little person's voice is literalized in David's

Figure 2. Mr. Peggotty and Mrs. Steerforth
Drawing by Phiz for *David Copperfield* (Oxford: Oxford University Press, 1987).

response to Miss Mowcher. David finds her face in this second manifestation "so earnest" and finds himself so pleased by the "afflicted manner" in which "she wrung her little hands" that, as he tells us, "I rather
inclined toward her" (376). That inclination is here complicit with sympathy calls both into question: of course David must incline—physically—toward the short woman, and, in writing his sympathy as a matter
of inclination, Dickens just makes another short joke. It is the joke's
somewhat resentful implication that Miss Mowcher's body demands the
sympathy (the production for checking off of that feeling) no less than
the inclination; David's or Dickens's understanding of that demand—and
David's and Dickens's response to it—render Miss Mowcher's body as
itself a kind of blackmail, certainly as no body to love.

And yet, as explanation of her vaunted volatility and of her extension
of the blink's involuntarity into the elaborately willful gesture that is
her wink, Miss Mowcher's suggestion that—no other task presenting
itself—she makes herself her own jest does finally assert something over

the weakening and disempowering function of explanation as apology. Making a jest of herself, Miss Mowcher—like Rosa Dartle—makes self-consciousness into the (painful and powerful) detachment of self-owner-ship and into a useful and half-confident self-possession. As David writes of his reaction to her in her earlier manifestation (winking, volatile, demonstrative of a coy vulgarity), "I never beheld anything approaching to Miss Mowcher's wink, except Miss Mowcher's self-possession" (267).

For *David Copperfield*, Miss Mowcher is one of those characters who pose the problem of the demand of the body (one's own or not one's own) to be dealt with. That problem and her solution (the conversion of body into language) are—by the ambiguity of the genitive—Dickens's; in *David Copperfield*, the scar is *of* Dickens (he is its possessor and source), according to the logic—recurrently displayed in corporal relations in his text—by which the mark one makes becomes one's own. Dickens's con-version of body into language involves making on characters marks that are supposed, within the fiction, to be read as physical; but it is an aspect of his necessary recognition of their linguistic status that, for Dickens, the written bodies consequent upon these markings imply a certain speech. The speech of the Dickensian eccentric—in mimicking a kind of talking back—registers Dickens's recurrent conviction that the marked body's correction is merely temporary and phantasmatic. The Dickensian eccentric becomes characteristic (establishes the Dickensian identity of the Dickens text) in facilitating Dickens's oscillation between the dis-comforts of bodily involuntarity and the consolations of legibility.

Phiz's Rosa Dartle, attendant on Mrs. Steerforth, bears on her lower face what seems at first—even or perhaps especially for one half-obsessed—a peculiar mouth: a downturned slash, slightly off center (fig. 2). Her scar occupies the place of Rosa Dartle's mouth in this rendering, Phiz's astute representation of Dickens's inability finally to satisfy himself that language is not in possession of the body. If the marking of bodies in his text begins for Dickens as a way anxiously to show the body its place—to subordinate it to the needs of legibility and to display its corrigibility—the marking of bodies ends with the anxious attribution to the corrected body of a language peculiarly its own. If that language is produced by anxieties of which Darwin's work indicates real people have sometimes been—are sometimes still—painfully the objects (anxieties about class, for Dickens, about race for Darwin, about gender and sexuality, about the body),[33] it is nevertheless possible to imagine exploiting that language—whatever its irritations—for its consolations, saying sometimes "I only ask a question" (351) in order sometimes to risk, "I want to know" (352).

Chapter Five The Mechanics
of Confusion

*T*he use of the blush in the nineteenth-century novel, as the preceding chapters describe it, can be thought of as articulating the tension between a sense of the blush as expressive of a deep personal truth (expressive of character, of self, of the body) and a notion of the blush as the appropriate local response to and inevitable product of the pressure of social circumstance—as a mechanism, that is, the workings of which forward the grander social work of legibility and manners: Jane Bennet's blushing revelation of her feelings for Bingley or Elizabeth Bennet's mortification versus their socially obliged blushes for an unblushing sister. Austen's negotiation of this tension in *Pride and Prejudice* resolves itself in determining that the blush's convincing performance of its social work is in fact dependent upon understanding the blush as expressive; the accurate functioning of the mechanism is dependent on its naturalization. Still and conversely, the pleasure of Austen's blush inheres in its performance in excess of its social function; Austen is able to harness the energies of the blush's famed duplicity, knowing and showing that Elizabeth Bennet's blush for her sister—while it displays the resigned accession of her body to the demands of legibility and virtue—also permits her actively to access the pleasures afforded by the experience of that body. Taken as I am by Austen's erotics of mortification, I emphasized in my discussions of *Pride and Prejudice* and *Persuasion* Austen's forgery of expressive pleasures from the deployment of social mechanism, and, by implication or by my own performance, I wanted to outline the ways in which an active reading practice might (if only ephemerally) convert the social work of the novel into less prescribed and less proscribing energies. In this chapter, I mean to explore some ways in which a self-conscious understanding of the blush as product or as mechanism disrupts a fantasy of its expressivity and alters the novel's intimate dependence on the blush as index of character and signifier of the erotic.

The last two chapters considered novels by Elizabeth Gaskell and

Charles Dickens in order to pursue the ways these Victorian writers took up the challenge of Jane Austen's legible and compelling blush. Because it seems involuntarily to tell the truth of character and of the body, the blush is potentially invaluable to the novelist, who can exploit its apparently reluctant witnessing as the most credible of testimonies. In working with the blush, Gaskell, like Austen, must establish a relation between the blush as mechanism and the blush as expression. Gaskell's fantasy of the expressive blush in *North and South* is disrupted by the interference of class and of artifice. In striving to preserve for Margaret Hale a natural and visible gentility, Gaskell is disturbed by the possibility that manufactory can reproduce manners and troubled by the inescapable recognition that Margaret's blush is of course not somatic: Gaskell begins to recognize that the blush is a mechanism of signification, and to see that the blush in her fiction is the product of willful authorial agency and untrustworthy novelistic intention. By substituting the blunder for the blush as a natural and involuntary sign of gentility and virtue, Gaskell reinvokes involuntarity by valorizing the mistake. While her recuperation of linguistic and somatic error permits Gaskell to efface a potentially disabling and self-conscious recognition that the body in the novel is most fundamentally *written,* it also grants access to a deep fantasy about the body: that the physiological events and somatic accidents that culture understands as signs of the body (the blush of course—among other things—and the physical blunder) are its intentional acts, the products of its agency. And in reproducing or generating this fantasy in her fictions, Gaskell restores the body, if not the blush, to expressivity.

Dickens seems more in touch than Gaskell does with Austen's sense of the blush's excess. But where that excess offers iridescent (now you see them, now you don't) liberatory pleasures to Austen and her readers, it proves the site of anxiety for Dickens. In their apparent expressivity, the marks of the body threaten to escape the management of Dickensian signification. Replacing the disturbing instability of the blush with the ostensible fixity of the scar in *David Copperfield,* Dickens plans that his new sign will work mechanistically: always and everywhere to signify, always and everywhere to render body and character legible. But in making this substitution, Dickens merely displaces his anxiety, and Dickens's scar comes to have the transitory properties of the blush in addition to its signifying capacities. If reading Jane Austen permits one in fortuitous and isolated moments to tap the excess of the body, reading Dickens might do the same: but only in anxious figuration, unless against Dickens's will and through an against-the-grain reading practice that resists his fixating nervousness about the body and about the forms (the scarred and exasperating woman, the rough-skinned and insinuating worker, the eccentric minor character) with which he has figured threatening illegibility.

Austen's pleasing use of the blush is based on a complex and adaptive manipulation of the tension between an expressive and a mechanistic blush. Reading *Persuasion* showed with what difficulty (if also with what brilliance) Austen sustains her erotics of mortification. The strains of working with the blush, still more visible in *North and South* and *David Copperfield,* are also evident in the work of other and later nineteenth-century novelists, for some of whom the terms of the debate between the expressive and mechanistic blush become simpler than they proved for Austen and Dickens. Rather than focus on successful and stimulating modulations of the blush (into blunder, for example, and scar), this chapter begins by considering some instances in which the blush proves disappointing and troublesome for novelists who want—despite decreasing faith in its expressive capacity—nevertheless to retain the blush in order to exploit its obvious appeals as legible sign of character and as source of erotic charge. Turning from these examples to Henry James and then briefly to Salman Rushdie, the chapter considers the connection between the troubled expressive blush and a recognition of the blush's mechanistic social utility.

Dubiety

To begin, a seemingly unmotivated passage in Mary Elizabeth Braddon's *Lady Audley's Secret.* Describing the melancholy Robert Audley's contemplative train travel, *Lady Audley's* narrator reports on the other traveler who disembarks at Robert's station—"a burly grazier, who had been to one of the theatres to see a tragedy." Though the grazier is never

referred to again, and though theater-going is not an interest much in-
dulged by any of the novel's central characters, the narrator comments
at length on the theatrical tastes of "country people," who—rejecting
"flimsy vaudevilles," "gauzy productions," and "your pretty drawing-
room moderator lamp and French window pieces"—"always go to see
tragedies." Country people, Braddon writes, prefer

a good monumental five-act tragedy, in which their ancestors have seen Garrick
and Mrs. Abington, and in which they themselves can remember the O'Neil, the
beautiful creature whose lovely neck and shoulders became suffused with a crim-
son glow of shame and indignation, when the actress was Mrs. Beverley, and
insulted by Stukeley in her poverty and sorrow. I think our modern O'Neils
scarcely feel their stage wrongs so keenly; or, perhaps, those brightly indignant
blushes of to-day struggle ineffectually against the new art of Madame Rachel,
and are lost to the public beneath the lily purity of priceless enamel.[1]

Braddon's discussion of "the blushes of to-day" takes the form of a conventionally nostalgic lament for life in a simpler time (when the great
O'Neil strode the boards) and among simpler people (whose unsophisticated tastes engender their natural preference for what is simply if
implicitly the best). In the simpler time posited, simpler people might
have numbered among themselves such thoroughly unmodern women as
would have rejoiced in the keen perception of their wrongs and gloried in
the display of their sensitive feelings; uncorrupted by modern artifice, the
blushes of these women would have been neither produced by cosmetics
nor hidden beneath them. But however fully they embody their roles,
"our modern O'Neils" would (as O'Neils) be actresses, and it is on this
point that Braddon's longing for simplicity stumbles, proving to be anything but simple itself.

For Braddon's excavation of a self-evidently felt and effectively com-
municative blush contents itself with uncovering the stage blush, which
in its iterability (its invariable production in response to nightly cues) is
necessarily mechanistic. The delusively absolute language with which
Braddon indicates identification ("when the actress was Mrs. Beverley")
and possession ("and insulted . . . in her poverty and sorrow") eliminates
the mediation of acting to suggest that what she prizes in O'Neil is

the expressivity of O'Neil's blush for O'Neil-who-is-Beverley. Though seeming to preserve the expressive blush in her recollections by protecting it from the harshness of modernity and makeup, Braddon's narrator does not contrast nature and art or expression and mechanism; displaying her preference of a "natural" to a made-up art of the blush, Braddon always understands the blush as a performance for "the public" and grants that the personal expressivity of the blush is already compromised. Braddon's fantasy of the stage blush might be better articulated as a Foucauldian perception about the social blush: every blush is a response to circumstantial cues; every blush would involve acts of recognition, identification, and self-nomination; blushing, I become one-who-would-blush under such conditions as these, and the only character my blush reveals is the character outlined by the pressures of circumstance.[2]

Braddon's digression on the stage blush marks a problem of representation for Braddon with respect to Lady Audley, whose ambivalent status as heroine is characterized in part by an ambivalent relation to the blush.[3] If Lady Audley's blushes do not *mean* goodness or indicate her embodied acceptance of Robert Audley's code of values, neither can they mean a refusal to recognize a moralized account of the circumstances that produce them. As an actress of the blush, Lady Audley may be more O'Neil than she is one of O'Neil's modern counterparts, but that means no more than that she blushes on cue.

Braddon's anxieties about the blush are hidden wisely in plain sight; discussing the blush in performance, she neatly deflects by nearly naming the recognition that the blush *is* a performance. Braddon's privileging of the stage blush evokes (as it evades acknowledging) the specter of color that, in being both somatic and artificial, collapses natural into unnatural. In *The Eustace Diamonds*, Anthony Trollope fantasizes more explicitly than Braddon does a body that can produce at will effects that have been thought to signify involuntarily. Describing the "person and habits" of Lizzie Eustace,[4] Trollope turns to complexion and finds it lacking:

Her face was oval,—somewhat longer than an oval,—with little in it, perhaps nothing in it, of that brilliancy of colour which we call complexion. And yet the shades of her countenance were ever changing between the softest and most transparent white, and the richest, mellowest shades of brown. It was only when she simulated anger,—she was almost incapable of real anger,—that she would succeed in calling the thinnest streak of pink from her heart, to show that there was blood running in her veins. (1:17)

The logic of his odd and striking equation of complexion with "brilliancy of colour" suggests that Trollope understands complexion more narrowly than definition (appearance, color, texture of facial skin) would have it. In refusing to accept Lizzie Eustace's "ever changing" shades of white and brown as complexion, Trollope determines that the first requisite of complexion is that it be pink, and, in suggesting that without that essential characteristic, Lizzie is without complexion, Trollope suggests as well that she is without character: there is no there there; "there was no reality about her" (2:203). Trollope's contrast of Lizzie's brownness with the brilliancy of color that constitutes Trollopean complexion invokes such racial terms as those in which Darwin casts his debate about the moral status of complexion.[5] Its shaded variations indicate that Lizzie's skin as Trollope writes it might be exploited for the signifying capacity that novelistic characterization has come to depend upon, but Trollope refuses to afford the signifying capacity of Lizzie's brown-and-white skin admission to acknowledged moral status in his novel. Like the rough skin of sailors for Sir Walter Elliot in *Persuasion*, Lizzie Eustace's brown-tinged skin for Trollope signifies without variation just one thing: a correspondingly compromised character. It comes as no surprise, when he describes Frank Greystock's attraction to Lizzie Eustace as an "ill-used woman" despite evidence of her "other traits" (1:320), that Trollope reminds readers "that beauty reclining in a man's arms does go far toward washing white the lovely blackamoor" (1:320–21). Trollope's clichéd denial that he has recuperative plans for Lizzie's character reinforces his jointure of brown skin with bad character: "There shall be no whitewashing of Lizzie Eustace. She was abominable" (1:321).[6]

Trollope's racist construction of Lizzie Eustace's complexion and character permits him to work at maintaining a connection between these features even as his fearful and titillated fantasies break it in considering Lizzie's relation to anger. Putting embarrassment and modesty out of the question, Trollope replaces the blush with the angry flush in his novel's system of legibility. "Almost incapable of real anger" and thus morally incapable of the righteousness with which indignation rejoices in coupling itself, Lizzie is imagined as still (if just barely) able to use her body for its assistance in righteous and angry display. Simulation's work as the origin of somatic stimulation depends on Lizzie's surrender of her body to its seductive and convincing grip: by acts of will and of imagination ("she actually did not know that she was lying" [1:198]), Lizzie can "succeed in calling the thinnest streak of pink from her heart." The voluntary of Lizzie's achievement evacuates the flush of its expressive credibility and suggests the prospect of a body-manufactory that produces and supplies on demand a physiologic cosmetic.

Trollope does not pursue this fantasy of Lizzie's frighteningly controlled body with much consistency, and indeed no one in the novel seems to believe Lizzie or believe in her body's signs for too long. Lizzie is found to paint at the end of the novel: "Lizzie, since the reader first knew her, had begun to use a little colouring in the arrangement of her face, and now, in honour of her sickness, she was very pale indeed. But still, through the paleness, there was the faintest possible tinge of pink colour shining through the translucent pearl powder. Any one who knew Lizzie would be sure that, when she did paint she would paint well" (2:364). The willful self-delusions of the later Lizzie ("she knew, or half knew, that the man was a scheming hypocrite" [2:367]) are saddest here, in her loss of faith in the body that Trollope's narrative had promised for her; Lizzie's painting is a vulgar excess only because she once seemed to have access to her body's cosmetology. But her painting is Trollope's comforting degradation of that knowledge, a containment of the threat he raised himself in imagining the body as a cosmetic mechanism.

Mrs. Carbuncle serves *The Eustace Diamonds* as a nightmare version of what one might expect Trollope to prefer. Her inflammatory nature—as readable in her high coloring ("the wonder of her face was its complexion") as in her name—is an index of her temper: "Though that too brilliant color was almost always there, covering the cheeks but never touching the forehead or the neck, it would at certain moments shift, change, and even depart. When she was angry, it would vanish for a moment and then return intensified" (1:329). But Mrs. Carbuncle's volatility makes her beautiful ("People said,—before they knew her, that . . . she had been made beautiful forever") and its effects are often misperceived as the work of paint: "There was no chemistry on Mrs. Carbuncle's cheek; and yet it was a tint so brilliant and so little transparent, as almost to justify a conviction that it could not be genuine" (1:329). Frightening enough for Trollope that, imagining Lizzie's cosmetic simulations mistaken for the signs of righteous anger, he imagines a natural simulation. Mrs. Carbuncle's complexion works by a still more sophisticated and decadent mechanism: her genuine anger is so little transparent as to seem cosmetic; the natural and ugly disguises itself as the unnaturally beautiful.

Lizzie's endeavors "to restrain the telltale blood" (1:186) and her ability, caught, to have "about her . . . none of the look of having been found out" (1:179) take part in Trollope's efforts to distinguish her from her rival Lucy Morris, the domestic angel who is "above any sort of trick" (1:123). If Lucy cannot of course rely on her body to protect her from embarrassment, she can count on its involuntary testimony to the fact of her reliable legibility: "Lucy was as red as fire, although she had especially made up her mind that she would not blush when the communication was made" (1:305).[7] Lucy's blushes figure as expected in the story of the deserving heroine who waits for the wrongs of neglect to be righted by notice. (Such heroines have a place and offer their pleasures, though more satisfactorily—witness Fanny Price and Lucy Snowe—when their desserts are set against an erotic or resentful edge.) But, in so neatly fulfilling the expectation of circumstance, the responses of Lucy Morris's complexion are a dull reminder that convention (the aesthetic produced mechanically) can recuperate the incendiary pleasures of the blush for well-behaved utility.

George Eliot's use of the blush in *Middlemarch* is similarly complicated by matters of distinction and convention that are generated by Eliot's sense of the difficulty involved in retaining a notion of the expressive blush, given the frequency with which novels have exploited it for that very quality. In suggesting that the blush is sometimes a tic of character—rather than a deep expression of it—*Middlemarch* begins to register the way the blush can be a tic of characterization and of writing.

Eliot's descriptions of Dorothea Brooke note the infrequency of Dorothea's blushes. Introducing the Brooke sisters, for example, Eliot writes that "unlike Celia, she rarely blushed, and only from high delight or anger."[8] The very rarity of Dorothea's blushes seems itself to function as an expressive distinction (the blush's absence takes on the blush's expressive dimension); unblushing, Dorothea would be "unlike Celia," who "sometimes seemed to blush as she breathed" (46), unlike flirtatious Rosamond whose complexion is "beyond anything" from infancy (526), and even unlike Mary Garth, the self-described "brown patch" (92) who nevertheless reddens with modesty, with indignation, and with the riled delight of the readily teased. (Dorothea's exemption from the blush is half about the sororophobia[9] that would distinguish her from the familial sister as well as from those figurative sisters who, as characters in Eliot's novel, are rivals for centrality in its narratives of courtship and marriage.) And unblushing, Dorothea would be revealed as that admirable heroine whose character is to be established and expressed more by its elaborate exclusions ("She likes," notes Celia, blushing, "giving up" [16]) than by what in writing or in fact it bodies forth.

But Dorothea blushes quite a bit. She colors "deeply," for example, from annoyance (71), temper (25), and exercise (23, 225). Her face brightens (646, 660); her cheeks bloom (518); she colors and glows with pleasure (19, 669) and with surprise (354). "A little flushed" (172) and "colouring deeply" (182), Dorothea answers accusations from her husband Casaubon and from Will with some eagerness to elide her own anger and "to exaggerate her own fault" (172). (Her skin also indicates with its regularly noted "sudden" pallor that Dorothea has had "a shock of alarm" or that she has spent exhausting time in vigilant contemplation [237, 269, 386, 392, 651]). Observers may experience Dorothea's beauty as in part a consequence of her coloring: Naumann, Ladislaw's painter friend, admires "the breathing blooming girl" (155) who rivals in life and color "the marble voluptuousness" of sculpture; and, while allowing that Dorothea never was "high-coloured," Tantripp pays Dorothea's usual complexion the tribute of her expertise and pride, as a devoted servant, in the attributes of her beloved mistress ("Well, not to say high-coloured, but with a bloom like a Chiny rose" [393]). Sometimes, like *Persuasion*'s Anne Elliot, Dorothea seems especially aware of her blushes as felt events of the body ("the blood rushed to Dorothea's face and neck pain-fully" [400]), but, like the narrator, she nevertheless conceives of herself as someone who does not blush ("What was Will Ladislaw thinking? Would he hear of that fact which made her cheeks burn as they never used to do?" [406]). Finally, despite having early limited to anger and "deep delight" (16) the emotional conditions conducive to Dorothea's blush, the narrator records Dorothea's experience of the most intense embarrassment: "she coloured deeply under the double embarrassment of having expressed what might be in opposition to her husband's feeling, and of having to suggest this opposition to Will" (302).[10]

Given that Dorothea's complexion, then, seems no less responsive than that of any other heroine and her blushes no less frequently noted by an attentive narrator, the narrative's defensive insistence on the rarity of Dorothea's blush is peculiar and telling. Commenting on one of Dor-othea's blushes, Eliot describes it as Celia perceives it: "It seemed as if something like the reflection of a white sunlit wing had passed across her features, ending in one of her rare blushes" (39). No ordinary blush, the response of Dorothea's skin to "the reflection of a white sunlit wing" seems the reconciliation to embodiment and flesh that follows on a sa-cred transfiguration. In evoking her notion that "souls have complexions too" (12), this rarity emphasizes precisely by means of its delicacy that Dorothea's blushes are as clearly expressions of soul as they are products of physiology. And yet what this extraordinary blush tells is what the silliest of novelistic blushes have long been known to tell. As her body's answer to the announcement that the unlikely object of a mortifying crush will come to dinner, Dorothea's blush apprises her sister of roman-tic information: "For the first time it entered into Celia's mind that there might be something more between Mr. Casaubon and her sister than his delight in bookish talk and her delight in listening" (39).

In writing for Dorothea a sacred blush, Eliot seems at first able to preserve a one-to-one correspondence between blush and character: nei-ther Celia nor Rosamond, different yet alike in their immersion in the social world, could blush this blush, expressive as it is of Dorothea's white intensity and her reluctant if powerful embodiment. But as a blush that proclaims even the oddest accession to the demands of the marriage plot,

Dorothea's is undistinguished from a thousand others. And Eliot's desire to assert the rarity of Dorothea's blush registers her own irritation with a blush that has been debased and robbed of expressivity by convention:[11] *these* blushes (Eliot's, Dorothea's), she seems eager to say, *mean* something.

But what blushes might mean, another question, is elsewhere for Eliot less clear than that they mean contextually, doubtfully. Caught looking at Daniel Deronda and caught in thinking about him, Gwendolen Harleth "felt herself blushing."[12] Eliot writes of Gwendolen's feelings at being caught (looking, thinking, blushing):

Her annoyance at what she imagined to be the obviousness of her confusion robbed her of her usual facility in carrying it off by playful speech, and turning up her face to look at the roof, she wheeled away in that attitude. If any had noticed her blush as significant, they had certainly not interpreted it by the secret windings and recesses of her feelings. A blush is no language: only a dubious flag-signal which may mean either of two contradictories. Deronda alone had a faint guess at some part of her feeling; but while he was observing her he was himself under observation. (474)

In considering the blush a matter of interpretation, this passage from *Daniel Deronda* begins from within the perspective of Gwendolen Harleth, who—if she is made available for interpretation by her blush—is nevertheless protected from incriminating self-evidence by the blush's dubious signification: only those with intimate and difficult access to the "secret windings and recesses" of the feelings that both produce and follow upon the blush (and only those whose cohabitation of context entitles them to share reference) can offer a "faint guess" as to its meaning. Still, Eliot's lament that the blush is "no language" speaks less in appreciation of its sheltering dubiety than in evident disgruntlement at its ambiguity and inexpressiveness. As a "flag-signal," Eliot seems puzzlingly to think she is explaining, "the blush may mean either of two contradictories." If, in its dubiety, the blush is no language, ought language by comparison be clarity itself? Or is the blush "no language" in the poverty of its choices (just *two* contradictories) and the supposed comparative inadequacies of its opportunities for the accumulation of

interpretive error and interpretive riches? And which two are the contradictories of the blush (can contradictories move together in a single
teleology?): guilt and innocence; knowledge and ignorance; anger and
embarrassment; flush and pallor; red and white; white and brown; S and
Z? Declaring the blush no language, Eliot cannot find the *not* in the
unconscious, performing with her declaration the conversion of her blush
into a festival and a nightmare of significatory excess, the blush into
language.[13]

Braddon's blushes, Trollope's, and Eliot's participate, variously, in a
shift in the suspicious attentions of the nineteenth-century novel. If still
in demand as the registry by which mistrusted character is made legible
in the novel, the blush itself becomes an object of mistrust. More visible
as mechanistic response to circumstance and inescapable as novelistic
convention, less reliable as characterological signifier, liable in fantasy or
in the world to cosmetic simulation, always in literal or metaphoric contiguity with the unstable body, the blush takes on the anxiogenic attributes of whatever instability it has been meant to stabilize and render
legible. What is a novelist to do?

Confusion

The suspect integrity of the blush, while abstractly a matter of its dishonor, is literally a matter of the failures of its self-consistency, its disintegrations of identity and boundary, its known duplicity understood specifically as self-division (*two* contradictories). Considering the ways in
which novelists respond to their increasingly troubled understanding of
the blush, I will turn to Henry James, but only by way of a fantasy—the
fantasy of confusion—persistent in novelistic thinking about and use of
the blush. While "confusion" is used in the English novel to refer to a
state of embarrassment or discomfiture (a dictionary's example, from Jane
Austen: "his sister [was] overcome with confusion and unable to lift up
her eyes"),[14] it tends to do so metonymically: confusion (as something
with which colloquialism indicates one might be "covered") names the
experience of blushing, describing its ruptures of integrity and its cele-
brations of perplexity.

Let a bizarre story told by Darwin introduce what he describes as "confusion of mind" and what the novel sometimes envisions as a confusion of bodies:

I will give an example of the extreme disturbance of mind to which some sensitive men are liable. A gentleman, on whom I can rely, assured me that he had been an eye-witness of the following scene:—A small dinner-party was given in honour of an extremely shy man, who, when he rose to return thanks, rehearsed the speech, which he had evidently learnt by heart, in absolute silence, and did not utter a single word; but he acted as if he were speaking with much emphasis. His friends, perceiving how the case stood, loudly applauded the imaginary bursts of eloquence, whenever his gestures indicated a pause, and the man never discovered that he had remained the whole time completely silent. On the contrary, he afterwards remarked to my friend, with much satisfaction, that he thought he had succeeded uncommonly well.[15]

Darwin's narrative of the embarrassed dinner scene has a fantastical or even fictional quality, exhibited in its being just a little too good a story and evident in the force with which Darwin renders it triply unassailable ("a gentleman, on whom I can rely, assured me . . . "). It is both painful and easy enough to identify with the solitude of Darwin's sensitive man in his embarrassment and confusion, his sad eagerness for celebration betrayed by those heart-felt lessons that prepare as inevitably the anticipated embarrassment as they prepare for the speech. And yet the man alone seems *un*confused: well-rehearsed, indeed, he offers his speech; graciously accepts applause; recalls the event with uncommon satisfaction. A vision of self-consciousness (incapacitating embarrassment), he is yet unselfconscious (unself-aware); and, unselfconscious, he offers his audience of friends a spectacle of self-consciousness and confusion in which social thermodynamics compel them to participate. Confusion (as perplexity, as embarrassment) is an attribute of the scene rather than of the man. (Darwin's mistake is his allocation of it to the man alone.) And this scene offers an opportunity that Austen's Lydia and bad comedians make somatically familiar: a dinner in honor of the sensitive man is a festival of confusion, of blushing *for*.[16]

The rupture of felt selfhood and the blurring of subject and object that constitute blushing *for* (the embodied assumption of a social obligation) fantasize confusion as entailing as well the disintegration of bodily boundaries for which the circulation of embarrassed blood has no respect. But the disintegrations of the made scene are dissolutions *into* something: the fantastical constitution of a social body is a formation wrought by confusion, and the union of separated bodies facilitates sometimes a kind of social work.

The English novel repeatedly invokes the fantasy of somatic confusion, which involves seeing the couple, the pair, or the group as a machine, powered by hydraulic relations and in search of homeostasis. Exploiting as it does its notion of confusion as the experience of psychosomatic disorder through blushing, the novel generates evanescent visions of perceptible mechanical relations between and among people— sometimes for the purpose of enforcing conventional unions that perform the work of social maintenance, sometimes (in a way disruptive of such maintenance) to facilitate the hallucination of otherwise inarticulable relations.

Of the flirtation between Lydgate and Rosamond in *Middlemarch*, for example, George Eliot writes of "that peculiar intimacy which consists in shyness." Their lookings and lookings away create an "unpleasant" consciousness for which there is "no help . . . in science": for "that intimacy of mutual embarrassment, in which each feels that the other is feeling something, having once existed, its effect is not to be done away with" (219). Embarrassment's odd intimacy—if it cannot be expunged by science—works yet by a kind of scientific law that determines the relative motion of bodies: if Lydgate one day looks "down, or anywhere, like an ill-worked puppet," Rosamond must look down the next day, their respondent and corresponding gestures yielding (in addition to the nearly tangible products of increased consciousness and premarital relation) the very correspondence and mutuality that produce the motions. Confusion attends readily upon courtship and marriage for Eliot, as it has for Jane Austen, whose erotics of mortification insists upon mutuality: the inequality of social relation between Elizabeth and Darcy, in *Pride and Prejudice,* is balanced by the fluid exchange of mortifying reproaches.

While mutuality powers the coupling of Elizabeth and Darcy, Anne Elliot and Captain Wentworth in *Persuasion* need balance righted before balance is achieved. Austen rewards Anne Elliot's forbearance under disadvantage ("the years which had destroyed her youth and bloom had only given him a more glowing, manly, open look" [61]) with Wentworth's acquisition of discomfort and a blush: "He was more obviously struck and confused by the sight of her, than she had ever observed before; he looked quite red. For the first time, since their renewed acquaintance, she felt that she was betraying the least sensibility of the two. She had the advantage of him, in the preparation of the last few moments" (175). The embarrassment of Wentworth's manner ("she could not have called it . . . anything so certainly as embarrassed" [175–76]) initiates his compensatory and complementary response to Anne's extensive mortification. In *North and South,* the confusion of heroine and hero over the appearance of her public defense of him against the striking workers of Milton is rendered by the twinned spectacles of wound and swoon: as Margaret Hale's blood flows with a "heavier, slower plash than even tears" (235), "all the blood in [Thornton's] body seemed to rush inwards to his heart" (236); Margaret's insensibility inspires Thornton to sensation and exclamation ("Dead—cold as you lie there, you are the only woman I ever loved!" [236]). And when George Eliot—against the evidence of her text—asserts that Dorothea Brooke does not blush, her asseveration is perhaps in service of a similar complementarity established and facilitated by the ready blushes of Will Ladislaw. Their blushes (his frequently noted, hers broadly dismissed) establish some relation between the imagined bodies of Dorothea and Will: an almost sexy complementarity, or a supplementary Fred-and-Ginger give-and-take (she gives him depth / he gives her sex).

If the English novel's mannerly erotics tend most often to manage desires and bodies by containing them within marriage, its parlor hydraulics exercise the bodies of characters (and of some readers) the better to control the oscillations of vice and virtue within a system of social obligation. Blushing for Lydia Bennet, her sisters accept with their bodies the dictates of legibility and manners. But, as a recurrent fantasy of the English novel, the confusion of bodies can also facilitate the expression of some resistance to and subversion of the social institutions and social systems it works largely to maintain. If the labors of Mrs. Croft's body (walking "for her life") are seen finally to be in aid of Admiral Croft ("to do him good" [*P,* 168]), the marriage as machine is shown as strained by the imbalanced working of its parts. And while Captain Wentworth's account of his unhealthful bond with Louisa Musgrove ("she would not have been obstinate if I had not been weak" [*P,* 183]) can only forward the trajectory of a heavily moralized plot, *Persuasion*'s coupling of Anne's body with Louisa's achieves a vengeful balance of which morality and manners ought to disapprove: Austen's plot enlivens and rejuvenates the mournful and neglected Anne, while producing Louisa's fall at Lyme effectively to convert Louisa's heretofore lively energy into fretful neurasthenia.[17]

Considering confusion as the tendency exhibited by "some sensitive men"—their unstable sensitivity presumably to be distinguished from the reliability of his witness—Darwin assents to the nineteenth-century novel's use of the confusion of bodies as a way to envision and half-articulate erotic relations between men. Wickham and Darcy encounter one another in Austen's novel, memorably, under the confusion by which "one looked white, the other red" (*PP,* 73). The mutual permeability with which confusion configures their two bodies suggests that other and unwritten novel in which proud Darcy relinquishes self-possession under the sway of young Wickham, the handsome cad from the dangerous classes; at the same time, it articulates the charged competition that informs their disputes over the financial remains of a patron and father. And *David Copperfield* similarly extends the field of its erotic charge beyond David's relationship with Steerforth to include his uncomfortable encounters with Uriah, the "detestable Rufus" (314) whose cheek ostensibly invites David's blow but leaves his fingers tingling, and to include the pained struggles in which his bite is coextensive with the abuses of a sadistic step-parent. But if the confusion of men's bodies in the English novel enables the vision of an erotic relation between men,[18] the confusion of bodies facilitates the novel's project of containing this erotic, without asking and without telling, and within the confines ("but aren't they just angry?") of a plausible deniability.

Confusion, that is to say, is about the maintenance and propagation of confusion. The confusion of bodies invokes visions it refuses to identify, enabling and sustaining confusion of mind. Saying without saying quite, the language of confusion is extrapolated from the iridescent signification of the blush and the insinuative signification wrought by the scar. What the confusion of bodies begins to articulate is a series of perceptions about personal relations (their desperate dependence, their eager vampirism, their disrespect for prohibitions in the name of sex and gender) that the novel is sometimes reluctant or unable to name aloud. Given its own reliance on a notion of expressive individuality, the novel resists knowing what else (by means of its fantasy of confused somatic interactions) it nevertheless portrays: that expressive individualism is a fantasy in support of an organic social mechanics, and that its prized sign—the blush—may mark less the body's betrayal and assertion of a unique and powerful self than its surrender to the needs and determinations of a larger inorganic corpus.

Hydraulics

No surprise, perhaps, that Henry James's troubled sense of the blush resembles that of George Eliot, perhaps derives from it. Like other novelists writing later in the nineteenth century, James expresses a sense of dissatisfaction with the blush (a cultivatedly resigned dissatisfaction, in his case) that coexists with frequent recourse to its significant capacities. In *The Portrait of a Lady,* for example, James writes of Isabel Archer that, when told by Mr. Touchett that she is beautiful, she "instantly rose . . . with a blush which was not a refutation."[19] The narrative, of course, joins with Mr. Touchett in gallantry by turning his compliment with its greater skill and delicacy (far from undercutting Touchett's point, suggests the narrative's flattery, Isabel's blush proves it), but at the same time registers a need that yields a Jamesian habit: the identification of blushes by what they do and say. When describing Ralph Touchett as having "blushed a little," the narrator explains the blush (one might not know it otherwise) as "the sign of an emotion somewhat acute" (181). James's blushes certainly refer to something in excess of Eliot's proclaimed "two contradictories" (hers do too, of course), but they seem nevertheless to require the help of translation, even if only by dubious narrative sema-phore. Like Gaskell, James sometimes assumes a disingenuous and dis-tanced vantage from which to regard the blush; when Lord Warburton (shaking a challenged hunting crop) announces his fear of Isabel's "re-markable mind" (116), James writes—of his own position with respect to the complexion whose responses are after all the products of his linguistic engineering—that "our heroine's biographer can scarcely tell why, but the question made her start and brought a conscious blush to her cheek" (116).

James's trouble with the blush—like Eliot's in this way as well—sometimes involves questions of meaning and expressivity versus fre-quency and convention. Caspar Goodwood is the equivalent of Dorothea Brooke in expressing "no embarrassment" (498), though very much his good wooden self in presenting "rather a hard surface" (498): "When he was touched he rarely showed it, however, by the usual signs; he neither blushed, nor looked away, nor looked conscious" (499). When Good-wood's hard surface softens to a blush, therefore, within paragraphs ("'How do you know what I care for?' he cried with a big blush" [500]), its softening serves James's desire to distinguish this blush for signifi-cance, the better to restore that surface to unblushing firmness. But all this is also to say, as if for Goodwood, that he is no Will Ladislaw—no "woman's man" (in James's notorious evaluation) with "transparent skin" (*M*, 492) and "girl's complexion" (*M*, 497) but, as an ambulatory phallus maximizing the size of its flush, capitalist successor to the "hussar" more suited than Will to James's fancy.[20] Allowing Goodwood his big blush, James constructs for him an imaginary realm of unsubtle but expressive masculinity—the blush understood in genital terms as a "mild erection of the head"—while defending it against the incursions of those more fre-quent, more delicate, and "smaller" blushes James would construe as feminine.[21]

Of the married Isabel Archer, who contemplates direct opposition to the wishes of her husband, James writes: "The prospect made her heart beat and her cheeks burn, as I say, in advance" (504). Isabel's burning cheeks appear in James's prose in odd sequence and in conjunction with the telling locution "as I say"; Jamesian colloquialism and slang ("as I say," "as who should say," "hung fire")—occupying as they do a notably casual space in otherwise mannered and elaborated prose—indicate by inflection what is vexed for James. (Here the colloquialism inflects the fraught recognition that burned cheeks are said rather than felt.) James's "as I say" refers back to the narrative discussion his digression interrupts: Isabel had been considering the "decencies and sanctities of marriage," and "the idea of violating them filled her with shame as well as with dread" (503). His use of a somatic specificity ("cheeks burn") to explain and to substitute for the antecedent and abstractly embodied emotion ("filled with shame") highlights the thoroughness and clarity with which James knows that the fiction of the blush has collapsed into language: as he says (and by his saying) the blush is made figure of speech rather than somatic incident.

This instance of high self-consciousness accompanies in James's work considerable skill in manipulating the troubled and confused nature of blushing. If Daisy Miller's habitual (though not absolute) failure or refusal to blush participates in a crisis of understanding for Winterbourne, it does not create a crisis of signification for James. James's adaptive construction of the blush reverses its conventionally presumed epideictic functioning, pointing to observer rather than observed; Winterbourne's attention to the inconsistencies of Daisy's blush ("the name of little American flirts was incoherence") tells about Winterbourne, renders him legible; its shame is on him.[22]

But, supremely the novelist of relation, James is at his best in seeing that the work of confusion lies in making lasting or (more often) temporary social mechanisms of bodies in social relation. (Isabel Archer's "perceptibly pale surprise" [312] makes a scene by answering and compensating for the abrupt intrusion and excess of Lord Warburton, "splendidly sunburnt" [313].)[23] James uses the blush to trace the confused relation of bodies in his story "The Middle Years," while demonstrating that the blush is what permits and effects their confusion. In the story, when Doctor Hugh sees that Dencombe has been writing in Dencombe's copy of the text both have been reading and the doctor has been admiring, he is startled by that act of revision, not yet realizing that Dencombe is (and, as his revisions of the published text suggest, will not stop being) the book's author. The doctor's mystification at seeing the writing and his consequently disordered consciousness reflect themselves in a blush ("Dencombe saw him suddenly change colour"), but if Dencombe is half-amused at being caught rewriting his own text (he is "a passionate corrector, a fingerer of style"), he responds as vividly to what he perceives as the doctor's reproach: "for an instant it made him change colour."[24] Confusion overwhelms the odd scene, including books with bodies under its influential sway: the doctor has confused Dencombe's copy of the book with his own (the red books—caught up in the confusion—reflect the men's blushes), and James's account of Dencombe's habits of revision ("the last thing he ever arrived at was a form final for himself") offers as well an assessment of Dencombe's responsive sensitivity to confusion's revisions of the self. Stimulation to the doctor-reader proves stimulating to the author, and, in his ill health, Dencombe is overcome by the vitality of his youthful partner in the scene:

He was amused at the effect of the young man's reproach; for an instant it made him change colour. He stammered at any rate ambiguously, then through a blur of ebbing consciousness saw Doctor Hugh's mystified eyes. He only had time to feel he was about to be ill again—that emotion, excitement, fatigue, the heat of the sun, the solicitation of the air, had combined to play him a trick, before, stretching out a hand to his visitor with a plaintive cry, he lost his senses altogether.

Later he knew that he had fainted. (246)

Distancing himself from himself, Dencombe relinquishes the integrity of "a form final for himself" in favor of confusion, and the system produced by his connection with the doctor (having played the trick of confusion on so ready and so vulnerable a form) collapses under the intensity. And James's outline of this confused relation of author and reader characters sketches in fantasy any text's production of a fragile somatic relation between author and reader under the sign of embarrassment and confusion.

As interested as Henry James is in the experience of somatic confusion and personal relation from within, he is perhaps more interested in the experience of seeing them at work. But if seeing bodily relations at work (perceiving confusion) replicates that somatic confusion as confusion of mind in the perceiver, such confusion is sometimes able to resolve itself into a breathtaking clarity: Isabel Archer's experience of *The Portrait of a Lady*'s primal scene has its genesis in her recognition of something telling about the "relative positions" of Osmond and Madame Merle (443). The language with which James explains Isabel's perception suits my own experience of perceiving English fiction's ephemeral conjunction of novel bodies and its visionary construction of social bodies, even as it describes the flashes of the Jamesian observer: "The thing made an image, lasting only a moment, like a sudden flicker of light. . . . But it was all over by the time she had fairly seen it" (443).

In *The Sacred Fount*, James confronts for himself and for his narrator the predicament of articulating the movements of such a flicker while stabilizing (by naming them) the oscillations by which confusion is perceptible. Discussing *The Sacred Fount*, I want first and perversely to take seriously what it is that James's nameless narrator sees in social relation. James's narrator is readable as a social neurasthenic: hypersensitive, hyperaware, hyperinterpretive. But the neurasthenic, like the paranoid, while noticeably not quite right as a reader of social stimulations is also not quite wrong.

Traveling to a house party at Newmarch, the narrator formulates the novel's central metaphor, the sacred fount, to describe couplings as he sees them at work. Noticing first that another traveler, Mrs. Brissenden, has undergone an Anne Elliot-style transformation ("she had changed so extraordinarily for the better"), he wonders "what in the world, in the year or two, had happened to her? . . . How could a woman who had been plain so long become pretty so late?"[25] What has happened in the world is Mrs. Brissenden's marriage, and the narrator later observes a complementary change in what had been her baby-faced young husband: "He had grown old, in fine, as people you see after an interval sometimes strike you as having grown rich" (15). Having thought in the past that his traveling companion Gilbert Long "was a fine piece of human furniture—he made a small party seem more numerous" (3), the narrator observes him again, becoming this time "proportionately more conscious of the change in him" (6). Finding Long much improved, the narrator seeks a fourth, whose decline might explain the change in Long, while making a proportion of the parallel. Throughout the rest of the novel, the narrator extends his attentions beyond these first four to members of the house party, mentally arranging and rearranging his fellow guests in closed-system pairs, the dynamics of which he subjects to relentless and imaginative examination.

James's narrator understands the complementary relations between the pairs he studies as operating by liquid means: "She keeps her wit then, . . . in spite of all she pumps into others?", he asks (8); of a characteristically unspecified antecedent, he points out, "you speak of it as if it were cod-liver oil. Does she administer it, as a daily dose by spoonful?" (8); finally, "Mrs. Briss had to get her new blood, her extra allowance of time and bloom, somewhere" (19). He imagines the source of this liquid that affords a literal refreshment as a "sacred fount" of limited resources that resembles the "'awkward' dinner dish" in offering "sometimes too much for a single share, but it's not enough to go round" (19). And, entertaining briefly the possibility that his fancies do not correspond with the realities of social relation, he yet retains his fluid metaphorics, implicating his own partnership-in-speculation with Mrs. Brissenden in his fantasies of liquidity: "We put it, the whole thing, together, and we shook the bottle hard" (153).

As metaphor, the sacred fount construes the relation between persons as a relation between bodies ("Mrs. Briss had to get her new blood . . . somewhere") and, further, understands the relation between bodies to operate hydraulically.[26] In positing this sense of hydraulic connection between bodies, the notion of the sacred fount marks James's full turn to a mechanic account of what I have been calling confusion. Watching Mrs. Briss and Gilbert Long (and colluding, this time, with yet another partner for himself—Lady John), the narrator explains the "impulse" that leads them to watch in fascination: "And we could ostensibly have offered each other no explanation of that impulse save that we had been talking of those concerned as separate and that it was in consequence a little odd to find ourselves suddenly seeing them as one. For that was it—they *were* as one; as one, at all events, for *my* large reading" (107–8). The uncanny for James's narrator inheres in this alluring and disturbing perception of separate beings as a single entity, but his *eureka* ("that was it")—even if it descends into the self-qualification that occurs at "all events"—indicates a discovery the nineteenth-century novel has made time and again, each time it reproduces and recognizes its vision of the couple as a machine.

If confusion as it is visible in nineteenth-century novels before James is less clearly and less absolutely a matter of repletion and depletion than is the sacred fount (the "bloated state" versus the "shrunken" [41]), this is because—in their ideological advancement of the marriage plot, which depends upon a fantasy of homeostasis—so many of these novels end by choosing marriage over the erotic (separating the two with the finality of narrative closure) and prove largely intolerant of fluidity's erotic imbalance, made anxious by it both in attractive and in unattractive forms. *Middlemarch*'s own metaphors of absorption are an exception in registering fluid imbalance: "Many who knew" Dorothea Brooke as Dorothea Ladislaw "thought it a pity that so substantive and rare a creature should have been absorbed into the life of another" (680); and, contemplating the love one might feel (love Dorothea felt) for someone other than a husband, Dorothea tells Rosamond that "marriage drinks up all our power of giving or getting any blessedness in that sort of love" (651). *Pride and Prejudice*'s assessment of Wickham and Darcy comprises another exception: "Attention, forbearance, patience with Darcy, was injury to Wickham" (89). The narrator's perception of relation in *The Sacred Fount* endangers the homeostatic and motivating fantasy of the couple; doing so, it proclaims itself a perception afforded the outsider, the uncoupled, the excluded, the exiled, the sensitive single gentleman:[27] social pressures compel the narrator's departure from Newmarch before the party's end.

But, precisely as unattached outsider, the sensitive narrator is always available for momentary couplings or for vicarious participation in those couplings to which he attends; James's narrator seems to have erotic and fluctuating relations with all the guests ("If I had wanted to hold him, I held him. It only came to me even then that I held him too much" [127]), relations constituted by confusing conversations and eroticized by his own sensitive susceptibility to the influence of connection. If some conversations in the novel (their frequent broken sentences left unfinished or completed by an interlocutor) sound a little like the dinner speech of Darwin's shy and sensitive man, this is because in the confused union of

Jamesian conversation—as in the confused union of Darwin's speaker with his auditors—there is no boundary: no need to say what the other as oneself must (the need and the demand are palpable) already know.[28]

Readers of *The Sacred Fount* attracted to the novel's central image have tended to describe it as vampiric, and indeed its late-century images of drainage and excess make this an entirely appropriate reading.[29] And yet a ratcheted down account of the novel's blood as less violently and more discreetly expressive suits better the lawns and balconies, the drawing rooms and train compartments that are its principal settings. *The Sacred Fount* is a warped example of that genre—the novel of manners—in which the blood so enlivening to vampires and to the unrejuvenated circulates by means of the blush. (Telling the artist Ford Obert that Obert fails to understand what he has claimed to understand, the narrator locates the discourse of obstacle within the purview of manners, while Obert articulates the circulation of social feeling: "No, you don't! Not at all yet. That's just the embarrassment!" "Just whose?" [128].)[30] James's novel offers a systemic and provisional answer to the question of what novelists are to do with their troubled and self-conscious relation to the blush. For James, that answer lies in eliminating dependence on the blush as a legible sign of character while retaining a fantasy of the mannerly blush in the book's central conceit and preserving the structural relation it has helped to outline. In its conception of the sacred fount, *The Sacred Fount* employs the dynamic structure of confusion to articulate social and sexual relations between characters (as well as to articulate textual relations between a self-conscious narrator and the fantasy of a neurasthenic reader) while it largely dismisses the blush as the narratable somatic phenomenon that generates confusion.

Characters *do* blush and color in *The Sacred Fount*. Of his part in a conversation with Mrs. Brissenden, for example, the narrator reports, "I literally blushed for her" (44). And if, encountering her husband, the narrator's "whole sense of the situation blazed up at his presence," causing "a bright confusion" (132), the narrator reveals Brissenden's hydraulically complected response: "he let his white face fix me in the dusk" (134). But the rare blushes in the novel—neither signal flags nor telegraphy—for the most part do not even gesture toward legibility. Though this late-century/new-century novel is notably less reliant on the blush than the nineteenth-century novel has been,[31] the narrator expresses (near the end of the novel) his sense that the loss of the blush is unimaginable. Increasingly irritated by the narrator's hydraulic visions—whether because they seem to her so inaccurate or (as he might think) so apt—Mrs. Brissenden tells him, "You see too much" (153). Reminding Mrs. Briss of her participation with him in speculation ("we shook the bottle hard"), the narrator contemplates what her assessment would mean for the bottle's contents: "'I'm to take from you,' I wound up, 'that what it contains is a perfectly colourless fluid?'" (153). The narrator's disbelief in the clarity of the bottled fluid of the fount reveals with a different kind of clarity that he takes that fluid to be red: the narrator's bottle preserves the blush of scandal—and thus preserves the novel's blush—but metaphorized as a figure within a figure. Not that the novel's blush has ever been anything but a figure within the figure of fiction; but here, abstracted and contained, the blush is disembodied and denaturalized, recast, no longer vehicle: now tenor. *The Sacred Fount*'s self-conscious figuration of the blush is *to be found* in the narrator's bottle ("that was it" [108]), and my readerly *eureka* matches the narrator's in calling neurasthenic attention to the status of this blush as written language rather than involuntary speech of the body.

Characters in James's novel come to regard the narrator as mad ("My poor dear, you *are* crazy . . . !" [187]) and critics have concurred in questioning the sanity of his imaginative interpretations. But the narrator's social neurasthenia merely marks the end to which well-mannered reading (attentive reading, that is, of the novel of manners or of those novels that exploit its conventions) always might lead: manners' insistence on the claims to attention of the legible body and its social obligations commands into existence a vigilant and obsessive readership. And, for the narrator of *The Sacred Fount,* the sight of bodies in confused relation yields a corresponding confusion of mind: excessive in its sensitivity, excessively attached to its formulations, unable to make itself clear. Common usage offers "self-consciousness" as the well-worn name for such confusion. And James's narrator is commonly thought to be an aspect of James's self-conscious comment on his own novelistic practice. As one of those *unheimlich* terms that manages in alternation and confusion to mean both one thing and its opposite, self-consciousness expansively includes mortification in its sense of mastery. Though literary critical discourse has tended to privilege and to praise the self-conscious in writing—even when self-deprecating, it makes a display of control over that which warrants deprecation—the voices that nudge adolescents ("stop being so self-conscious") articulate more readily the understood connection of self-consciousness to the habit of mortification. And if in *The Sacred Fount,* a sense of the mechanistic and hydraulic blush is articulated in the structure of relations outlined by the narrator's fantasy of the fount, a sense of the expressive and mortified blush is retained in the abstracted form of literary self-consciousness.

James's letters famously reflect his self-consciousness about *The Sacred Fount.* A joke, an accident, "the merest of *jeux d'esprit,*" this novel is an embarrassment for James, who, responding to Mrs. Humphry Ward's praise of it, would "almost blush to have made you suppose that, for the thing that it is, any at all were necessary."[32] James accepts "ruefully and blushingly" the work's metamorphosis from proposed story of "'eight to ten thousand words'!!"[33] to a novel that "makes exactly 77,794 words—say, more roughly, about *seventy-eight* thousand."[34] James's epistolary explanations of how *The Sacred Fount* came to be itself are sensitive rehearsals of embarrassment, remarkably alike accountings of verbiage, of blushing, of *jeux,* that seem as they would explain the book away. James's understanding of *The Sacred Fount*'s development, like his understanding of the blush, is both organic and mechanic. The novel, he writes to William Dean Howells for example, "*grew* by a rank force of its own."[35] But he writes to Morton Fullerton, who seems to have expressed reservations about *The Sacred Fount:* "*That jeu d'esprit* was an accident, pure and simple, and not even an intellectual one; you do it too much honour. It was a mere *trade*-accident, *tout au plus*—an accident of technics, pure and simple—brought about by—well, if you were here I could tell you."[36] Offering again the familiar story that explains this novel embarrassment, James eroticizes the telling with an epistolary half-whisper ("if you were here I could tell you") that duplicates the novel's obscurity and its seductive promises to tell. But his embarrassed and apologetic self-consciousness (it was an accident) is linked this time with the mechanics of literary production. "A mere *trade*-accident," *The Sacred Fount* is perhaps a financial miscalculation but also "an accident of technics," what follows when the self-perpetuating techniques of literary self-consciousness overwhelm the text to produce (the object, the experience) an embarrassment.

Where Austen's "all" ("Mr. Darcy is all politeness" [26]) represents stylistically her phantasmatic understanding of the body's possession by a virtue or by its opposite; where Gaskell's "as if" signifies the reluctance of her commitment to the fiction of the body in the novel; where *Copperfield*'s insinuations represent Dickens's association of a mode of speech with the marks of the body; and where Eliot's emphatic denial ("no language") emphatically asserts that the blush works as somatic signification; James's self-consciousness converts the informing memory of an expressive and legible blush into the perception of a mechanic social structure and the production of a literary mode. Following the nineteenth-century novel, the textual resonances and somatic energies of the blush—I mean speculatively to suggest—are enlisted in the formation of literary self-consciousness.

The somatic blush in many of the texts discussed in this book is associated with characterological self-consciousness, and I have argued that nineteenth-century novelists sometimes used the blush in ways that might colloquially be described as self-conscious. But a project that moves beyond this one would also have to move beyond the nearly idiomatic understanding of self-consciousness appropriate to the nineteenth-century novel in order to wonder, as I wonder now, what the blush looks like when it is enclosed within the set of textual practices that define the mode of writing also known as self-consciousness. Would such a blush—understood perhaps as *deprived* of the naturalizing power attendant on the compelling fiction of somatic habitation—lose its social, erotic, and incendiary force? Could it, construed alternatively as *liberated* from naturalization, highlight the ways in which the incorporation of ethical codes enlists the involuntarities of bodies in the performance of state social work? I have chosen for it to be beyond the scope of this book to respond to these questions with the amplitude and detail a fit answer would insist upon, but I do want to think briefly about a spectacularly self-conscious image with which Salman Rushdie represents blushing as a social obligation in his 1983 novel *Shame* in order to suggest what it is possible for the blush to look like in late-twentieth-century fiction.[37]

Rushdie's novel features a character, Sufiya Zinobia Hyder, who blushes "uncontrollably" (131) and whose "stinky blushes" (147), "like petrol fires" (130), smell of burning and radiate a heat that scorches those who try to kiss her. Born blushing, Sufiya Zinobia embodies her mother's shame at not having produced a boy child and assumes with her intrusive blushes the social obligations of a husband raised to be without shame. Yet, while Rushdie's narrator indicates that Sufiya Zinobia's obligations extend beyond the domestic and even beyond gender and politics ("she also, I believe, blushed for the world" [131]), he neglects to articulate her still more obvious relation to the self-consciousness with which he explains her origins in news accounts and fantasies ("My Sufiya Zinobia grew out of the corpse of that murdered girl" [124]). Sufiya Zinobia is, in Rushdie's word, an "idiot" (129), and, as the character without self-conscious self-awareness, she exists in a confused relation to *Shame*'s self-conscious narrator; separating from himself as narrator and assigning to Sufiya Zinobia the task of representing self-consciousness as mortification or shame, Rushdie tries—with more and less success—to reserve for narrative effect the display of self-consciousness as inescapable self-knowledge and sadistic authorial control: "I did it to her, I think, to make her pure."[38]

Discussing Sufiya Zinobia's capacity to blush "for the world," Rushdie wonders what happens to "emotions that should have been felt, but were not," asking of real and imagined readers, "where do you imagine they go?" (131). In pursuit of an answer to his own question, Rushdie finds an image that speaks to James's metaphorization of the blush as a bottled fluid:

Imagine shame as a liquid, let's say a sweet, fizzy tooth-rotting drink, stored in a vending machine. Push the right button and a cup plops down under a pissing stream of the fluid. How to push the button? Nothing to it. Tell a lie, sleep with a white boy, get born the wrong sex. Out flows the bubbling emotion and you drink your fill.

In converting shame's liquid—the blush—into the pop product of mechanic commerce, Rushdie literalizes as the workings of a machine the social and somatic mechanics that produce the blush and that result in the confusion of blushing *for:*

> Then what happens to all that unfelt shame? What of the unquaffed cups of pop? Think again of the vending machine. The button is pushed; then in comes the shameless hand and jerks away the cup! The button-pusher does not drink what was ordered; and the fluid of shame spills, spreading in a frothy lake across the floor. (131)

As the contemporary manifestation of James's bottling process, Rushdie's vending machine figures the blush as a socially systemic rather than physiologic phenomenon. When the functioning of the machine is disrupted by those who, acting without shame, "refuse to follow" the "simple instructions" (131) that ensure smooth running, humans are introduced into Rushdie's figurative system, though in a subordinated capacity:

> But we are discussing an abstract, an entirely ethereal vending machine; so into the ether goes the unfelt shame of the world. Whence, I submit, it is siphoned off by the misfortunate few, janitors of the unseen, their souls the buckets into which squeegees drip what-was-spilled. We keep such buckets in special cupboards. Nor do we think much of them, although they clean up our dirty waters. (131–32)

Rushdie's notion of social mechanics enlists and includes the labor of the body in service of the machine. Sufiya Zinobia's absorptive blushes, then, understood as attendant upon the machine, are finally not expressive of her nature (Rushdie's blushes do not mean to be expressive of character) or even of her body; their textual obligation is to render legible the system that produces Sufiya Zinobia and that her janitorial social work maintains. If this resembles the somatic operations that occur in Jane Austen's morning room (the blushes of Elizabeth and Jane Bennet for unblushing Lydia make visible the mannerly workings that produce them), it is nevertheless also very different. While the body is not only the sustaining metaphor by which social relations are understood in the novel of Austenian manners but first among its preoccupations, the body is elided in Rushdie's version of contemporary social mechanics; *Shame*'s systemic efforts substitute sweet pop for sticky blushes.[39]

In effecting this substitution—in retaining a figural and conceptual blush that has been dislocated from the body—Rushdie emphasizes the blush's work as a mechanism that constructs a system of social relations by producing signification—by generating, that is, the tantalizingly legible fluctuations that take place at the intersections of Sufiya Zinobia's S and Z. At the conclusion of Rushdie's novel, Sufiya Zinobia's repressed shame and internalized blushes explode into mass destruction and final "reckoning" in "the fireball of her burning" (317); in representing apocalypse as consequent upon self-consciousness, Rushdie restores to Sufiya Zinobia a limited degree of difficult self-knowledge, even as he entertains a grandiose fantasy of incendiary significatory powers for the disembodied if not wholly denatured blushes of novelistic self-consciousness. In Rushdie's imagination of disaster, the blush puts an end to the novel: awaiting inevitable self-immolation, Sufiya Zinobia stands, "blinking stupidly, unsteady on her feet, as if she didn't know that all the stories had to end together" (317).

Announcements

*B*ut literary self-consciousness—despite periodic apocalyptic pretensions—has put an end neither to all stories nor to all blushes. The blush in contemporary literary and popular culture appears regularly enough, if in a form diluted rather than infusive, locally expository rather than everywhere informative. The soft-boiled mystery novel, for example, inherits the blush along with other preoccupations from the Victorian novel, but its blushes are largely conventional and uninvested: if the blush in the standard mystery novel identifies the detective nature of personal attentions ("Catherine felt herself colour up just as the inspector looked up"), it reveals little more than what has already been naturalized by and as genre.[1]

References to the blush in the dominant forms of contemporary culture—film, television, video—serve more often, though, as reminders of their otherwise usual absence. When Marianne in the 1995 film version of Austen's *Sense and Sensibility* pinches her cheeks in anticipation of a potential suitor's call, her decisive manipulation of her cheeks replaces but recalls the blush's involuntary transformations. The gesture seems wrong for Austen's Marianne, who seems incapable of its self-interested and artful calculation. But if her cinematic pinch seems out of character for Marianne, it seems nonetheless responsive to the characteristic nature of Austen's attraction to the blush. Getting something right about Jane Austen, this moment in Ang Lee's film seems simultaneously to reveal something about the conditions of the film's own making: to "do" Jane Austen, you have to do the blush, but to do the blush on film is to remake its presumed involuntarities and revelations as art and as finger-tip cosmetic. If even the unmade-up look requires makeup, the blush is impossible; and if in the late twentieth century it is no longer desirable—despite the equations made by star billing ("Jane Seymour *is* Dr. Quinn, Medicine Woman")—to believe in an actress's embodiment of character (in a modern O'Neil's suffusion with shame and indignation), Marianne can be shown to be red but she cannot credibly be shown, take after take, to redden. Kate Winslet's gesture as Marianne makes clear, then, what we already know—that realist film is happy to neglect a somatic blush, that other movies don't include the blush and can't—but it does so by recording that omission.

Responses to or registrations of this absence typically take shape as a proud or sad or cynical announcement: "You're making me blush." Judd's warning in *Clueless* is finally an announcement, not a blush. And when *Star Trek*'s Q, discovered in a single "redeeming virtue," wonders in a *Voyager* episode "Am I blushing?" his ostensible checking serves rather to identify and to proclaim a condition of his omniscience. The blush announced misses embodiment, and calls for by calling out a blush presumed evidentiary of a self made and grounded in the body. Announcements of the blush are, first, acknowledgments of loss.

Acknowledging such loss, Don DeLillo's *White Noise* recuperates it for the replications of postmodern fantasy. In DeLillo's novel, though the "furtive" Winnie Richards avoids "contact" with a world that "struck her with the force of some rough and naked body—made her blush in fact," the narrator seeks her out in part for the pleasure to be taken in producing and watching her blushes.[2] In the denatured and commodified world of *White Noise*, Winnie's blush, while it is readable as a remnant of the natural and a thing to be prized, is also immediately reconceivable as a material resource for production: "Some of the New York émigrés liked to visit her cubicle and deliver rapid-fire one-liners, just to see her face turn red" (184). "Overrunning the world," her "awkwardness" the "sign of an intelligence developing almost too rapidly" (228), Winnie and her blushes support and enact a simultaneously natural and mechanical reproduction, the novel's nightmare and fantasy of "technology with a human face" (211).

Its frequent flyer program voted number one in an airline magazine's poll, United Airlines, too, paints the face of technology, not only announcing the modest reluctance of its pleasure in consumer compliment but having its portrait taken for the occasion of a 1995 advertisement:[3] the head-on view of an airplane against a dawn or twilight sky fills the advertisement page, as, well above the plane's nose (language in complicity with the portraitist), two high bright spots of reddish pink make cheeks of metal panels just below and to either side of the eyes suggested by light-flecked cockpit windows. "We're tickled pink," states the ad, with a smug aplomb (always the problem with "tickled pink") for which the state of being tickled cannot possibly allow. The airline's enlistment of the blush in its coy self-presentation as kindly faced humanity literalizes an unsurprising announcement of corporate incorporation: "Stop, you're making us blush." Dislocated from the body, the blush as announcement tries to construct a legible body in language, and does so the better to make or to claim or to assert an identity that *is* embodiment, *is* the capacity to blush.

In their removals from the body, the blushes of contemporary literary and popular culture—serving as a context for this writing—make it possible for me to see, in them as in the embodied fictions of nineteenth-century England, a fantasy that always underwrites the blush. Considering that fantasy, I turn for its articulation to the place I learned it first and where I still can see it most nakedly rehearsed. Though it now seems too predictable that the nurses' cheeks would have been crayoned red in the aged copy of *Cherry Ames, Student Nurse* that I retrieved on my last visit to my parents' home, I do not recognize myself as the child who colored them, preferring to blame another of my inscriptive sisters or to credit her with an attentive reading. Cherry Ames's complexion (and her pluck) bring her often to the notice of school and hospital authorities, and the book's plot depends upon the mistaking of Cherry's pluck for impertinence and of her rosy cheeks for rouged ones. Responding to the chief surgeon's commands to "wipe off that rouge!" Cherry counters, wailing, "But it isn't rouge. . . . It's me!"[4]

What announcements of the blush want to do is what Cherry Ames does. Announcing the blush is about using the blush to make an announcement (of the embodiments, accessions, and resistances that constitute identity); but what an understanding of announcing the blush reveals is that the deepest fantasy about the blush is that it is an announcement. Offering itself as the culturally acceptable way to resist acculturation—to imagine escaping culture through the embrace of somatic identity, while praying no one notices you've been gone—the blush makes into a just-audible proclamation the indelicate assertion "that's me."

Notes

Introduction

1. Jane Austen, *Emma*, volume 4 of *The Novels of Jane Austen*, ed. R. W. Chapman, 6 vols. (Oxford: Oxford University Press, 1933; reprinted 1988), 459. Subsequent references will appear in the text.

2. *Clueless*, a film written and directed by Amy Heckerling, Paramount, 1995. Josh is played by Paul Rudd and Cher Horowitz by MTV icon Alicia Silverstone.

3. I first noticed this series of Estée Lauder magazine advertisements in 1991.

4. A First American Bank advertisement thanks readers of the *Bryan-College Station Eagle* in this way for voting it "favorite bank" in the Texas newspaper's annual Reader's Choice poll, 21 June 1995.

5. James Ridgeway, *Blood in the Face: The Ku Klux Klan, Aryan Nations, Nazi Skinheads, and the Rise of a New White Culture* (New York: Thunder's Mouth Press, 1991), 8, 27. In Ridgeway's documentary of the same title (Right Thinking Productions, 1991), an unidentified participant in the film's conversations about racial and species distinctions slaps himself in the face to demonstrate his connection to the biblical Adam, whose name he believes refers to Adam's ability "to show blood in the face." The man (serving in the context of Ridgeway's documentary as the village explainer) separates himself, along with Adam and along with his own imagined listeners ("that's us") from "the other people—the colored and the other races," who, he claims, "were not considered as man" in biblical times because unable to blush. "And," he continues, laughing, "you don't have a conscience you're not gonna blush."

6. In his introduction to *Pride and Prejudice* (Harmondsworth: Penguin, 1972), Tony Tanner notes that "Norman O. Brown, following Freud, suggests that blushing is a sort of mild erection of the head" (35). Brown makes the connection between the blush and the erection as part of a meditation on the king's body as "a sublimation of the male member," which for him involves "displacement from below upwards. The erection is in the head, as in the case of virginal blushing" (*Love's Body* [New York: Random House, 1966], 134).

7. The absence of the lesbian from this conventional listing says something about the difference of invisibility from legibility as responsibility and burden. So when the narrator of Leslie Feinberg's novel *Stone Butch Blues* (Ithaca: Firebrand Books, 1993) notes her own frequent blushes and burnings ("I just wondered if I'd ever stop blushing" [122]), her record serves as much to paint into involuntarily expressive

visibility a distinctive face for the stone butch as to articulate the tensions between earned sentiment and protective distance as values within the stone butch ethic ("I blushed with pride and pulled away in embarrassment" [87]).

8. Bernard Weinraub, "A Surprise Hit Movie about Rich Teen-Agers," *New York Times,* 24 July 1995.

9. "The Long Hot Summer: Summer Movie Preview," *Entertainment Weekly,* 26 May 1995, 14–57. (The prudery is *Entertainment Weekly*'s.) Heckerling's film remains in many ways quite faithful to the distresses and vexations Austen's novel imposes on its heroine, and it is not least faithful to the novel in this attention to complexion. But Cher's discussion of her skin's failures becomes the blush on the cutting room floor: her response to Josh, while featured in the television advertising for *Clueless,* loses to the announcement of his blush and does not occur in the film itself. At least one other reference to the blush remains: when Caucasian Cher complains to her African American friend Dionne, who is helping her apply cosmetics before a date, that she still looks too red, Dionne replies that she's making Cher as white as she can.

10. The blush's temporal status, which signals its origin in physiology, is at the root of its appeal for the novel. Discussing Sherlock Holmes's reading of facial features and (contorted) facial expressions, Rosemary Jann writes: "Physiognomical conventions were more important than pathognomical ones since they were presumably more permanent, while enjoying the same kind of sanction." The value of physiognomy's permanence in the sphere of criminal detection is matched by an appreciation of blushing—grounded firmly in its impermanence—in the novel of manners, which exploits blushing's responsiveness and its ability to register change in and over time. See Jann's essay "Sherlock Holmes Codes the Social Body" in *ELH* 57 (1990): 685–708.

Nevertheless, the nineteenth-century novel's interest in the blush speaks to the literary tradition of attending to fixed marks on the body, just as this book notes the critical tradition made by attending to literature's focus on marks on the body. Considerations of the place of the marked body in literature include Erich Auerbach's discussion of Odysseus's scar in *Mimesis: The Representation of Reality in Western Literature* (Princeton: Princeton University Press, 1953); John Freccero on Manfred's scar in *Dante: The Poetics of Conversion* (Cambridge: Harvard University Press, 1986); Bruce Robbins's rereading of Odysseus and Auerbach in *The Servant's Hand: English Fiction from Below* (New York: Columbia University Press, 1986); Laurie Langbauer's discussion of George Meredith's "brutal stigmatization of women" in *Women and Romance: The Consolations of Gender in the English Novel* (Ithaca: Cornell University Press, 1990). See also Lee Edelman's discussion of the phantasmatics by which the homosexual body is imagined culturally and literarily to be marked and legible in his

Homographesis: Essays in Gay Literary and Cultural Theory (New York: Routledge, 1994).

11. Charles Dickens, *Our Mutual Friend* (Harmondsworth: Penguin, 1985), 891. Elaine Scarry's *The Body in Pain: The Making and Unmaking of the World* (Oxford: Oxford University Press, 1985) has been profoundly influential for critics interested in the nineteenth-century novel's encounters with materiality. For other recent and significant discussions of the novel and the body, see Eve Kosofsky Sedgwick, *Between Men: English Literature and Male Homosocial Desire* (New York: Columbia University Press, 1985); Helena Michie, *The Flesh Made Word: Female Figures and Women's Bodies* (New York: Oxford University Press, 1987); D. A. Miller, *The Novel and the Police* (Berkeley: University of California Press, 1988); Langbauer, *Women and Romance;* Ann Cvetkovich, *Mixed Feelings: Feminism, Mass Culture, and Victorian Sensationalism* (New Brunswick, N.J.: Rutgers University Press, 1992); Lawrence Rothfield, *Vital Signs: Medical Realism in Nineteenth-Century Fiction* (Princeton: Princeton University Press, 1992); and Peter Brooks, *Body Work: Objects of Desire in Modern Narrative* (Cambridge: Harvard University Press, 1993).

12. Ruth Bernard Yeazell begins her discussion of modesty by thinking about its connection to time and to narrative. Yeazell writes: "What we think of as a virtue can perhaps only be understood as a story. By adopting the modest woman as a subject for narrative, the novelists were able to represent modesty not as a set of rules but as a series of changing responses—not as a fixed condition but as a passage in time" (*Fictions of Modesty: Women and Courtship in the English Novel* [Chicago: University of Chicago Press, 1991], ix). Yeazell's insights about blushing support her discussion of modesty, as Christopher Ricks's underwrite his consideration of embarrassment, and as Eve Kosofsky Sedgwick's fuel her work on shame's role in constituting queer identity. In foregrounding the blush itself, I mean to energize my discussion of the fancies, delights, and struggles that constitute the novel's encounters with the body. In addition to Yeazell's book, see Ricks's *Keats and Embarrassment* (New York: Oxford University Press, 1976) and Sedgwick's essay "Shame and Performativity: Henry James's New York Edition Prefaces" in *Henry James's New York Edition: The Construction of Authorship*, ed. David McWhirter (Stanford: Stanford University Press, 1995), 206–39. See also Sedgwick and Adam Frank, "Shame in the Cybernetic Fold: Reading Silvan Tompkins," *Critical Inquiry* 21 (Winter 1995): 496–522.

13. Michel Foucault, *The History of Sexuality. Volume I: An Introduction*, trans. Robert Hurley (New York: Random House, 1980), 59.

14. See the following texts, which (with varying degrees of separation from Foucault) consider the ideological work of the English novel: Nancy Armstrong, *Desire and Domestic Fiction: A Political History of the Novel* (New York: Oxford University Press, 1987); Sedgwick, *Between Men;* Mary Poovey, *The Proper Lady and the Woman*

Writer: Ideology as Style in the Works of Mary Wollstonecraft, Mary Shelley, and Jane Austen (Chicago: University of Chicago Press, 1984); Terry Castle, *Masquerade and Civilization: The Carnivalesque in Eighteenth-Century English Culture and Fiction* (Stanford: Stanford University Press, 1986); Miller, *The Novel and the Police;* Catherine Gallagher, *The Industrial Reformation of English Fiction: Social Discourse and Narrative Form* (Chicago: University of Chicago Press, 1985); Joseph Litvak, *Caught in the Act: Theatricality in the Nineteenth-Century English Novel* (Berkeley: University of California Press, 1992); Ann Cvetkovich *Mixed Feelings;* Jeff Nunokawa, *The Afterlife of Property: Domestic Security and the Victorian Novel* (Princeton: Princeton University Press, 1994); and Laurie Langbauer, *Women and Romance.*

15. In noting some literary and cultural critics whose work seems to me always to involve an active and writerly reading process, I mean really to be acknowledging those critics whose work has taught me something about writing and the body. These include D. A. Miller; Scarry; Litvak; Sedgwick; Edelman; Garrett Stewart (see *Death Sentences: Styles of Dying in British Fiction* [Cambridge: Harvard University Press, 1984]); Naomi Schor (see *Reading in Detail: Aesthetics and the Feminine* [New York: Methuen, 1987]); and Michael Fried (see *Realism, Writing, Disfiguration: On Thomas Eakins and Stephen Crane* [Chicago: University of Chicago Press, 1987]).

16. Thinking about literature and the body as a way of thinking about the English novel in the nineteenth century can entail negotiating between two accounts of that relation that can be understood in terms of their denominations of literature. Articulating the relation between literature and the body as the body's connection to *narrative,* which one might loosely construe as following Barthes, involves thinking about literature as writing and thinking about writing's capacity for representing, enacting, and stimulating desire. In privileging, too, the pleasures and intimacies of reading as an encounter with a text, critics who see themselves as working with somatic *narrative* eroticize the connection between literature and the body.

Articulating the relation between literature and the body in terms of the body's relation to *the novel,* as this more historicized formulation suggests, has tended to mean emphasizing the novel's place as a contextualized social institution, articulating its relation to the body in terms suggested by Foucault: the novel performs the work of recuperating privacy and pleasure for surveillance and a normatizing ideology while teaching the body to know its social place, and the novel does all this without acknowledging the coercive processes that effect such placement.

What it means to negotiate between these two positions is, with some resistance to absolute immersion in the persuasive pleasures of textuality, to find ways to examine the manipulation for ideological ends of the desires and pleasures one values in narrative, while, at the same time, to permit the acknowledgment that textually induced pleasures and pains can sometimes afford incitements and opportunities to formulate alternatively powerful resistance to the restrictive pressures and productive impulses wrought by the novel.

1. Austen's Blush

1. *Jane Austen's Letters*, ed. Deirdre LeFaye (Oxford: Oxford University Press; 3rd ed., 1995), 1. Subsequent references will appear in the text.

2. John Halperin, *The Life of Jane Austen* (Baltimore: Johns Hopkins University Press, 1984), 62. Subsequent references will appear in the text.

3. *Rebecca*. Dir. Alfred Hitchcock. United Artists, 1940.

4. The power of Rebecca's body is evinced by its invisible presence in the film: when Lawrence Olivier as de Winter describes the encounter with Rebecca that leads him to strike and kill her, Hitchcock's neurotic camera follows, as if simply doing its job, the movements he describes but that no one is there to make.

5. Jane Austen, *Pride and Prejudice*, volume 2 of *The Novels of Jane Austen*, ed. R. W. Chapman, 6 vols. (Oxford: Oxford University Press, 1932; reprinted 1988), 141. Subsequent references will appear in the text.

6. George Henry Lewes, "The Novels of Jane Austen," *Blackwood's Magazine* 86 (1859). Reprinted in *Jane Austen: The Critical Heritage*, ed. B. C. Southam (London: Routledge & Kegan Paul, 1968), 157, 158. Subsequent reference will appear in the text.

7. In his introduction to *Pride and Prejudice* (Harmondsworth: Penguin, 1972), Tony Tanner notes that this tendency of Austen's "society" exists alongside a tendency to minimize even "the possibility" of a transcendental dimension (37). Summarizing critical condemnations of Austen's supposed failure to acknowledge the body, John Wiltshire writes, "It has usually been understood that the body in these condemnations is a metaphor or metonymy, and that what is felt to be missing is overt ardour or warmth or intensity of desire" (*Jane Austen and the Body: "The Picture of Health"* [Cambridge: Cambridge University Press, 1992], 2). Wiltshire reads Austen's novels as "pictures of health" and suggests that Austen "framed her interest in the moral life and in imagination . . . through seeing how these are enacted in and by the body, not only through picturing a string of hypochondriacs and invalids, but in the more subtle ways that structure the novels, in the facilities of care and attentiveness that make up in fact a large part of what we call community" (22–23). As one such sign, for Wiltshire, the blush "does, in all its varieties, represent clearly a form of the juncture between the body and culture, and functions as a miniaturised version of hysteria, the embodied correlate of social affect" (19).

The critical tradition that there is no body in Jane Austen leads Susan Morgan to wonder "Why There's No Sex in Jane Austen's Fiction" (*Sisters in Time: Imagining*

Gender in Nineteenth-Century British Fiction [New York: Oxford University Press, 1989]). For Morgan, if Austen's novels "do have sex and passion" (37), "the romantic encounters between Austen's leading characters are not literally sexual" (38). Morgan's suggestion that this is Austen's response to an eighteenth-century tradition which has represented "character change as sexual violation" (30) personalizes Austen's writing and implicitly portrays Austen as touching in her protectiveness of her heroines and of herself. Morgan seems in a way to contradict herself: she wants "to be absolutely clear about insisting that [Austen's] novels do have sex and passion" (37) but can refer with casual comfort to "the absence of sex in Austen's work" (50). This confusion seems the product of a tension in Morgan's thinking between what might be more expansive understandings of embodiedness and sexuality, and limiting notions played out in the eighteenth-century novel that in identifying she seems sometimes to adopt: Austen's fiction "redefines the nature of power and the power of nature in British fiction, by turning away from their physical, and therefore masculine-dominated, base" (51). Morgan discusses the appeal of *Mansfield Park*'s Henry Crawford: "Is Henry sexy? Only if a woman is a masochist, which is to say, totally imbued with patriarchal values" (48). But what, for instance, if a man is a masochist, or what if he finds Henry Crawford sexy? And what if a woman *is* a masochist or what if she can imagine using Henry Crawford and then losing him? Morgan goes on to quote Susan Kneedler: "We can measure how lost our sense of liberation has become if sex in any form is interpreted as liberation for women, and restraint in any form is maligned as conservative prudery" (48). True. But women lose something, too, if physicality (masochistically fantasized or not) is understood as inherently anything, let alone as masculine-dominated or patriarchally valued.

8. Discussing *Mansfield Park* in *Jane Austen and the Body*, Wiltshire makes a similar point albeit to a different end, writing of Fanny Price that her "face signals her body's treason." For Wiltshire, though, while Fanny's "blushing manifests her desire to the reader (and her shame)," because it is "confined to a signal on the envelope of her body, desire remains mute, inoperative, passive" (83). My sense of Austen's blush is that it is less confined than Wiltshire suggests and more expressive and functional in its activation of somatic pleasures.

9. Inept, Jane evades the charge of false modesty that Tassie Gwilliam considers when she notes that, in *A Father's Legacy to His Daughters* (1775), Dr. John Gregory "directly confronts the problem for a woman of *seeming* to be modest while encouraging admiration, but he also explicitly justifies duplicity: deliberate concealment lures the masculine imagination" (109). Gwilliam's interest in Gregory chiefly involves the way his pursuit of the female blush engenders a comparison between men and women. The sensibility that produces a young woman's blush, writes Gwilliam of Gregory, "which in his sex is a 'weakness and encumbrance,' becomes in hers 'pecu-

liarly engaging'" (110). See Gwilliam's "*Pamela* and the Duplicitous Body of Femininity," *Representations* 34 (Spring 1991): 104–33.

10. That it is Elizabeth who observes her sister's blush supports Robyn R. Warhol's contention about one of Austen's later works that "looking at physical detail in order to read interior significance is constructed in this novel as a distinctly feminine thing to do" (9). See Warhol's essay "The Look, the Body, and the Heroine: A Feminist-Narratological Reading of *Persuasion*" [*Novel* 26 (1992): 5–19] for a discussion of gender in relation to Austen's focalization through the consciousness of Anne Elliot in *Persuasion*.

11. It is not quite right to call Elizabeth's smiles appropriate since it is their very appropriateness that vexes those who would grasp her social sarcasms: "'Mr. Darcy is all politeness,' said Elizabeth, smiling" (26).

12. Dim memories of my own first experience of *Pride and Prejudice* inform my sense that the body work in this scene is pleasurably confusing, as do the responses of students with whom I have read Austen. I have also been told that on the *Victoria* network, a query once asked for help in determining which of these men is doing what.

Wickham and Darcy seem elsewhere linked in a single entity within which good shifts, goods circulate. Telling Jane what she has learned of relations between them, Elizabeth describes the association of Darcy and Wickham in this way: "There is but such a quantity of merit between them; just enough to make one good sort of man; and of late it has been shifting about pretty much. For my part, I am inclined to believe it all Mr. Darcy's, but you shall do as you chuse" (225). And, at the ball which must seem to the absent Wickham not big enough for both of them, Elizabeth considers her attentions to Darcy and Wickham as circulating within a closed system, drawn to Darcy only in being pulled from Wickham: "Attention, forbearance, patience with Darcy, was injury to Wickham" (89).

13. Thomas Edwards points out that while "more commonly and successfully, the reader's embarrassment is shared by one or more of her characters" (74), sometimes in Jane Austen "only the reader is embarrassed, as when in *Persuasion* Austen quite cruelly warns us not to be moved by Mrs. Musgrove's grief for her scapegrace son who died at sea" (74–74). Edwards writes of his response to this scene, "I don't know what to say except that I wish she hadn't said it, or that she had lived to revise the passage as she reportedly intended to do" (74). Edwards's complete embarrassment at this scene makes him feel that his "freedom as a reader has been intolerably abridged" (74); but being embarrassed by Jane Austen highlights an issue of greater consequence for readers of fiction, according to Edwards: "In reading any novel we accede to a loss of freedom which is at least structurally an embarrassment: the book is not *our* book, while reading it we submit to another mind, whose interests and purposes are not

identical to ours" (79). See "Embarrassed by Jane Austen," *Raritan* 7.1 (Summer 1987): 62–80.

14. "And it is just because Louisa has her modesty, all the authorities would agree, that the men will wish to marry her," writes Ruth Bernard Yeazell of Reverend John Bennett's "pattern young woman" in his 1789 *Letters to a Young Lady* (43–44). The conduct literature Yeazell discusses in *Fictions of Modesty* (Chicago: University of Chicago Press, 1991) includes a powerful sense of modesty's incitement to other somatic pleasures. Discussing what she calls modesty's "thermal model of female attractions," Yeazell notes that "if one of the paradoxes of modesty is that the clothed body entices more than the naked one, another is that a well-insulated vessel retains the heat that a warm surface dissipates" (47). Yeazell finds that Fanny Price's blushes work within this model for Henry Crawford in *Mansfield Park:* "He persists in reading the language of her body for the promise of erotic responsiveness it obliquely betrays" (146). The resistance that characterizes the textual relationship of Darcy and Elizabeth can certainly work as an incitement to imagine their sexual relationship; a friend reports it incited poverty-stricken graduate student fantasies of the money to be made from pornographic versions of Austen's novels.

15. In *Sense and Sensibility,* Marianne Dashwood doubts her sister's love for Edward Ferrars precisely because Elinor does not exhibit the signs of appropriate romantic incivility and embarrassment: "When is she dejected or melancholy? When does she try to avoid society, or appear restless and dissatisfied in it?" ([Oxford: Oxford University Press, 1932; reprinted 1988], 39). While this erotic belongs to the narrative in *Pride and Prejudice,* its attribution to Marianne Dashwood in *Sense and Sensibility* can seem lightly to ironize it. Yet if Austen makes it relentlessly clear that Elinor Dashwood's "self-command" is "invariable," she is also at some pains to demonstrate that it is invariably challenged, maintained by Elinor only at some cost and under some strain.

16. According to Robert M. Polhemus in *Erotic Faith: Being in Love from Jane Austen to D. H. Lawrence* (Chicago: University of Chicago Press, 1990), the appeal of dance for the novelist lies in its capacity for "representing physical attraction and of aestheticizing erotic drives" (41). Allison Sulloway writes in *Jane Austen and the Province of Womanhood* (Philadelphia: University of Pennsylvania Press, 1989) that "in Austen's fiction, the balance between dance as dance and as a sanctioned and delightful erotic pleasure, on the one hand, and on the other, as an introduction to a business deal in which all the advantages lie with the initiating partner, is often shifted in favor of the benevolent and mythic qualities in the human art of the dance" (138). Richard Handler and Daniel Segal's *Jane Austen and the Fiction of Culture* (Tucson: University of Arizona Press, 1990) is interested in dance as "serious play" (100) and in dance's relation to "metacommunication" (91) in Austen, whose "exem-

plary characters" (99) are able "to discuss and analyze cultural conventions even as they participate in them" (91). Because dance is recognized by these characters as a metaphor for courtship ("the larger process of which [dance] is so often a part") and marriage ("the telos of that process"), its conventions are potentially manipulable (91).

17. Austen's systemic notion of social sensation depends upon the phantasmatic possession of bodies by virtues, each body momentarily and exclusively a vessel for what has been attributed to it: invited to dine, Bingley is "all grateful pleasure" (103); seeing Wickham and Darcy change color, Elizabeth is "all astonishment" (73); agreeing to dance, Mr. Darcy may be "all politeness" (26), even if, in describing him so, Elizabeth means to suggest that he is all arrogance. And when Wickham stays away from a ball at which each of three women "meant to dance half the evening" with him (87), his absence saves from rupture a social system that, barely able to manage the circulation of passions between Wickham and Darcy, is potentially unable to contain the excesses of desire represented by plans for three-halves of a man's time.

18. Darcy seems to have been given by Austen erotic and epistemological advantages, in addition to his more obvious social and financial ones. His emotions function, from the start, logically and strategically to his romantic benefit, as if based on some impossible comprehension of a novelistic alignment of the erotic with the mortifying. Austen describes in this way his initial appreciation of Elizabeth: "No sooner had he made it clear to himself and his friends that she had hardly a good feature in her face, than he began to find it was rendered uncommonly beautiful by the beautiful expression in her dark eyes. To this discovery succeeded others equally mortifying" (23). In Darcy, Austen writes a hero for whom attraction is experienced only through and as mortification. As he eliminates the elements ("hardly a good feature") by which he might have constructed reasoned admiration, Darcy clears space for their rendering as "uncommonly beautiful." No new strategy if, as Mr. Bennet suggests, as habit Darcy "never looks at any woman but to see a blemish" (363).

19. In *Some Words of Jane Austen* (Chicago: University of Chicago Press, 1973), Stuart Tave discusses the "happy ending" of *Pride and Prejudice* as "earned by two properly humbled people" (157). The language with which Tave discusses mortification highlights his sense that its processes are painful; for Tave, mortification, "a source of touching, piercing emotion" (143), is a thing inflicted, "a force that cuts into" self-esteem (142). Endorsing a kind of mannerly machismo (worthy Austen characters learn to "accept the blow" [145], while the unworthy are found "incapable of the pain" [144]), Tave demonstrates with paraphrase the thoroughness with which he has permitted Austen's writing to inhabit his own; sometimes little more than tense separates Tave (of Elizabeth and Collins, "The moment of release from him is ecstasy" [151]) from Austen ("The moment of her release from him was exstasy"). Not able, really, to

separate myself as I might wish from Tave—not least because neither of us wants, really, to separate from Austen—I mean rather to acknowledge in describing his work the ways in which, writing about Austen, I too have come, however problematically, to want seen the assiduity with which I have learned my lessons at her hands.

20. Mr. Bennet continues to comment on his sense of Lydia's need for exposure: "We can never expect her to do it with so little expense or inconvenience to her family as under the present circumstances." The exposure of one of its members is conceived by Mr. Bennet, as it has been by Elizabeth, as a family expense. Elizabeth's painful fantasy, and the novel's, even in Mr. Bennet's more matter-of-factual account, is a fantasy of the family's embarrassment by the family.

21. Eve Kosofsky Sedgwick argues, in "Jane Austen and the Masturbating Girl" (*Critical Inquiry* 17.2 [1991]: 818–37), that "repressive" and "antirepressive" critics of Jane Austen are interested in exacting from her novels "the spectacle of a Girl Being Taught a Lesson" (834, 833). According to Sedgwick, both kinds of critics—the former more likely to imagine Austen's heroines as on the lesson's receiving end, the latter more likely to enact it themselves on some idea of Austen—make "a lot of Austen criticism [sound] hilariously like the leering school-prospectuses or governess-manifestoes brandished like so many birch rods in Victorian sadomasochistic pornography" (833). The "must's" and "have to's" Sedgwick finds so prevalent in Austen criticism suggest that she is right about the polite fascination of ballroom fascism for some of us who work on Jane Austen, but Sedgwick forgets, I think, the extent to which Austen passes her lessons on: if Austen critics tend to imagine those behaviors best that have been enforced by obligation, it is because they have deduced from Austen—with chastened anger and with angry identification—their fantasies of the force and pleasure to be found in the experience of chastening mortification. Sedgwick's own famous association of poetry with spanking (in childhood, she writes, "the two most rhythmic things that happened to me" ["A Poem Is Being Written," 114]) suggests that she understands elsewhere that the conversion of spanking's rhythms into writing's might be a spectacle orchestrated by invitation, by Jane Austen's no less than "Eve Kosofsky's" "claim for attention to her intellectual and artistic life" ("Poem," 110). See Sedgwick's "A Poem Is Being Written," *Representations* 17 (1987): 110–43.

Sedgwick reads the blushes and distractions of Marianne Dashwood in *Sense and Sensibility* as indicators of an erotics of masturbation in Austen. My reading configures surface/depth relations in Austen somewhat differently, suggesting that blushes and distractions are themselves the erotic in Jane Austen, signs of themselves rather than superficial manifestations of a sexuality under cover. See Sedgwick's "Jane Austen and the Masturbating Girl."

22. In using the first person plural, as I have sometimes done in this chapter and

elsewhere, I risk evoking the universal and prescriptive "we" of literary criticism in hopes instead of naming and specifying a precise segment (those of us who blush) of that middle-class readership that has too often and too powerfully fantasized its particularity into a disembodied general rule. Even within that readership, we who have learned to blush in and from reading Jane Austen do the work of embodiment, gratified by the signs of our inclusion in and incorporation by the story of manners.

2. Mortifying Persuasions

1. Austen's notorious acceptance and subsequent rejection of the marriage proposal of Harris Bigg-Wither (she slept on it, the story goes) might be understood as constituting precisely a recognition that courtship need not end in marriage. Discussing the more likely "sleepless night" that Austen would have passed in contemplating Bigg-Wither's offer, Deborah Kaplan, in *Jane Austen among Women* (Baltimore: Johns Hopkins University Press, 1992), finds it "plausible to conjecture" that Austen's refusal was made "in order to avoid the heaviest burdens of domestic femininity and to preserve some time and liberty to write" (109, 119); Kaplan finds—in Austen's contentment in circles of female support—reason to think that Austen may have been satisfied with her decision.

2. Thomas H. Burgess, M.D., *The Physiology or Mechanism of Blushing; Illustrative of the Influence of Mental Emotion on the Capillary Circulation; with a General View of the Sympathies, and the Organic Relations of Those Structures with Which They Seem to Be Connected* (London: John Churchill, 1839), 182. Burgess's treatise combines his dermatological expertise with a strong religious sense (for Burgess, blushing—which "could never be the effect of chance" [11]—is evidence of design or of divine authorship, a proof of the existence of God) and a sense of what I can only describe as wacky curiosity ("Can the Blush be produced after the head is severed from the body?"). The latter query, prompted by rumors about the posthumous blush of Charlotte Corday, leads Burgess to conclude that, if a blush could be produced under such conditions, it would have to be a moral phenomenon (viii, 156–57). Burgess later writes a somewhat less quirky dermatology text, *Eruptions of the Face, Head and Hands with the Latest Improvements in the Treatment of Diseases of the Skin* (London: Henry Renshaw, 1849).

3. Charles Darwin, *The Expression of the Emotions in Man and Animals* (Chicago: University of Chicago Press, 1965; originally published in 1872), 311. Subsequent references will appear in the text. While for Burgess the blushing family has been part of a discussion of mixed emotion (the youngest of the family cries when blushing) as well as of diseased sensibility, for Darwin the family constitutes a proof that "the tendency to blush is inherited."

4. Darwin's survey and its role in his attempt to understand blushing "in the various races of man" (315) are considered further in chapter 4.

5. Darwin's reports of responses to his survey and anecdotes from diaries and correspondence register peculiarities and horrors that originate with his travelers but that Darwin disregards: Mr. Scott's observations of "the Lepchas of Sikhim" occur "when he has accused them of ingratitude" (315); Mr. Forbes's observations, which include his feeling a rise in temperature, occur "even in the dark" (317); "Lady Duff Gordon remarks that a young Arab blushed on coming into her presence" (316); Darwin himself recalls a "young Fuegian, Jemmy Button, who blushed when he was quizzed about the care which he took in polishing his shoes" (317); a Maori blushed when Mr. Stack laughed at him; "Capt. Osborn . . . , in speaking of a Malay, whom he reproached for cruelty, says he was glad to see that the man blushed" (316).

6. Jane Austen, *Persuasion*, in volume 5 of *The Novels of Jane Austen*, ed. R. W. Chapman, 6 vols. (Oxford: Oxford University Press, 1932; reprinted 1988), 5. Subsequent references will appear in the text.

7. In a world in which complexion inflects characterization, it is easy enough to imagine a direct relation between the vulgarity and the freckles, the spottedness of skin suggesting an inconsistency of nature; Mrs. Clay's attachments prove fickle.

8. The goods not perhaps having yet gotten together, this is a generous gesture between women in the world of Jane Austen.

9. Chapman points out that while critics have tended to assume that Lady Russell extends her head *from her carriage* (which he agrees "seems right"), the passage does not specifically place Anne and Lady Russell in a vehicle (294–95): an odd and disembodying dislocation.

10. D. W. Harding, ed., *Persuasion* (Harmondsworth: Penguin, 1965), 394–95. Chapman notes that A. C. Bradley, too, believes Lady Russell's account of her observations, emphasizing what in the passage would lead Anne to laugh at herself: "Anne is extremely agitated to observe Lady Russell gazing intently from her carriage at the long-lost lover, and finds that she was really examining some curtains." And my most sophisticated friend agrees. I agree with Chapman, who finds that the direction of Anne's smile of "pity and disdain, either at her friend or herself" (179) is inexplicable unless it includes the possibility that Anne at least suspects Lady Russell of prevaricating. Bradley's essay on Austen in *Essays and Studies by Members of the English Association*, vol. 2 (Oxford: Clarendon Press, 1911), 33, is quoted in Chapman (294–95).

11. D. W. Harding, "Regulated Hatred: An Aspect of the Work of Jane Austen," in *Critics on Jane Austen*, ed. Judith O'Neill, 42–49. Harding's defense of Austen against a colleague's "too extreme" charge that "she *hated* people" separates the regulated hatred from that which he might be more willing to prize in Austen: "The urbanity,

the charm, the wit and lightness of touch, the good humour, are there as they always were, but the other aspect which readers nowadays notice means that for full enjoyment we have to appreciate a more complex flavour" (introduction to *Persuasion*, 7). I am not sure that—despite his sense of a fuller flavor—Harding understands that Austen's "regulated hatred" is not an aspect of Austen's work that is entirely "other" to her urbanity.

12. Anne is like Elizabeth Bennet in this. When Darcy looks at Elizabeth, early in *Pride and Prejudice*, she imagines it is only because he is fascinated by what in her is "wrong and reprehensible, according to his ideas of right" (51). See my discussion of this passage in chapter 1.

13. *Pride and Prejudice*, 20.

14. Maaja A. Stewart notes that empire yields differently for "metropolitan women and the imperial adventurer," writing of *Persuasion* that "the market economy . . . is brought back into the text to emphasize an unexpectedly ironic gender differentiation: the political situation has deprived Mrs. Smith of access to her West Indies returns while it has enriched Captain Wentworth through the wars specifically fought to ensure Britain's colonial possessions" (*Domestic Realities and Imperial Fictions: Jane Austen's Novels in Eighteenth-Century Contexts* [Athens: University of Georgia Press, 1993], 81). See also Suvendrini Perera's discussion of *Persuasion* in *Reaches of Empire: The English Novel from Edgeworth to Dickens* (New York: Columbia University Press, 1991).

15. Though Anne understands Mr. Elliot's bad practices to include "Sunday travelling" and past carelessness "on all serious matters" (161), Mrs. Smith conveys a sense that they involved dissipations not so mild.

16. Mrs. Smith's profit is in the narrative and information she acquires: the money is for charitable uses. Acquiring thus "the means of doing a little good to one or two very poor families in this neighbourhood" (155), Mrs. Smith retains the benefits to self and place entailed in exercising genteel condescension, to shore against the advent of such resentments as might be entailed in her needing also to accept it.

17. That Austen may have found plotting to be a precarious occupation—or that pleasure is to be found in thinking so—is demonstrated by Austen lore, which passes on the story that she would not permit repairs of the squeaky door that guarded her sitting room at Chawton, to keep from being caught working (Halperin, 113).

18. Letter of Friday 9–Sunday 18 September 1814 to Anna Austen, in LeFaye, ed., *Jane Austen's Letters*, 275.

19. Nina Auerbach addresses related issues in *Romantic Imprisonment: Women and Other Glorified Outcasts* (New York: Columbia University Press, 1985), writing of Austen's "limitation" that "both Romanticism and Jane Austen express a profound awareness that the questing spirit is bowed down by indelible manacles, of its own

and society's making" (21). Auerbach's conclusion emphasizes limitation's end in "delicate desperation."

20. Flattery can modify Sir Walter's estimations. The strategic revelation by Mr. Shepherd (the lawyer hoping to arrange the Admiral and Mrs. Croft's rental of Sir Walter's property) that Sir Walter was "known, by report, to the Admiral, as a model of good breeding" helps produce this extraordinary compliment: "Sir Walter, without hesitation, declared the Admiral to be the best-looking sailor he had ever met with, and went so far as to say, that, if his own man might have had the arranging of his hair, he should not be ashamed of being seen with him any where" (32).

21. Darwin argues "that the consciousness that others are attending to our personal appearance" leads to blushing and "that attention directed to personal appearance, and not to moral conduct, has been the fundamental element in the acquirement of the habit of blushing" (326). This insistence on the observer raises for Darwin questions about "the fact that blushes may be excited in absolute solitude" (334). The idea of an implied or imagined observer resolves these questions for him: "But when a blush is excited in solitude, the cause almost always relates to the thoughts of others about us—to acts done in their presence, or suspected by them; or again when we reflect what others would have thought of us had they known of the act" (335).

22. As I suggested earlier, Darwin's reference to the family is motivated by his need to support a claim that "the tendency to blush is inherited" (311).

23. Writing of *Mansfield Park,* Edward Said has suggested that "in order more accurately to read works like *Mansfield Park,* we have to see them in the main as resisting or avoiding that other setting, which their formal inclusiveness, historical honesty, and prophetic suggestiveness cannot completely hide" (*Culture and Imperialism* [New York: Vintage, 1993], 96). Read against Austen, the hardly inaudible colonial narratives of Burgess's and Darwin's texts are nearly repressible; Austen did not travel with the Portmans, and the products of empire are made present in her novel by the hints (orange, mahogany) of a colorful pre-Joycean diction. Still issues of race-understood-as-color are finally inseparable from the fantasy of the travel cure. The same metaphorics that suggests blushes work by contagion would figure the skin of the traveling family as taking on the darker hues of people in the "desirable but subordinate" worlds beyond England (Said, 52); the cure for their excessive blushing would end in their blushes being made illegible against brown skin. See my discussion of Darwin's consideration of blushing "in the various races of man" (315) in chapter 4.

24. Responding to Mrs. Musgrove's observation about "what a great traveller" she must have been, Mrs. Croft comments with geographic specificity:

"Pretty well, ma'am, in the fifteen years of my marriage; though many women have done more. I have crossed the Atlantic four times, and have been once to the East Indies, and back again; and only once, besides being in different places about home—Cork, and Lisbon, and Gibraltar. But I never went beyond the Streights—and never was in the West Indies. We do not call Bermuda or Bahama, you know, the West Indies." (70)

Eager as any tourist to assert her insider knowledge ("you know" marking its awareness that of course you don't), Mrs. Croft also notes with a scrupulous honesty that escapes Mrs. Musgrove what it is she does not know; articulating the extent of her circle, Mrs. Croft suggests what lies beyond it.

25. Judy Van Sickle Johnson's contention that *Persuasion* is "the most unreservedly physical" of Jane Austen's novels is supported by her account of Louisa's accident, which emphasizes its beginning in a leap rather than its ending in a fall. In her essay "The Bodily Frame: Learning Romance in *Persuasion*" (*Nineteenth-Century Fiction* 38.1 [June 1983]: 43–61), Johnson describes *Persuasion* as "a novel in which a young woman leaps off a sea wall because the sensation of being in a man's arms is delightful to her" (60). Of the novel's blushes, Johnson writes that "they are delicately controlled manifestations of physical discomfort and repressed sexual desire" (46).

26. Darwin asks, "Does shame excite a blush when the colour of the skin allows it to be visible?" (15).

27. Describing Anne as "having been 'restored' instead of 'improved,'" Jill Heydt-Stevenson locates Austen's treatment of Anne's complexion in the context of debates about the nature of the picturesque in landscape. See Heydt-Stevenson's essay "'Unbecoming Conjunctions': Mourning the Loss of Landscape and Love in *Persuasion*," *Eighteenth-Century Fiction* 8.1 (October 1995): 51–71.

28. Chapman cites an advertisement for Mrs. Vincent Gowland's lotion, found in *The Bath Chronicle*, 6 January 1814. The lotion promises "pleasant and effectual remedy for all complaints to which the Face and Skin are liable" and is available for the needy complexions of Bath "in quarts" (*Persuasion*, 294).

29. Anne's return to beauty also works some revenge on her family. By acclamation, "the ladies of Captain Wentworth's party" in Bath defy convention in confessing that "though it is not the fashion to say so" they "admire her more than her sister." Their sense of her effect, though, is qualified: "The men are wild after Miss Elliot. Anne is too delicate for them" (177–78). Perhaps Austen's fantasy for Anne picks up Anne's own reluctance to want too much; or perhaps Austen is awarding Anne rights to that rare fantasy in the rivalrous world of the English novel's understanding of the marriage market: beautiful, Anne is yet liked by women.

30. Wentworth's reassurance takes this form in *Persuasion*'s canceled chapter. I will discuss later Austen's revision of Wentworth's assertion.

31. As one might expect, the experienced and knowing Mary Crawford is *au fait* as to the dermatological consequences of exposure to sea air. When Fanny Price visits

Portsmouth, in *Mansfield Park,* Mary offers Fanny the benefit of her expertise, warning her by letter of the deleterious effects of wind (Austen, *Mansfield Park,* volume 3
of *The Novels of Jane Austen,* ed. R. W. Chapman, 6 vols. [Oxford: Oxford University
Press, 1932; reprinted 1988]): "My dear little creature, do not stay at Portsmouth to
lose your pretty looks. Those vile sea-breezes are the ruin of beauty and health. My
poor aunt always felt affected, if within ten miles of the sea, which the Admiral of
course never believed, but I know it was so" (416).

32. In dermabrasion, a cosmetic procedure often undergone for its rejuvenating
effects on the complexion, a tiny wire brush scrubs and bloodies aging, scarred, or
pitted cheeks in order to wear away the imperfections of complexion.

33. James Joyce, *A Portrait of the Artist as a Young Man* (Harmondsworth: Penguin,
1964), 151. It is not surprising that Stephen's expertise in the pleasures of mortification
and embarrassment extends to his appreciation of flushed skin. His diary fantasy of
"girls demure and romping" articulates their erotic qualifications: "All fair or auburn:
no dark ones. They blush better" (250–51).

34. Nathaniel Hawthorne, *The Scarlet Letter and Selected Tales* (Harmondsworth:
Penguin, 1970), 268, 167.

3. Gaskell's Blunders

1. In his introduction to *North and South* (Harmondsworth: Penguin, 1970), Dodsworth writes that "the novel starts three times—in Harley Street, in Helstone, and in
Milton—and only really gets under way at the third attempt" (12). The Harley Street
beginning, he finds, strikes "a very calculated false note." Dodsworth's comment on
Gaskell's calculation continues:

One is likely to take care *especially* with the beginning of a story, and Mrs. Gaskell does not
normally have difficulty in her openings. It seems to me that she *deliberately* sets out to
confuse her reader in the first chapters of *North and South,* and that she does so with two
objects in mind to make clear, first, the sort of novel she is *not* writing, and second, the sort
of novel she *is* writing. (10)

All references to *North and South* will be made to this edition of the novel; page
numbers will be included in the text.

In her discussion of *North and South,* Hilary M. Schor notes that "not only does it
open in London society, move to rural England, then move again, abruptly, to the
industrial northern city of Manchester but its thematic concerns seem to change as
rapidly." Schor sees these changes as reflections of "the intense changes of industrial-
ization," connecting them to Gaskell's ability to see "the usefulness of the heroine's

plot for the representation of industrial transformation." See Schor's *Scheherezade in the Marketplace: Elizabeth Gaskell and the Victorian Novel* (New York: Oxford University Press, 1992), 124–25.

2. In *The Politics of Story in Victorian Fiction* (Ithaca: Cornell University Press, 1988), Rosemarie Bodenheimer writes that Arnold Kettle, A. B. Hopkins, and W. A. Craik have discussed *North and South* as evidence of Gaskell's literary descent from Austen. Bodenheimer herself describes the way the novel "reaches back to Jane Austen both for its depiction of strong-minded domestic virtue and for the social optimism of its *Pride and Prejudice* plot structure" (53). While some critics have seen Austen's influence at unabashed work in *North and South*, some are interested in the influence only insofar as it is demonstrably rejected by Gaskell. In noting the comment of Gaskell's narrator on the consoling capacities of delicacies, I echo Deirdre David, who cites the comment in her book *Fictions of Resolution in Three Victorian Novels* (New York: Columbia University Press, 1981) while discussing Gaskell's evocation of Jane Austen:

The ironical tone suggests that we are in the world of Jane Austen, as does the note that Mrs. Shaw's "friends" are people she happens to dine with more frequently than others; however, the resonances of Austen's acerbic prose do not continue beyond Chapter 1 and Margaret's departure from the house. This is not to be a novel of manners, and Gaskell's abandonment of London society and the ironic mode indicates, on the one hand, that Margaret has no place in the South, and, on the other, that she is not to be treated ironically by Gaskell. (12–13)

In his introduction, Dodsworth does not have to name Jane Austen as the source of what he suggests Gaskell is rejecting in the first chapter of *North and South;* his characterization of an "orthodoxy" that "straitjackets the author in the attributes of charm, tenderness and feminine sensibility" (10) is sufficient reminder of the cultural "Jane Austen."

Among Austen critics, Ann Banfield identifies *North and South* as a novel that replicates the social visions and formal solutions of Jane Austen. For Banfield, "Austen's form is only superficially rejected" in the novel; she sees *North and South*'s resemblance to *Mansfield Park*, "for Margaret, like Fanny [Price] confronts a new place as an outsider" and "the novel is built on the same contrasts of place, now seen on a larger scale" (44, 45). See Banfield's essay in David Monaghan, ed., *Jane Austen in a Social Context* (Totowa, N.J.: Barnes & Noble Books, 1981), 28–48.

3. Mrs. Thornton's drawing room is critically notorious. Deirdre David discusses "the museum-like quality of the room": "[Mrs. Thornton] lives in an interminable devotion to the past, and turns her house into a monument where everything is frozen in cold tribute to her son's power to overcome disaster. And even when the covers are

removed, the room is overwhelming, comfortless, a fully revealed display of acquisition and achievement." For David, the room is "to be viewed in a symbiotic relationship to what is to be seen from its windows": Mrs. Thornton's pleasure in her room is in its contiguity to the mill, the products of which have furnished the room. See *Fictions of Resolution*, 22–24.

4. Emily in *David Copperfield* similarly embodies her family's desire, and is similarly a by-product of her family's class aspirations. See chapter 3, "Dickens's Scar."

In her industrious relation to her trousseau, Fanny is blissfully ignorant that she pursues the family occupation ("she would choose and superintend everything herself" [441]), while her mother, more troubled by labor, would farm labor out ("she heartily wished Fanny had accepted her brother's offer of having the wedding clothes provided by some first-rate London dressmaker"). While seeming to disapprove of it, the novel nevertheless rewards Fanny's unabashed love of clothing with significant pin money by way of a marriage that gives her "ample means for providing herself with the finery, which certainly rivalled, if it did not exceed, the lover in her estimation" (441).

5. A 1991 Estée Lauder print ad is based on just this assumption. Its copy commands, "Just Blush," as if one could (one can with Estée Lauder), as if that's all one has to do, once freed by Estée Lauder to bear only the burden of being ornamental.

6. This anxiety about distinction reflects, of course, anxieties about shifting and unstable class positions that make the cartography of class more difficult. Mr. Thornton is repeatedly difficult for people to place, and his own rejection of class in favor of gender as essential determinant of character (his "true man" to replace "gentleman" as the highest complimentary classification) suggests his own anxieties about status. When Frederick Hale takes Thornton for a shopman, he undercuts Thornton's power in Milton, by understanding that power as purely, literally physical (Thornton is "a great powerful fellow" [324]), rather than as metonymic of his influence and standing. Margaret's embarrassed response to what, by this later point in the novel, she wants to see as Frederick's mistake also suggests that her understanding that taking Thornton for a shopman depends on "but a natural impression."

7. The chapter called "Angel Visits" (198) describes Margaret's attentions to Bessy Higgins in her sick-bed.

8. Telling Fanny from Margaret's cousin Edith might easily be more of one. The two are similarly serviceable in the narrative as comparisons for Margaret; as the less worthy but more fortunate, they are foils against which Gaskell displays Margaret's earnestness and strength (rather than their giddy dependence), her stoicism and commitment (rather than their self-indulgent liability to distraction). What distinguishes Edith from Fanny is purely the direction of sympathy in the novel toward her rather than toward Thornton's sister. Gaskell's handling of Fanny and Edith may

indicate that she subscribes to a notion of sympathetic distinction as ultimately arbitrary, a matter of liking that might as well go one way as another. Or it may (less surprisingly) suggest that the expected indulgences of gentility are likely to charm; while the wasteful indulgences of the manufacturing class are morally suspect.

9. Schor's discussion of Margaret's difficult lessons in reading customs and clues in Milton-Northern leads her to the insight that "misunderstanding is eroticized" in Gaskell's novel (127–28).

10. In expressing to Nicholas Higgins her disappointment in Thornton as a manufacturer and "master" of working men, Margaret seems to have blundered; Thornton overhears her. But this blunder is fortuitous, like her blundering offer of money, in that it leads to a good end: if Margaret's realization that Thornton has heard her seems "to fill up the measure of her mortification," it shames Thornton (who, if he "dreaded exposure of his tenderness" was "equally desirous that all men should recognize his justice") into offering Higgins work (403).

11. Bowing repeatedly to Wayne's improbably glamorous girlfriend, Wayne and Garth (in the *Wayne's World* movies) chant—ostensibly in her praise—"we are not worthy."

12. In discussing the Statue of Liberty, Lauren Berlant writes that "her immobility and silence are fundamental to her activity as a positive site of national power and fantasy." Berlant notes that workers who built the statue responded to it as a fantasy of passive sexuality; one of them kissed it upon its completion and another suggested that all the workers were "in love with her." Berlant quotes a scholar's fantasy of, as Berlant puts it, "taking her off her 'pedestal' ": "Not as we see her, but as we know her, this decent woman takes on an altogether different character—for a fee she is open to all for entry and exploration from below." The fantasy of woman's monumental status seems to entail her willingness to exchange her "decency" for use. See Berlant's *The Anatomy of National Fantasy: Hawthorne, Utopia, and Everyday Life* (Chicago: University of Chicago Press, 1991), 22–28.

Rosemarie Bodenheimer discusses Margaret's sexuality as an aspect of Gaskell's refusal to permit a reading of Margaret's attempt to rescue Thornton as "an act of social idealism that is merely misinterpreted by a conventionally minded world." Bodenheimer writes that Margaret's shame about the incident "suggests that Margaret has been seen by crude eyes in an act that unwittingly reveals her secret passional life—one that we have already begun to read as a firmly repressed sexual interest in Thornton." Bodenheimer emphasizes Margaret's sexuality without denying what I call her monumentality: "The idealistic invocation of a myth of passive virtue covers up the act of impulsive emotion." See *The Politics of Story*, 65–66.

Both Deirdre David and Barbara Leah Harman comment on what Harman calls "the insistently sexual language of the strike scene" as part of her discussion of female public appearance in *North and South*. For David, the scene "symbolically suggests defloration" (*Fictions of Resolution*, 43). For Harman, Margaret's use of her body in the scene "confirms the physical and even sexual significance of female public appearance." Gaskell, she writes, "never reduces our sense that public life is dangerously thrilling." Harman sees Gaskell suggesting "both that female sexuality is almost unmanageably potent—affiliated with exposure, criminality, indiscretion, and immoral secrecy—and, at the same time, that this is emphatically not stigmatizing." See Harman's essay "In Promiscuous Company: Female Public Appearance in Elizabeth Gaskell's *North and South*," *Victorian Studies* 31 (Spring 1988): 351–74.

13. Furbank's brief, interesting, quirky essay, "Mendacity in Mrs. Gaskell," appears in *Encounter* 40 (1973): 51–55.

14. J. A. V. Chapple and Arthur Pollard, eds., *The Letters of Mrs. Gaskell* (Cambridge, Mass.: Harvard University Press, 1967), 324. Coral Lansbury reads Gaskell's epistolary consideration of this title as an ironic response to Dickens's changing Gaskell's proposed title "Margaret Hale" to *North and South* when the work began appearing in Dickens's *Household Words*. Lansbury comments on Gaskell's letter: "Elizabeth Gaskell was often malicious, particularly when angry, and this irony was directed at the butcher of Little Nell, and the acknowledged master of the death scene." See Lansbury's *Elizabeth Gaskell: The Novel of Social Crisis* (New York: Barnes & Noble, 1975), 96. I read Gaskell's remark as somewhat more significant with respect to the content of her novel, or I at least insist on Gaskell's responsibility for her joke.

15. Garrett Stewart's psychological account of Gaskell's notion of death as subject to variation considers "variations" matters of transition. Stewart writes:

When Gaskell writes to Dickens that she might have called her novel "Death and Variations," one assumes her to intend not only mortal episodes that serve as variations on a central theme (changes rung on the formulaic death scene) but also those systematic analogies drawn from dying that vary death into a symbol for some powerful transition in the proximate self, be it precipitous collapse, decay, or edification.

See Stewart's *Death Sentences: Styles of Dying in British Fiction* (Cambridge: Harvard University Press, 1984), 105.

16. In the same way that Gaskell's swoon masquerades as death, death, in *North and South*, can be mistaken for the swoon. The possibility of such a mistake teases Higgins into denial of Bessy's death: "Still he pondered over the event, not looking at Margaret, though he grasped her tight. Suddenly, he looked up at her with a wild searching inquiry in his glance. 'Yo're sure and certain she's dead—not in a dwam, a faint?—she's been so before, often'" (281).

17. In Samuel Richardson's *Pamela*, notably, Mr. B— anticipates the critical tradition of doubting the innocence and involuntarity of Pamela's swoons in commenting, of Pamela, that "she has a lucky knack of falling into fits, when she pleases." The

position occupied by the unconscious Pamela, visible through a keyhole, is doubly rendered as a position of accessibility; as somatic defense, the faint relies passively upon helplessness, but it depends as much upon the will of the defended against to keep vulnerability distinct from opportunity. Henry Fielding, of course, resolves doubts in his revision of Pamela's fainting as Shamela's "counterfeit" of a swoon. See *Pamela* and *Shamela* (New York: New American Library, 1986).

18. A song in Rodgers and Hammerstein's *Oklahoma* can help articulate cultural suspicions about the swoon. When the straightforwardly sexual Oklahoman Ado Annie explains her inability to say no, she explains as well that she "ain't the type that kin faint." Asserting that she ain't it, Ado Annie asserts the existence of such a type—innocent-seeming as a class, but able in a tight spot to exploit the ability to swoon. As a thing that can or can't be done, fainting seems a duplicitous resort. The sexual honor of the fainter is as dubious as Ado Annie's; the fainter's honesty is perhaps still more dubious.

19. A hasty sampling of Gaskell's prose in just the novel's first chapter includes these instances of her use of "as if": "But Mrs. Shaw said that her only child should marry for love,—and sighed emphatically, as if love had not been her motive for marrying the General" (37); "Margaret heard her aunt's voice again, but this time it was as if she had raised herself up from her half-recumbent position" (38); "[Margaret's aunt] sank back as if wearied" (38); "the minute lap-dog in Mrs. Shaw's arms began to bark, as if excited by the burst of pity" (38); "little Margaret . . . tried to lie quiet as if asleep" (39); "some of the ladies started back, as if half-ashamed of their feminine interest in dress" (40); "Margaret stood perfectly still, . . . looking at Mr. Lennox with a bright, amused face, as if sure of his sympathy in her sense of the ludicrousness at being thus surprised" (40).

Gaskell's fondness for "half-" ("Edith came back, glowing with pleasure, half-shyly, half-proudly" [44]) implies a similar resistance to commitment. That resistance seems in part an anxiety about ever being caught at not knowing (like my freshman French "peut-être," that word's hedging being my attempt to work into French compositions my fantasy of French sophistication, despite limitations imposed by gloriously unsophisticated language skills). Gaskell's "half-" answers hesitantly and carefully the careless abandon of Austen's "all." See chapter 1, "Austen's Blush."

4. Dickens's Scar

1. Darwin, *The Expression of the Emotions in Man and Animals*, 15. Subsequent references will appear in the text. See my discussion of Darwin's respondents in chapter 2.

2. Darwin excises from the survey as finally circulated his characterization of the

people to be studied as "savages." His sanitation leaves in place his barely less troubling concern about the place of races in a "mankind" constituted by its conformity to a particular moral sense demonstrable in blushing.

3. Burgess's discussion of the woman appears in his *The Physiology or Mechanism of Blushing,* 31–32.

4. Writing of Stanford University's handling of a white student's racist defacement of a poster of Beethoven (his riposte in an argument with an African American student about whether Beethoven "had black blood"), Patricia J. Williams examines her response to what she calls "the Beethoven injury": "The most deeply offending part of the Beethoven injury is its message that if I ever manage to create something as monumental as Beethoven's music, or the literature of the mulatto Alexandre Dumas or the mulatto Alexander Pushkin, then the best reward to which I can aspire is that I will be remembered as white." Williams suggests that while " 'white' still retains its ironclad (or paradigmatic) definition of 'good' . . . blacks, whom we all now know can be good too, must therefore be 'white.' " See Williams's *The Alchemy of Race and Rights* (Cambridge: Harvard University Press, 1991), 110–16.

Like the racist logic Williams discusses, the logic of Burgess and Darwin depends on a construction of moral response as always in some sense "white," in the same way that the description of acts of kindness as "Christian," with an ostensibly tolerant disregard of who performs them, depends on a similarly arrogant equation. Amazing in Burgess and Darwin is that whiteness is not purely a matter of metaphor; rather, it is the name assigned both the material pigmentation of those who chastise and examine the black woman and the injured pigmentation by which she is seen to display the alteration that chastisers and examiners would find in her. The circular logic of the examination is insatiable and reproductive: if people with black skin are moral only insofar as they are found to be white, then black people are denied access to goodness, and "blackness" has yet to be made to display for examiners a relation to moral status. See also note 33.

5. Add to this list the "celebrated painter" who reports that "the chest, shoulders, arms, and whole body of a girl, who unwillingly consented to serve as a model, reddened when she was first divested of her clothes" (314). Darwin finds this report in Lavater's *L'Art de connaître les Hommes.*

6. Charles Dickens, *David Copperfield* (Oxford: Oxford University Press, 1983), 240. Subsequent references will appear in the text.

7. In *David Copperfield,* it is Miss Mowcher who works to make over the blushes of her clients with the help of a product "unmentionable to ears polite" (269), and, indeed, the efficacy of the applied blush requires her to sustain with her chatter a mannerly silence for those imagined so polite they may not hear "rouge," if also able to imagine themselves so impolite as to need it. Among Miss Mowcher's clients,

rouge is always to be called something else, and the extensive fiction of makeup inspires its wearers to a frenzy of renaming. Miss Mowcher reports, "One Dowager, *she* calls it lip-salve. Another, *she* calls it gloves. Another, *she* calls it tucker-edging. Another, *she* calls it a fan. *I* call it whatever *they* call it." The women she supplies with rouge "make believe with such faces," Miss Mowcher says, "that they'd as soon think of laying it on, before a whole drawing room, as before me" (270). Miss Mowcher's best work depends on its own disavowal, and her best service is permitting (by seeming to share) the periodically untenable fantasy of those made over that the work of sponge or brush is less application than restoration or revelation. When they ask Miss Mowcher how they look ("Am I pale?" [270]), those who have been made up insist that even she does not know for sure, and demand of her a kind of reassurance ("how could anyone suspect you're wearing rouge?") that could only also distress ("looks like you could use some"): the natural look proves natural only in proving inadequate. To choose the fixity of blusher is to refuse the intermittence of blushing and to cede the signifying capacities of the exchange of pink for white or brown.

8. Balzac, "Sarrasine," in Roland Barthes, *S/Z* (New York: Hill & Wang, 1974), 252.

9. "When Darwin is struck," writes George Levine, "it will be with the force of self-exposure" (*Darwin and the Novelists: Patterns of Science in Victorian Fiction* [Cambridge: Harvard University Press, 1988], 217). Levine argues that Darwin's empiricism derives assurance of its capacity for accuracy from a conception of reality as powerful and compelling ("the all but physical pressure of observed fact" [Levine, 214]). Darwin's rhetoric of compulsion (Levine notes that Darwin thinks himself "struck" and "driven" [214]) permits evasion: "The verbs investing authority in what is observed disguise and diminish the activity of the observer and leave him blameless for the consequences of the vision" (214–15). Levine is right in his assessment of the lucky Darwin. If the accusations, provocations, and punishments by which he comes to record blushes recoil upon him—leaving what marks of self-exposure?—they will not discolor, not throb, not even heal or scar. In thinking about Steerforth as stricken with the force of self-exposure, I want to underscore the means by which a stricken Rosa Dartle comes to harness that force to empower herself. I mean to consider how Steerforth's violation operates upon his own aims in order to plot all the better the fantasy that subjects his blow to Rosa Dartle's deflections.

10. When Michael Slater writes of Rosa Dartle's relation to Steerforth's remarks about the Peggottys, he is able to assess her pleasure and pain only by imagining her as Dickens does—provocative of Steerforth's worst displays; if "herself a victim of Steerforth's brutal insensitivity," nevertheless "she derives a masochistic pleasure from provoking him to exhibit so blatantly this part of his nature" (*Dickens' Women* [London: J. M. Dent, 1983], 266). "Look," it seems hard not to say, "what she made him do."

Ned Lukacher describes Rosa Dartle as "Dickens's most brilliant sketch of a woman scorned." See *Primal Scenes: Literature, Philosophy, Psychoanalysis* (Ithaca: Cornell University Press, 1986), 319. Lukacher seems to respond to the way Rosa Dartle's scar appears to cut her lip on its appearance when he imagines the scar as made by Rosa's failure to "let go": "For Rosa, remembrance is destructive and disfiguring." If she is furiously the woman scorned, Rosa Dartle nevertheless seems in Lukacher's account a woman one might describe as clingy, if only to memory.

11. The action of the scar as writing (its starting forth) unites and alters Steerforth (start forth) and Dartle (dart forth). Despite its ever-presence, in what is nevertheless the intermittence of its starting forth (in its status as verb), the scar makes of Steerforth's steerage almost an obsolete past tense. If the scar comes to mean Rosa Dartle's character, it manages still also to mean—in Dickens's language—the story (Rosa's present, Steerforth's past) of how it has been made.

12. Helena Michie and Audrey Jaffe have discussed the role of the scar in establishing identity in Dickens's novels. Michie argues that female identity in Dickens is born of "illness, scarring, and deformity." "Pain," she writes, "works on both the level of the narrative's construction of character and the character's construction of self." See "'Who is this in Pain?': Scarring, Disfigurement, and Female Identity in *Bleak House* and *Our Mutual Friend*," *Novel* 22 (1989): 199–212. Commenting on Michie's essay, Jaffe argues that "the evidence of *David Copperfield* suggests that in the novel character is itself a scar, a 'marking' of identity by an effaced narrator." See *Vanishing Points: Dickens, Narrative, and the Subject of Omniscience* (Berkeley: University of California Press, 1991), 118n. As my reading suggests, I am in considerable sympathy with these arguments, but I would differ to the extent that Rosa Dartle's identity, if formed and founded in her scar, inheres for me more powerfully in the insinuations that are her adaptations of it and to it. In attending to the language of *David Copperfield*'s minor characters, I mean to explore the link between Dickens's notorious interest in establishing character by way of remarkable physical features or peculiar physiological tics and his consequent and correspondent interest in an insinuative mode of speech.

13. The erotics of David's discovery of blush as sign are woven intricately with the erotics of intermediacy. Murdstone expresses his attachment to David's mother by exploiting her son's own feeling ("I cannot wonder at his devotion" [15]). Enlisting Clara Copperfield in the search for meaning through the mediation of David's devotion, Murdstone enlists David as well. David the narrator profits by the lesson of Murdstone's example, enlisting readers in the search for significance in what he coyly and coercively withholds. Like Clara Copperfield, gently pressured to partake of the gratifications of discovery, readers may enjoy themselves in condescension to the young David and may find him touching: unlike him, I know already that to turn "a

beautiful color" is to blush; unlike him ("Confusion to Brooks of Sheffield!" [19]), I know that, when she takes on "such a beautiful color," his mother engages the discourse of the compliment. A festival of anxious mediation (young David *means* by means of "footstool," Mr. Murdstone means by means of David, the knowing narrator means by means of his unknowing young self), the passage replays the scene it describes: "and I was jealous that his hand should touch my mother's in touching me—which it did" (15).

14. Barkis—in his work as carrier, susceptible to the effects of weather—is only ambiguously able to make his face a register of significance. David recalls Barkis's response to Peggotty: "And he gave me a look as he shouldered the largest box and went out, which I thought had meaning in it, if meaning could ever be said to find its way into Mr. Barkis's visage" (109). As an invalid, Barkis is said to be "nothing but a face" (251), as if trying to compress from his stricken body a capacity to convey meaning that Garrett Stewart suggests he *is* able to render through "the self-conscious epitome of spoken last words." See *Death Sentences: Styles of Dying in British Fiction* (Cambridge: Harvard University Press, 1984), 16.

15. It is easy to note with complacence the patience and condescension with which David interprets Mr. Peggotty ("this was in allusion to his being slow to go"). More complicated to describe without acknowledging complicity would be the artfulness by which, even as I recognize the act of translation ("he meant snail"), I am made to feel my need of it ("reg'lar Dodman") and made to enjoy the maintainance of an amused distance from Mr. Peggotty. In his condescension, as in his attention to the improvements in Mr. Peggotty's skin, David as narrator recites and endorses the lessons he has learned through Steerforth's discourse on the Peggottys.

16. Astutely, or perhaps just assisted by cultural clichés at hand, Rosa Dartle outlines for Emily the way that Emily has been functional for the Peggottys in her involvement with Steerforth: "You were a part of the trade of your home, and were bought and sold like any other vendible thing your people dealt in" (586). In the harshness of her assessment, Rosa mistakes as monetary the source of Emily's value to the Peggottys, which, in the intricate plications of class with money, lies rather in the family's ability to keep her. Spent in unproductive relations with Steerforth and unable with him to reify her gentility in marriage, Emily does not yield value for her family. Her value for them would be greater in retention (this is the use of her betrothal to Ham), by which she may be prized, enjoyed, displayed as one prizes and displays the collectible with which one can afford not to part.

17. To use Emily in the process of production is also potentially to empower her, in the way the novel has with anxiety empowered its assemblage of unmarried women. Steerforth's use of Emily adds her as grace to the novel's assemblage of women who, not attached to husbands, threaten with the prospect of a frightening detachment:

Rosa Dartle ("edge-tool"), Miss Murdstone (who "like the pocket instrument called a life-preserver, was not so much designed for purposes of protection as of assault" [318]), Miss Mowcher (in her volatility an explosive, in her capacity to jest, "a sharp little thing" [379]).

18. Mr. Peggotty, trying to recall the name of young David's special friend, calls that friend "Rudderford" in what seems a proleptic or Adamic announcement of "bold" Steerforth's own erythristic capacities (113).

19. Talking about Jane Austen, it seems necessary sometimes to literalize the idiom of mortification in order to recall that the pleasures of manners are sometimes accompanied by a kind of violence. But it seems necessary here, discussing Steerforth and Dickens, to recall the inverse: that blushing is sometimes a pleasure and that the other's blush need not be called up by assault.

20. Discussing the link between shame and confusion, Robert Newsom notes shame's capacity to be "profoundly disorienting" but also to be useful in exploring "questions of the identity of things and the identity of self." See "The Hero's Shame," *Dickens Studies Annual* 11 (1983): 1–24. See also my discussion of confusion in chapter 5.

21. In the embarrassed novel of manners he fits within *David Copperfield*—the romance of David and Dora—Dickens enjoys the conventional blurring of confusions, of mix-up with embarrassment. On the eve of his wedding, David answers a tap at the door, "wondering who it is" there to meet "a pair of bright eyes and a blushing face." David comes to recognize them as Dora's, finally as Dora herself "in a delightful state of confusion" (515).

22. The novel finally punishes Uriah's offending hand for its perceived transgressions ("I felt ashamed to let him take my hand" [609]) when it tries to snatch in Wickfield's office Micawber's inevitable letter of accusation: "Mr. Micawber, with a perfect miracle of dexterity or luck, caught his advancing knuckles with the ruler, and disabled his right hand. It dropped at the wrist, as if it were broken" (613). *David Copperfield* writes Uriah's crime and its punishment in the secrecy of his hand and in the openness of David's as it strikes him.

23. When she considers Peggotty's disapproval of Murdstone, Clara Copperfield imagines that Peggotty harbors wishes similar to Rosa Dartle's: "Would you wish me to shave my head and black my face, or disfigure myself with a burn, or a scald, or something of that sort? I dare say you would, Peggotty. I dare say you'd quite enjoy it" (16). Dickens imagines disfigurement as something women can nearly ask of each other—or offer each other protectively—in this novel.

24. Cosmetics and prosthetics have complicated these twentieth-century manifestations of the scarred villain. The Joker in Tim Burton's film *Batman* and wicked David Kimble on the CBS soap opera *The Young and the Restless* make themselves up to pass without physical scars. The Joker's scars, though, come in part *from* the work

of a plastic surgeon, David Kimble's entirely from such a source; if cosmetics and prosthetics can fail ethics in successfully hiding the sign of villainy, they can also ethically produce it. The scars of Burton's Edward Scissorhands reverse convention to suggest supersensitivity rather than toughening. Audrey Jaffe connects Doyle's man with the twisted lip with the Joker in "Detecting the Beggar: Arthur Conan Doyle, Henry Mayhew, and 'The Man with the Twisted Lip'" (*Representations* 31 [Summer 1990]: 117n).

25. Mouthing need not be the language of abuse; one can imagine an empowered gentility choosing to mouth what it would signal but keep respectably silent ("cancer" or "breakdown" in one age; "AIDS" in this one). And, of course, in Dickens, it is not just women who resort to mouthing (it is Joe Gargery's primary way to communicate and to bond with Pip in the early domestic arrangements of *Great Expectations*) and not just women who live in domestic oppression (the bookseller to whom David brings Micawber's books is often found in bed "with a cut in his forehead or a black eye," their provenance unclearly either his "excesses over-night" or the wife who scolds him "violently" each morning [133]).

26. Rosa Dartle identifies herself as mediatrix in Steerforth's relationship with his mother. Since the flight of Steerforth's fancy she has been, she tells Mrs. Steerforth, "a mere disfigured piece of furniture between you both" (654); impossible, really, not to imagine that furniture a bed.

27. Brian Firth writes in "*David Copperfield* and Jeremy Diddler" (*Notes and Queries* 31: 489–90) that Rosa Dartle's "menacing and several times repeated 'I only ask for information'" is meant to echo the tag line of Jeremy Diddler in James Kenney's popular farce *Raising the Wind*. In a letter from which Firth quotes, Byron writes "I wish you would speak to *Perry* . . . and ask like Jeremy Diddler—not for eighteen pence—but for information on the subject." Byron's characterization of Diddler attributes a certain transparency to his efforts, and Diddler's use in popular reference seems to have been a way of saying "I know what you're after." The transparency of insinuation seems somewhat different and, at least in *David Copperfield*, not to preclude its efficacy.

28. *The Posthumous Papers of the Pickwick Club* (Harmondsworth: Penguin, 1986), 589. The Oxford English Dictionary cites this sentence as part of its entry for *corkscrew*.

29. Miss Mowcher is marked in the text by her body size, but also, later, by Littimer, whom she identifies and restrains for arrest: "He cut her face right open, and pounded her in the most brutal manner, when she took him; but she never loosed her hold till he was locked up. She held so tight to him, in fact, that the officers were obliged to take 'em both together" (700).

30. Wanting to know if she should leave with Steerforth and David a lock of her

hair, Miss Mowcher solicits her own body for leavings and reveals her connective project as mere exaggeration of the romantic ordinary.

31. With a biographer's resentment, John Forster tells of Dickens's receipt of a letter from an upset woman Forster calls "a grotesque little oddity among [Dickens's] acquaintance," who recognized aspects of herself in Miss Mowcher. Dickens, continues Forster, with greater sentiment, "was shocked at the pain he had given" and promised to alter his writing of Miss Mowcher in later numbers "so that nothing but an agreeable impression should be left." See *The Life of Charles Dickens*, volume 2 (London: J. M. Dent, 1966), 99. Fred Kaplan's briefer and more cynical account suggests that Dickens's reparations were a response to being "threatened by a lawsuit and his conscience." See *Dickens: A Biography* (New York: William Morrow, 1988), 261.

32. Miss Mowcher imagines herself unheard when in earnest and fantasizes a death consequent on that effective silencing. Saying of herself that "she might whistle for her bread-and-butter till she died of Air!" (378), she imagines a death that answers (the way God is said to answer all prayers) the desperation of the pursy.

33. Ridgeway entitles his book about white supremacist groups *Blood in the Face* because such groups determine Aryan status by one's ability or inability to blush, to show "blood in the face." The ambiguity with which the phrase attributes blood to one face or another is suggestive as well of the displacement by which prizing the blush can seem to justify spilling blood.

5. The Mechanics of Confusion

1. Mary Elizabeth Braddon, *Lady Audley's Secret* (Oxford: Oxford University Press, 1991), 405–6. Braddon refers to Madame Rachel's pearl tooth powder elsewhere in the novel as well. Skilton's note on Madame Rachel identifies her as Mrs. Rachel Levison, who from her shop in New Bond Street "marketed beauty products which she claimed could make women 'Beautiful for Ever!'" (452n). While "enamel" clearly identifies this Madame Rachel as the cosmetics vendor, whose tooth powder accompanied a tooth enamel, "Madame Rachel" may also play on the name of the actress Rachel Felix, a favorite reference for nineteenth-century novelists.

O'Neil is Eliza O'Neill, distinguished in nineteenth-century theater by her emphatic gesticulation and heavily physical acting style. See Julie A. Carlson, *In the Theatre of Romanticism: Coleridge, Nationalism, Women* (Cambridge: Cambridge University Press, 1994), for a discussion of "bodies politic and theatric."

2. In an essay in the *London Magazine*, Hazlitt suggests that O'Neill's theatrical distinction has its source precisely in her ability to display "what she, and every other woman, of natural sensibility would feel in given circumstances" (quoted in Carlson, *In the Theatre of Romanticism*, 169).

3. Since color constitutes an important part of Lady Audley's near-universal appeal as Braddon writes it and since Braddon is herself fascinated by the contrast between Lady Audley's innocent appearance and her less innocent character, Braddon needs Lady Audley's complexion to be colorful. (Chatting with her look-alike maid, Lady Audley suggests that "a pot of rouge" and "a bottle of hair dye" might heighten the likeness and improve Phoebe's looks: "It is only colour that you want. . . . Your complexion is sallow and mine is pink and rosy" [58].) Braddon's fascination indicates rather than extinguishes her anxiety about somatic characterization, and she sometimes uses the language with which she describes Lady Audley's blushes to suggest that something is perhaps not quite right about them. (That Lady Audley often pales in response to crisis is, I take it, another way to recuperate her complexion for the registry of moral status.) In a circumstance that calls for maidenly modesty, for example, the future Lady Audley "flushed scarlet to the roots of her fair hair" (8). But the efficacy of this language as equivocation is itself questionable, dependent as it is upon some already formulated notion of Lady Audley as a scarlet woman.

4. Anthony Trollope, *The Eustace Diamonds* (Oxford: Oxford University Press, 1983), 1:16. Subsequent references to *ED* will include volume and page number and will appear in the text.

5. See my discussion of Darwin in chapter 4.

6. The dubious cleansing of the blackamoor is a figure for doomed moral improvement elsewhere in the Victorian novel. Mr. Bradshaw's fulminations about Gaskell's fallen Ruth include the suggestion that Mr. Benson might have acquired the help of "sickly sentimentalists" in "washing the blackamoor white" (*Ruth* [New York: Oxford University Press, 1985], 349). Elsie Michie also notes this passage and connects it to Dickens's disguise of Tom Gradgrind in *Hard Times* as, in Michie's words, "a comic blackamoor who will have to be washed clean in beer." Michie identifies Dickens's image as a literalization of Bradshaw's phrase. See her *Outside the Pale: Cultural Exclusion, Gender Difference, and the Victorian Woman Writer* (Ithaca: Cornell University Press, 1993), 123–24.

7. John Kucich's *The Power of Lies: Transgression in Victorian Fiction* (Ithaca: Cornell University Press, 1994) called to my attention the specifics of the distinction between Lizzie and Lucy in their appraisals of truth and falsehood. While Lizzie "liked lies, thinking them to be more beautiful than truth" (*ED*, 2:367), Lucy "represents the extreme of truth-telling" (Kucich, 56) and, according to Frank Greystoke is "truth itself" (*ED*, 1:121). (Both passages from the novel are also quoted by Kucich.) As one of what Kucich describes as Trollope's " 'middling' characters" (55–56), Lucy exhibits a middle-brow taste for truth, whereas Lizzie proves herself an aesthete of the lie; an account of their relative attractions makes of Lucy ("truth itself") an untouchable monolith, in contrast to Lizzie, whose simulations offer the fascinations of variety.

8. George Eliot, *Middlemarch* (Oxford: Oxford University Press, 1988), 16. Subsequent references will appear in the text.

9. See Helena Michie's *Sororophobia: Differences among Women in Literature and Culture* (New York: Oxford University Press, 1992), which discusses the way the sister plot of *Middlemarch* (involving relations between Dorothea and Rosamond as well as Dorothea and Celia) exists as "counter-narrative" to the novel's romance plot (40–50). Michie also notes that as the "principle of realism" in *Middlemarch,* Celia is the locus of "interest in the body" (42).

10. Without intending that this list exhaust the amplitude of Eliot's references to Dorothea's complexion, I want to make clear that Eliot's interest in that complexion is evident and even habitual.

11. Eliot's irritation with the blush is an extension of Dorothea's impatience with Celia. In its embrace of an irresistible parenthesis—of Celia "(she sometimes seemed to blush as she breathed)" (46)—*Middlemarch* reveals a certain narrative testiness about the blush, and Eliot's free indirect dismissals of an annoying Celia as, for Dorothea, "no longer a cherub" and "a pink-and-white nullifidian" (31) exhibit the gratuitousness in dismissal or in insult that separates the contingent excuse for irritation (Celia's exasperating skepticism) from its lasting and irrational basis (a complexion that—imagined as less suited to the cherub than to the scamp—lets one get impishly away with murder).

12. George Eliot, *Daniel Deronda* (Harmondsworth: Penguin, 1967), 473. Subsequent references will be made in the text. Gwendolen is touring Sir Hugo's stables, which retain something of the character of the "beautiful choir" (472) from which they have been converted, when she is led by impulse to exclaim that they are "glorious" and to announce her preference of these stables (future ownership of which speculation attributes to Deronda) to those of her husband (473). "Consciousness" of "the reference of her thoughts" prompts Gwendolen to look at Deronda, who is looking at her.

13. In *Keats and Embarrassment,* Christopher Ricks, too, remarks that Eliot's characterization makes the blush sound more like language than not: "She is in danger of forgetting the extent to which this shows that a blush is like, not unlike, language" (London: Oxford University Press, 1974), 53.

14. *Webster's Third New International Dictionary,* s.v. "confusion." The phrase is from *Pride and Prejudice* (269).

15. *The Expression of the Emotions in Man and Animals,* 322–23. Darwin, too, notes the recognition by colloquial speech that blushing involves a "confusion of mental powers" in "such common expressions as 'she was covered with confusion'" (322).

16. That implication in the embarrassing scene (in blushing *for*) involves some pain is indicated in Darwin's story by the quick effort of the reliable gentleman who is

the source of the story to distance himself from participation in the scene: reporting it, he is merely the disinterested observer, the eyewitness.

17. Charles Musgrove reports to Anne that, while he finds his sister recovered from her fall, "she is altered: there is no running or jumping about, no laughing or dancing; it is quite different. If one happens only to shut the door a little hard, she starts and wriggles like a young dab chick in the water; and Benwick sits at her elbow, reading verses, or whispering to her, all day long" (*P,* 218). Pushing too hard on the subversive potential of confusion would falsify: here, for example, the energies of female rivalry produced by the confused relation between Anne Elliot and Lousia Musgrove are more readily available for harnessing to unattractive social purposes than they are for suggesting the possibility of interesting and somatic relations between women.

18. See Eve Kosofsky Sedgwick's discussion of the interest of *Our Mutual Friend* in the blurry struggles of Bradley Headstone and Eugene Wrayburn (*Between Men: Literature and Male Homosocial Desire* [New York: Columbia University Press, 1985], 161–79).

19. Henry James, *The Portrait of a Lady* (Oxford: Oxford University Press, 1981), 16. Subsequent references will appear in the text.

20. James complains of Will Ladislaw: "He is, we may say, the one figure which a masculine intellect of the power as George Eliot's would not have conceived with the same complacency; he is, in short, roughly speaking, a woman's man." James's taste in men perhaps is suggested in this comparison: "If Dorothea had married any one after her misadventure with Casaubon, she would have married a hussar." Quoted in Gordon Haight, "George Eliot's 'eminent failure,' Will Ladislaw," *This Particular Web: Essays on "Middlemarch"*, ed. Ian Adam (Toronto: University of Toronto Press, 1975), 34.

21. Tanner, introduction to *Pride and Prejudice* (Harmondsworth: Penguin, 1972), 35.

22. Henry James, *Daisy Miller and Other Stories* (Oxford: Oxford University Press, 1985), 62. Lynn Wardley wonders similarly if the "black little blot" Winterbourne ascribes to Daisy might not be "actually the diacritical mark of the blind spot in Winterbourne's reading of the pretty American flirt and not the sign of her innocence lost, like the X that follows the notorious Innocent's name" ("Reassembling Daisy Miller," *ALH* 3 [1991]: 232–54). See also Eve Kosofsky Sedgwick's "Shame and Performativity: Henry James's New York Edition Prefaces" for a discussion of activating the energies of "shame on you" for queer performativity (*Henry James's New York Edition: The Construction of Authorship*, ed. David McWhirter [Stanford: Stanford University Press, 1995], 206–39). Sedgwick's consideration of a phenomenon similar to what I would describe as blushing *for* construes shame as a source of identity: "One of the strangest features of shame . . . is the way bad treatment of someone else, bad

treatment *by* someone else, someone else's embarrassment, stigma, debility, bad smell, or strange behavior, seemingly having nothing to do with me, can so readily flood me—assuming I'm a shame-prone person—with this sensation whose very suffusiveness seems to delineate my precise, individual outlines in the most isolating way imaginable" (212).

23. My sense of the Jamesian scene is informed by Joseph Litvak's discussion of "James's veritable *theater* of embarrassment." Litvak is interested in embarrassment's relation to the theatrical ("the experience of making a spectacle of oneself"), understanding embarrassment as what he calls "a complex signifying *mechanism* within the Jamesian text." See Litvak's *Caught in the Act: Theatricality in the Nineteenth-Century Novel* (Berkeley: University of California Press, 1992), 195–234.

24. Henry James, "The Middle Years," *The Figure in the Carpet and Other Stories*, ed. Frank Kermode (Harmondsworth: Penguin, 1986), 245–46. Julie Rivkin's essay "Doctoring the Text: Henry James and Revision" brought this passage to my attention. Rivkin's essay considers the passage in light of the "anxiety reading represents" and that "revision attempts to waylay." See Rivkin's essay in McWhirter's *Henry James's New York Edition*, 142–63.

25. Henry James, *The Sacred Fount* (Harmondsworth: Penguin, 1994), 5. Subsequent references will appear in the text.

26. Peter Brooks notes that "*The Sacred Fount* is, to be sure, a somewhat 'perverse' example of the body in the field of vision, since it is so highly cerebral," but the subject of observation "returns us again and again to the body, and particularly to two bodies, in the relation of giver and taker, spender and getter, given its central expression in the metaphor of the sacred fount" (*Body Work: Objects of Desire in Modern Narrative* [Cambridge: Harvard University Press, 1993], 107, 110).

27. In his introduction to *The Sacred Fount* (New York: Grove Press, 1953), Leon Edel writes of readers' initial impressions of the narrator that "we must determine for ourselves, whether he is (as we suspect) a man" (ix). These suspicions might (or might not) be supported by such details as the narrator's presence, for example, in a roomful of cigar-smoking men. But it turns the book on its head—in ways I very much like— to think of the narrator's obsessed interpretations as a woman's or at least as interpretations ascribed to one.

28. Laurence Holland notes that, in these conversations, "virtual miracles of communication take place—as when the Narrator exclaims with glee and pride 'Then . . . you *could* tell what I was talking about!'" (*The Expense of Vision: Essays on the Craft of Henry James* [Princeton: Princeton University Press, 1964], 185).

29. Leon Edel is among those who offer this reading. See, for example, his introduction to *The Sacred Fount* (xi).

30. In *Caught in the Act*, Joseph Litvak notes that "the term *embarrassment* appears frequently enough in James's work, though it sometimes has the older meaning of

'obstacle' or 'impediment' rather than the newer one, current when James was writing, of 'abashment' or 'discomposure' " (199).

31. The first reference in James's notebooks to a liaison demonstrable by evidence of a "transfusion" from one partner to the other appears in 1894 (Leon Edel and Lyall H. Powers, eds., *The Complete Notebooks of Henry James* [New York: Oxford University Press, 1987], 88). Publication of the novel occurred in 1901.

32. Leon Edel, ed., *Henry James Letters*, volume 4, 1895–1916 (Cambridge: Harvard University Press, 1984), 185–86.

33. *Letters*, 4:251.

34. *Letters*, 4:154.

35. *Letters*, 4:251.

36. *Letters*, 4:198.

37. "The country in this story is not Pakistan, or not quite," writes Rushdie. "There are two countries, real and fictional, occupying the same space, or almost the same space" (*Shame* [New York: Random House, 1983], 23–24). In choosing to discuss Rushdie's novel in the context of the English novel and the culture it forms and reflects, I am responding to the constant allusiveness in Rushdie's text to English literature and the English novel. But Rushdie's book is more obviously interested in the status of women in Pakistani culture and in its own retelling of the politics surrounding the execution of Pakistan's president Zulfikar Ali Bhutto in 1978. For a discussion of *Shame*'s participation in the "othering" that "enables disparities between the power of men and women" in "both England and Pakistan," see Inderpal Grewal's essay, "Salman Rushdie: Marginality, Women, and *Shame*" (*Genders* 3 [Fall 1988]: 24–42). Grewal suggests, of Rushdie's novel, that "the logic of the narrative operates to show the need for addressing the oppression of women by the very process of establishing their subordination" (39). See Sara Suleri's discussion of *Shame*'s negotiation of problems of representation and history in her book, *The Rhetoric of English India* (Chicago: University of Chicago Press, 1992), 174–89. Subsequent references to *Shame* will appear in the text.

38. Suleri writes of the formal dislocations and narrative disjunctions of *Shame* that as the text "take[s] on as its fictional provenance a series of events so sensational, so violent in its currency as gossip, that the text is impelled to construct elaborate defenses against the lure of melodrama by focusing obsessively on its own literariness and its status as a formal artifact" (174). Suleri's diction suggests that her understanding of literary self-consciousness, like mine, includes a sense of its mortification: discussing *Shame*'s "nervous advertisement of self-conscious ideological rectitude" and its "neurasthenic idiom" (175), she writes that "its narrative self-consciousness suggests a deep embarrassment at the idea of political discourse, a nostalgic will to create apolitical pockets in the garments of such language" (174).

39. In focusing on the figure of the vending machine, I do not mean to suggest

that—as some critics have suggested that there is no body in Jane Austen—there is no body in *Shame*, which in some ways seems all body in its enjoyment of bodily gunk: decapitations and impalings, slaughters, illnesses, and pregnant suicides yield such products as "sheets turned yellow by perspiration and urine" (309), a "crackly" burqa "starched by the dried-on blood" (242), "the pestilential squashiness of . . . excrement" (309). But the body in Rushdie's novel is not so much a site of even these gross indulgences or pleasures for characters or readers as it is a means of illustrating—by means of its physical corruption—moral and political corruptions.

Announcements

1. This particular instance of the mystery novel's blush occurs in Jill McGown's *Murder . . . Now and Then* (New York: Fawcett Crest, 1993), 152.

2. Don DeLillo, *White Noise* (Harmondsworth: Penguin, 1985), 184–85. Subsequent references will appear in the text.

3. *The New Yorker*, October 23, 1995.

4. Helen Wells, *Cherry Ames, Student Nurse* (New York: Grossett & Dunlap, 1943), 34–35. Mabel Maney's parodies of the Cherry Ames and Nancy Drew books, in which nurse Cherry Aimless is romanced by amateur sleuth Nancy Clue, exploit Cherry's responsive complexion for its erotic possibilities. Cherry Aimless herself—nothing if not out of touch with her feelings—is often startled by what her blushes and flushes might portend: "Cherry checked her lipstick in the vanity mirror. She noticed how flushed her face was. Was it the afternoon sun, or her heart—suddenly beating at a frantic pace?" (*The Case of the Not-So-Nice Nurse* [Pittsburgh: Cleis Press, 1993], 171).

Mary Ann O'Farrell is Associate Professor in the Department of English at Texas A&M University.